Nostalgia, Nationalism, and the US Militia Movement

Nostalgia, Nationalism, and the US Militia Movement is an accessible primer on the contemporary US militia movement. Exploring the complicated history of militias in the United States, starting with the Revolutionary War period, this book leverages unique data from ethnographic fieldwork, in-depth interviews, and previously unseen archival materials from militia founder Norm Olson to detail the modern movement's origin and trajectory through the attempted insurrection of January 6th and beyond.

This book uses the lenses of nostalgia and settler colonialism to explain militia members' actions and beliefs, including their understandings of both nationalism and masculinity. This approach situates militias in a broader political landscape and explains how and why they will continue to be relevant actors in American politics.

A general audience will find this book approachable, and it will be of particular interest to people studying militias or other social movement organizations whose vision of an ideal nation rests on a nostalgic image of the past and potentially encourages political violence.

Amy Cooter, PhD, is Director of Research, Academic Development and Innovation at Middlebury Institute's Center on Terrorism, Extremism, and Counterterrorism. Prior to joining Middlebury, Professor Cooter was a senior lecturer in sociology at Vanderbilt University.

Nostalgia, Nationalism, and the US Militia Movement

Amy Cooter

NEW YORK AND LONDON

Cover image: Zach D. Roberts

First published 2024
by Routledge
605 Third Avenue, New York, NY 10158

and by Routledge
2 Park Square, Milton Park, Abingdon, Oxon, OX14 4RN

Routledge is an imprint of the Taylor & Francis Group, an informa business

© 2024 Taylor & Francis

The right of Amy Cooter to be identified as author of this work has been asserted by them in accordance with sections 77 and 78 of the Copyright, Designs and Patents Act 1988.

All rights reserved. No part of this book may be reprinted or reproduced or utilised in any form or by any electronic, mechanical, or other means, now known or hereafter invented, including photocopying and recording, or in any information storage or retrieval system, without permission in writing from the publishers.

Trademark notice: Product or corporate names may be trademarks or registered trademarks, and are used only for identification and explanation without intent to infringe.

ISBN: 978-1-032-42198-8 (hbk)
ISBN: 978-1-032-42197-1 (pbk)
ISBN: 978-1-003-36165-7 (ebk)

DOI: 10.4324/9781003361657

Typeset in Sabon LT Pro
by Apex CoVantage, LLC

Contents

Acknowledgments   viii
List of Acronyms   ix

Introduction   1

Research for the Book 2
Understanding the Militia 3
Plan for the Book 5

1   The Modern US Militia Movement: Member's Motivations, Beliefs, and Practices   8

What Are Domestic Militias? 10
Centrality of the Second Amendment 11
Who Are Militia Members? 12
What Do Members Believe? 15
   Racism 15
   Citizenship and Politics 19
   Nationalism and Nostalgia 21
Boy Scouts or Extremists? A Militia Typology 23
   Typological Blurring 26
   Distinctions and Overlaps With Other Nostalgic Groups 28
   Nostalgic Group Interconnections 30
   Political Winds 32

2   Militia History in the United States: Contextualizing the Modern Movement   40

Colonial Roots and Catalysts 40
Nineteenth-Century Militias 44
Militias of the 1900s 48

vi Contents

3   **Militia Origins: The Gospel According to Norm Olson**   55

    Sowing the Seeds: Crucial Events in the Militia Movement's Formation 58
      The Weaver Family in Ruby Ridge, Idaho 58
      David Koresh and the Branch Davidians in Waco, Texas 61
      The Brady Bill 63
    Tending the Flock: From Fear to Action 64

4   **The Oklahoma City Bombing and Militia Decline: A Floundering Father**   71

    Oklahoma City and a Nation's Tribulation 71
    The Japan Allegation 74
    Impact on the Movement 76
    Olson's Transformation 79

5   **Settling for Nostalgia: How Nostalgia and a Rural Mentality Shape the Militia Movement**   91

    A Rural Mentality 91
    Nostalgic Nationalism 97
    Weaponizing Nostalgia 99
      Racial Threat 101
      Racism or Cultural Exclusion: A False Dichotomy 103
    Settler Colonialism 105
      Nostalgic Memories 107
      The Legacy of the Frontier 108
    Nostalgia and Stated Motives for Membership 110
    Nostalgia's Influence on Action 112
      Firearms and Mythic Nationalism 114
      Sheriffs Within the Nostalgic Settler Worldview 116

6   **The Movement's Trajectory: The Early 2000s, the Trump Era, and Beyond**   126

    Recent Militia Trajectory 126
    Movement Evolution 130
      Millenarianism and Accelerationism 130
      Boogaloo's Emergence 134
      Boogaloo's Influence 135
      Militias in the Trump Era 136
    Case Studies 137
      The Hutaree 138

  The Crusaders 144
  The Wolverine Watchmen 149
 January 6, 2021 153
 Future Militia Action 157

7 Conclusion: Signals of Violence and Informed Best Practices 169

 Behavior and Beliefs 171
  Target Specification 171
  Cavalier Training Practices 172
  Open Discrimination 172
  Conspiracism 173
  Secrecy 174
 Network Characteristics 175
  Strict Hierarchy 175
  Leader Worship 175
  Inverted Expertise 176
  Stolen Valor 176
  Isolation 176
  Familial Relationships 177
  Network Characteristics in Practice 177
 What Can We Do? Suggested Best Practices 178
  Legal Strictures 178
  LEO Rapport 180
  Confidential Informant Movement 182
  Tidy Prosecutions 183
 Other Best Practices 185
  Lower Barriers to Contact for Legitimate Concerns 186
  What About Communities? 187
  Structural and Long-Term Solutions 188

Index 196

Acknowledgments

This book would not have been possible without the enormous support of my newest colleagues and oldest friends. I appreciate early readers who all gave valuable feedback on draft material, especially Dustin Faeder, Matt Kriner, Sam Jackson, and Mike Gibson.

The cover photo from Zach D. Roberts (*ZDRoberts.com*) and photos in these pages from Daniel Hud help bring militia members and their concerns to life, and I am grateful for their generosity in sharing their talent.

Thanks to my family (the worst coauthors but the best human beings, especially J, P, S, and G) and to the Anderson family, who have been a constant source of simultaneous support, grounding, and entertainment. Thanks, too, to Mr. Davenport, who helped me not be another brick in the wall.

I also appreciate the Nashville Public Library and its dedicated workers. Much of this book was drafted at my local branch. Librarians here and nationally are at the forefront of fighting disinformation and preserving access to early voting and other resources central to democracy's preservation.

Last but not least, I appreciate the militia members and their families who spent their time and trust sharing their concerns, activities, and goals with me as I've attempted to capture the full range of the movement.

Acronyms

ATF (also BATF)	Bureau of Alcohol, Tobacco, and Firearms
CI	Confidential Informant
CRT	Critical Race Theory
DHS	Department of Homeland Security
FEMA	Federal Emergency Management Agency
FBI	Federal Bureau of Investigation
KKK	Ku Klux Klan
LEO	Law Enforcement Officer
MMCW	Michigan Militia Corps of Wolverines
NFAC	Not Fucking Around Coalition
NRA	National Rifle Association
UN	United Nations
US	United States

Introduction

"It doesn't look like *that* big of a deal to me. 'Not very many people involved, just a few crackpots getting a lot of media attention," a colleague told me about 2 p.m. CST on January 6, 2021. We didn't know it yet, but Ashli Babbit had just died inside the Capitol building, having been shot after refusing a police order to stop trying to access the Speaker's Lobby through a broken window. We were starting a Zoom call to discuss a possible change in an undergraduate program, but it was difficult to avoid talk of the ongoing mob in DC. I had been monitoring the day's events as closely as possible, and even with my partial view from afar of the developing events at the Capitol, I knew that dismissing the insurrectionists in both size and intention was a mistake.

In contrast to my colleague's assessment, more than a thousand people have now been charged (Hall et al., 2023) for their actions that day, while more than twice that number are believed to have breached the building (Rubin et al., 2022). As many as 10,000 total people may have been at the rally outside before the violence began (Mascaro et al., 2021). In addition to Babbit, several other people died during the insurrection or shortly after, including four police officers who died by suicide, and more than 100 other officers were injured (Farley, 2022). What is even more concerning is that many people continue to believe that the Presidential election was "stolen" and that Joe Biden illegitimately attained the office. That belief, shared by as many as 71% of Republicans (Hagen, 2021), underscores how political and social tensions are likely to continue in the coming years and demonstrates the need to understand how supposedly fringe beliefs can become mainstream.

My colleague's early response nonetheless reflects the general attitude that many people shared at the time about the militia movement as a whole: that militia members are scant social outcasts on the fringes of society, "crackpots" who have little importance or social influence. There has been a complementary tendency in academic circles to downplay the study of militias and similar groups, and that tendency has historically also existed in law

DOI: 10.4324/9781003361657-1

enforcement circles. Even when militia plots have been foiled by arrests, we've collectively tended to think about them as social flukes rather than examining how they may fit with broader patterns of political support. Failure to do so has impaired our ability to anticipate and prevent militia violence.

It has only been in the last few years that our discussion of national security and terrorism has started to consider the role of domestic extremists—those radicalized within—rather than thinking about extremism as something that could only originate from an outside or a "foreign" influence. The first concerted development of new policies and programs to address domestic extremism came on President Biden's first full day in office, just 15 days after the attack on the Capitol, when he identified it as our "most urgent terrorism threat" (The White House, 2021). His 2022 *United We Stand* initiative is a developing but unique effort to address how domestic extremism negatively influences social media, information streams, and social unity.

Research for the Book

I have been systematically studying the militia movement for much longer than these recent concerns, since 2008, and have been arguing since that time that militia members are barometers for political currents that extend well beyond those groups' official membership ranks. Based on my research, I believe that many members have traditionally been not more fervent but merely more comfortable publicly espousing ideas that are shared by many political conservatives and that are deeply embedded in our collective national mythos. Pundits continued to laugh at the prospect of a Donald Trump Presidency well into election night in November 2016, but I told my previous spring semester students in a class titled "The Social Psychology of Prejudice" that they should prepare themselves for that inevitability. Trump, of course, did win his election, galvanized militias and related actors, and dramatically reshaped the Republican Party.

There were clear indications among militias and similar groups that this outcome was likely long before it came to fruition. My own insights came from direct interactions with militia members, rather than assessments merely of their online activities or analyses of only the militia units that have been arrested and charged with various crimes. I conducted more than 300 hours of ethnographic research with various militia groups—primarily in Michigan—across different types of events that allowed for nuanced, longitudinal observations. Some events were open to the public and the media while others were private. From 2008 to 2011, I observed members respond to a variety of both social and personal issues and talked with them about how they processed each event. I observed how they interacted with each other, with the media, with their families, and, occasionally, with law enforcement or politicians. I conducted 40 formal, in-depth interviews with members during that time and countless informal interviews with other members and non-member family and friends. Militia members also gave me a trove of unique archival data. Some data included training and other tactical information, especially from the Southeast Michigan Volunteer Militia, whose materials have been modified or outright copied by many militia organizations across the country. Some of the data came directly from major militia founder Norm Olson and concerned the founding of the modern militia movement and his influence within it.

After 2011, I continued to monitor many of the groups and individual members I had interacted with during my fieldwork, but my observations moved more explicitly into militias' online activities. Online spaces became more crucial to these groups during this time as militia units increased their coordination and communication across state lines. Facebook was most groups' platform of choice until they were forced off of that site in 2020. I have also continued case study analyses of some militias while consulting with United States (US) Congress, lawyers, law enforcement agencies, action groups, and journalists seeking to understand militias and their risks.

Understanding the Militia

People usually want to know how I became interested in studying these groups, and that information is also important for framing my own positionality relative to the data in this book. When taking social science classes as an undergraduate, I noticed that very little serious work existed on groups broadly labeled "right-wing." My background had, in many ways, been a liability on Vanderbilt University's wealthy campus where, even a decade into a program designed to bring first generation and other underrepresented students to campus, the average family income of students who benefit from that program is 174% of the US median household income (Rothbaum & Edwards, 2019; Ten Years of Opportunity Vanderbilt, 2019). I had limited friend groups because I couldn't afford regular excursions off campus and was often reticent to speak up in classes because my examples and cultural reference points were so different than those of most of my peers. When I began studying social movements, I nonetheless started to understand that my background was in fact a powerful cultural tool that I could use to ask questions from a different standpoint than many other researchers. My background continues to give me a greater and more organic understanding of the cultural scripts underlying conservative values and practices that many social scientists can only approach from a pure outsider perspective.

I grew up in rural East Tennessee, where, in the mid-1980s, my family's electricity might be off for more of the day than it was on, and where there were high odds of waking up to discover that my grandfather's cows had again slipped their fence to graze in our yard. Although my parents had aspirations for me to attend college from a young age, neither was able to clearly communicate what that meant. My father did not have running water in his house for many years, growing up in a building that had originally been a two-car garage before my grandfather converted it, only years later adding a bathroom and a sitting room. Today, my father lives in that house once more with a portrait of Jesus and a sign for Hornady ammunition hanging above the kitchen table on the wood-paneled walls. My mother's farming family was better off, having inherited land originally obtained as a grant to an ancestor who was a Union officer in the Civil War, land likely stolen from the Cherokee. My mom attended college, but not until after she was already married at 18 years old. She never lived on campus nor had many of the usual experiences of most college students.

Neither of my parents could have envisioned where my academic trajectory would lead, but both were adamant that they wanted me to have better educational experiences than their own in that community. They saved and spent nearly every spare cent to send me to a small Christian school run by a Southern Baptist church, where I stayed through middle school. There, I learned many lessons that resonate in other rural, conservative areas—lessons about hard work, individualism, and the need to acquire a variety of competencies because there are very few people you can ever truly count on besides yourself.

An emphasis on self-defense is a natural outgrowth of this kind of thinking, and, perhaps especially in places with more cows than people, conversations about self-defense rapidly turn to firearms. There were several firearms in my house growing up, and from a very young age, I was shown how to safely handle them, but only ever under adult supervision. My father carried his sidearm fairly regularly, keeping it tucked in his waistband on more than one occasion when people drunkenly came into our property well after dark, but only firing it once to kill a rabid coyote that was trying to eat my pet rabbit through its hutch. Some of my other relatives still hunt to put food on the table, bagging deer and turkeys, mostly, and freezing some of it for year-round use. I never hunted but did obtain my concealed carry permit in Tennessee as soon as I was legally able to do so. I rarely carried a pistol but admittedly felt relieved to have access to it when my neighbor and his friends sometimes pretended to confuse my apartment door with his when I was living alone after college.

Well before that point, however, I had started questioning many of the principles my hometown community had tried to instill, perhaps in part because some of those lessons were so extreme. In third grade, for example, my small, parochial school's class was made to watch a film that argued the Gulf War was a clear sign of the End of Times, using an interpretation of the biblical book of Revelations that insists that the prophesied return of Jesus Christ will occur through social strife and violent apocalypse. My class, as eight- and nine-year-olds, was told that we needed to ensure our own salvation and prepare for the world to end. When the US instead withdrew troops from the Gulf, effectively ending active hostilities, no explanations, corrections, or even follow-up predictions came from the school. This lack of consistency, alongside the supposed urgency of the original prediction, made me skeptical of future messaging not only from the school but also from the broader community that echoed similar ideas and underlying moralizing.

My skepticism evolved to outright rejection in future years when certain community leaders expressed blatant hypocrisy on topics like gender: when, for example, I was 14 and the pastor at my parents' church held a sermon about the proper place of women, insisting it was acceptable for women to go to college and to work but that they should stop and be full-time mothers once married. This lecture was directed at a congregation where the pastor's own wife fit that description, but other families were financially unable to make that transition even if they had wanted to do so. Yet no one in the congregation seemed to take issue with the sermon or their inability to follow this divine command. Even though I rejected much of the messaging from this environment, being surrounded with it for so long still allows me to see and analyze relevant cultural patterns in which many individuals who have never been part of organized conservative groups participate. Many are the same patterns that are now increasingly understood to be fostering exclusionary white Christian nationalism in our national politics.

My own perspective continued to broaden when I attended public high school, where not every student was so embedded in evangelical culture. The school was especially strong in basic science classes that taught logical reasoning, evidence evaluation, and critical thinking skills. My Advanced Placement US History teacher there nonetheless still taught that the Civil War was absolutely not about slavery, a reminder of how certain narratives remained fundamental to the cultural scripts in my hometown.

My goal is not to demonize this teacher, others from my hometown, or the militia members I have studied. Rather, I think it's crucial to present them all as both real and complicated individuals who are in part shaped by their environments, just as we would tend to do when studying groups with whom social scientists are more likely to be politically aligned. This nuanced approach helps us better understand militia motivations, contradictions, and potential dangers. It also helps us understand what we have in common with them, thus—hopefully—giving us potential in-roads for lessening polarization and potential violence.

Plan for the Book

It is nonetheless important to emphasize that different militia units, and even individuals within a given unit, can have different motivations or base characteristics from one another. My goal is to focus on both overarching patterns and "magnified moments" (Hochschild, 1994)—ungeneralizable but meaningful instances that help us better understand the militia movement as a whole. In Chapter 1, I define modern militias, analyze their key ideas and practices, and assess some of the core characteristics of militia groups versus other, similar groups. I introduce this material first so that readers can have a shared understanding of these concepts before approaching the more historical and theoretical material. Chapter 2 details the history leading up to the modern militia movement. While in many ways the modern movement is its own conceptual beast, there are important historical events and earlier groups that are essential for understanding why militias look and function the way they do in the contemporary United States.

Chapters 3 and 4 use unique data that I received directly from Michigan Militia founder Norm Olson and his personal archive to revisit the birth of the movement. Examining how key events played out from his perspective allows a fuller understanding of the movement's early actions and goals. I analyze how Olson and other actors engage with events that were necessary for the movement's foundation in Chapter 3 and, in Chapter 4, events responsible for its near dissolution following the Oklahoma City bombing. Both chapters show how Olson's personal religious framework, which centers America as a Christian nation uniquely favored by God, was important to the early movement's identity,

Chapter 5 analyzes how the concepts of nostalgia and settler colonialism influence militia understandings of nationalism. Nostalgia is a wistful reembrace for a past that never was and, when wedded to archetypes of strong and brave white men who are at the center of our mythologized national origin story, explains much of the ideological underpinnings of militia practices. Settler masculinity and a rural mentality provide a framework that avoids reductive explanations that attribute all militia action merely to overt racism and help better predict militia activity and threats in the future.

Chapter 6 turns to the recent years of the militia movement, building on the theoretical framework of the prior chapter to help contextualize its actions and tracing its development after Olson's direct influence faded away. I detail three case studies of militias whose members were accused of various criminal activities both to explore the trajectory of the movement leading up to January 6th and to detail the potential for violent plotting from militia actors. This chapter also considers likely future militia action in the context of their beliefs and political priorities.

In the Conclusion, I focus on potential practical lessons about managing dangerous militia actors. I suggest a set of risk factors based on my years of observation and my interactions with various law enforcement agencies that may help identify which units merit the most investigation and other resources. I also offer suggestions for some starting best practices for law enforcement and community actors who are worried about future militia violence.

Throughout this book, I use pseudonyms for my participants except in cases where they have already made their comments or actions public and are easily identifiable. Unless I note otherwise, readers should assume that interviewees I quote in these pages are both white and male because this demographic represents the majority of the movement and thus the majority of my interviewees. I generally refrain from identifying specific militia units or other groups by name unless there has been public coverage of their actions. This is for two reasons. First, some units I conducted fieldwork with operate privately and nonviolently, and naming them would breach the confidentiality afforded to most research participants through both federal and institutional policies. Second, there is a risk of amplifying the platform and reach of dangerous units. While it may be unlikely that readers of these pages will be looking for their own militia unit to join, avoiding specific identifications further limits that risk.

References

Farley, R. (2022, March 21). How many died as a result of Capitol Riot? *FactCheck.Org*. www.factcheck.org/2021/11/how-many-died-as-a-result-of-capitol-riot/

Hagen, L. (2021, December 28). Poll: A third of Americans question legitimacy of Biden victory nearly a year since Jan. 6. *U.S. News*. www.usnews.com/news/politics/articles/2021-12-28/poll-a-third-of-americans-question-legitimacy-of-biden-victory-nearly-a-year-since-jan-6

Hall, M., Gould, S., Harrington, R., Shamsian, J., Haroun, A., Ardrey, T., & Snodgrass, E. (2023, February 16). At least 1,003 people have been charged in the Capitol insurrection so far. This searchable table shows them all. *Insider*. www.insider.com/all-the-us-capitol-pro-trump-riot-arrests-charges-names-2021-1

Hochschild, A. R. (1994). The commercial spirit of intimate life and the abduction of feminism: Signs from women's advice books. *Theory, Culture & Society*, 11(2), 1–24. https://doi.org/10.1177/026327694011002001

Mascaro, L., Fox, B., & Baldor, L. (2021, April 10). 'Clear the Capitol,' Pence pleaded, timeline of riot shows. *Los Angeles Times*. www.latimes.com/world-nation/story/2021-04-10/clear-the-capitol-pence-pleaded-timeline-of-riot-shows

Rothbaum, J., & Edwards, A. (2019, September 10). Survey redesigns make comparisons to years before 2017 difficult. *Census.Gov*. Retrieved July 26, 2023, from www.census.gov/library/stories/2019/09/us-median-household-income-not-significantly-different-from-2017.html

Rubin, O., Mallin, A., & Steakin, W. (2022, January 4). By the numbers: How the Jan. 6 investigation is shaping up 1 year later. *ABC News*. https://abcnews.go.com/US/numbers-jan-investigation-shaping-year/story?id=82057743

Ten Years of Opportunity Vanderbilt. (2019, May 2). https://web.archive.org/web/20190502164205/https://giving.vanderbilt.edu/oppvu/ten-years/

The White House. (2021, June 15). FACT SHEET: National strategy for countering domestic terrorism. *The White House*. www.whitehouse.gov/briefing-room/statements-releases/2021/06/15/fact-sheet-national-strategy-for-countering-domestic-terrorism/

1 The Modern US Militia Movement
Member's Motivations, Beliefs, and Practices

Six men dressed in camouflage and carrying a backpack holding what I know is about 50 pounds of gear (including a pocket constitution, ammunition, and a first aid kit) jog across an uneven dirt path, pitted with potholes, soggy, and smelling slightly of rot under a cool October drizzle. The man at the front of the group turns his head slightly and jokingly tells the others, "This is Amy. Don't mess with her!" as I step off the side of the path into a dormant soybean field to give them ample room to pass. I'm not entirely sure if he is trying to tell them that I can protect myself or that he would stand up for me if need be, but I laugh and raise my hand in brief greeting to the others who are attempting to complete a timed 2-mile run as part of the requirements for membership in a Michigan militia unit.

I continue my trek toward this unit's main training ground, smoke from the struggling campfire already reaching my nose well before I can see it. When I arrive, one member is near the fires, setting up a camp stove where he'll later cook a meal of hamburgers and canned baked beans to share with most of those in attendance. Two members are casually listening in to an interview that another is having with a major news outlet's crew that has come to do a report on the modern militia movement. Another half dozen or so people are milling about, chatting, or showing off newly purchased gear. Further away, one of the unit leader's children eagerly awaits her turn at the shooting range. She's an experienced shooter, though she still only pulls the trigger under heavy supervision. It looks like she may have to be extra patient today because two adult male members are obviously enjoying this month's special shoot, where targets are gory-printed zombies in honor of upcoming Halloween.

The joggers soon return to the campsite, one of them—slender, recently former military, but a heavy smoker—doubles over and struggles to catch his breath for several minutes. He and the others managed to pass this stage of the qualification. Later, they would also have to prove their shooting acumen by hitting at least eight of ten shots from 100 yards away with their personal rifle in under two minutes. They will have to leave the zombies to other shooters, however, and instead use a traditional nine-inch bullseye target to verify their accuracy. First though, everyone gathers for a basic compass training course.

DOI: 10.4324/9781003361657-2

Figure 1.1 Pumpkins—left over from Halloween—being repurposed as targets during a November training.
Source: Photo by the author.

A Navy veteran explains how to use a compass and a map together and gives everyone a short assignment to locate an empty backpack that he had previously placed on the property so that we could practice what he taught. I participate in this activity and watch as some groups complete the task quickly while others struggle. My own partner, a young guy in his twenties who is attending a militia gathering for the first time, keeps forgetting our goal and instead rambles at me about beer and his new business even though there seems to be no connection between those two topics. At least it has stopped raining.

After lunch, which, as it turns out, includes veggie burgers that the chef brought because he believed there were high odds that at least one of the news crew would be a vegetarian, two long-time members construct "field ready shelters" to demonstrate how they could protect themselves against the elements without full camping gear. One shelter is a poncho propped up with sticks. It passes unit leaders' approval, but barely, as one says he'd rather sleep in a waterproof sleeping bag that he didn't have to worry about blowing away. The other shelter is a sturdier version of the same concept. Its builder's pride at having taken advantage of trees and long grass to expertly camouflage it from the view of the dirt path quickly disappears when another leader points out he's positioned it so that wind will blow "all the goodness" from the latrine directly at it. Everyone gives a goodhearted chuckle before separating, with some preparing for more zombie culling and others for storytelling by the now-extinguished fire pit.

This selection from my field notes is a fairly standard representation of what most militia trainings looked and felt like during my ethnography with them. The aura is not typically one of anger or anxiety but instead of recreation and comradery. Long-time affiliates continue to participate and, in some cases, demonstrate their skills. Newcomers are looking for a place to belong. Bystanders are observing and being observed. All in attendance are engaged in different but complementary activities that may defy stereotypes of militias as they are usually presented in popular culture or news stories of their actions.

On the other hand, some militia members and units do much more closely fit the stereotypes. One meeting I attended at a different unit leader's house, for example, was much less relaxed. Everyone present spoke in hushed whispers and looked around suspiciously. They stopped talking altogether, and some stood at attention when their leader, who had no military experience or rank, entered the room. There were no organized activities, simply the promise of a meeting that never seemed to start even as the leader kept pointlessly drifting through the door, clearly enjoying the attention he garnered every time he did so. There was no joking, only an uneasiness that was as unmistakable as the aroma of dog urine that putrefied the room. The only child present, a nine-year-old girl, voiced the discomfort that everyone else was ignoring, whispering to me, "I don't want to be here. My mom doesn't like it when I come here."

What Are Domestic Militias?

Scholars prefer to have parsimonious definitions of concepts that they research, meaning definitions that make sense and that clearly capture some phenomenon in a way that does not overlap with other phenomena. Some concepts, like the militia movement with its remarkably disparate parts, escape these efforts, however. A classic example is the idea of consciousness. There are formal definitions of this term, but precisely how we define it and measure it continues to be a bit murky: how exactly do thoughts, dreams, and feelings emerge from the physical states of our gray matter? Some philosophers even debate whether plants have a kind of consciousness, depending on precisely how we characterize the idea (Marder, 2013).

Defining social concepts can have similar challenges. Socioeconomic status, for example, is a concept that reflects one's general social standing, largely with regard to one's finances, but it may nonetheless be measured in a variety of ways: through income, wealth, education, job type, or several other metrics. All these markers hit on similar ideas but have slightly different implications for what socioeconomic status means in a given study.

People are, in short, complicated and difficult to parsimoniously define, as are the societies, communities, and groups to which they belong. Group structures and values can change over time, while other groups can maintain consistency even as individual participants desist and new members join. As an outgrowth of this definitional complexity, some researchers define militias and their members very broadly, using the term to refer to almost any armed person or to many conservative political organizations whose members at least occasionally carry firearms. Other people define militias very narrowly, for example, by using the term only with groups who themselves identify as militias.

Centrality of the Second Amendment

I aim for a definition that takes a more nuanced approach such that, for me, militias are distinct groups within a broader ideological spectrum, yet the boundaries between militias and other similar groups remain both permeable and hazy, rather than fixed and easily identifiable. This is especially true over time as the salience of certain political and cultural issues ebbs and flows. What remains consistent and is the core defining feature of militias is how they centralize gun rights in their narratives of what it means to be a good American.[1] Militias prioritize the Second Amendment right to bear arms and exercise it joyfully at every opportunity. From their perspective, the Second Amendment crucially distinguishes the US from other countries because, they say, it allows citizens to defend themselves against the prospect of government tyranny. Tyranny in this framework includes not only the threat of illegitimate physical force against citizens but also various theoretical incursions on other inalienable rights, especially those likewise delineated in the Constitution and its amendments.

Militia members see themselves as super citizens, as true patriots who honor the Constitution and the Founding Fathers. They believe militias are civic-minded organizations whose fundamental goal is protecting not only themselves but also their broader communities and their nation from threats against the American way of life. Their identified threats include government overreach and even foreign invasion, but much of their preparation is more practical. It includes things like encouraging members to have plans to sustain themselves and help others during natural disasters, car accidents, and other emergencies that are comparatively mundane relative to the catastrophizing about governmental threats. Most militia members believe that community awareness of their activities helps encourage other non-militia citizens to remember their obligations and rights of citizenship, even as they distrust the general public to adopt or internalize these ideals en masse. As Jack, a 38-year-old farmer, told me regarding the role of his militia unit:

> There's a lot of humanitarian things that happen, charity, just taking care of your community, and other people. And education. Trying to educate the sheep, if you will, as to what's going on around them. And maybe get their gumption up a little bit, you know?

Militias are so invested in embodying and enacting the Second Amendment that they regularly and collectively train, practice, and have other group events where firearms have been both the key point and key outcome of the gathering. Some militia events, for example, feature not only target shooting practice and friendly marksmanship competitions but also carrying unloaded weapons across varied terrain while moving as a cohesive unit, an activity that is typically of special interest to men without prior military service. Other gatherings involve unit leaders, usually military veterans, hosting detailed demonstrations on how to break down certain weapons for cleaning, explaining the function of each part in the process. Lessons from all such events further solidify the importance of firearm handling not only for the stated militia goals of fostering self- and community defense but also for providing concrete activities and discussion points over which members bond through their shared action.

Who Are Militia Members?

Bonding is also facilitated by the fact that most members share core demographic characteristics, even though there can be large variation in their socioeconomic and educational statuses and in their general life experiences. Members are predominantly white men who range in age from about 18 to 65 or even a bit older in some units, though most members are in their twenties and thirties. Most militia members are "normal" people who have jobs, families, and other responsibilities. They are not the stereotypical off-the-grid hermits who are disengaged from society; instead, they are people who strongly want to influence their society—the way it looks, functions, and even thinks. This often leads to over- rather than under-engagement with certain societal structures, especially when members rely heavily on social media and dubious news sources to understand and influence the world around them. This makes them prone to both misinformation and echo chambers such that they find it increasingly difficult to accept challenges to their worldview.

Echo chamber effects are often amplified by the fact that most militia units are rather small and insular. Units can vary in size, ranging from just three people to several hundred, but most maintain somewhere between eight and twenty members who consistently attend unit functions. Very large militias like the Oath Keepers are the exception, rather than the rule, for how militias structure themselves. These large organizations often require members to pay dues and encourage them to purchase various group-branded merchandise so that core leadership can financially support themselves without working another job. Dues or other funding sources are incredibly uncommon in most community-based militias, where members are instead responsible for paying for their own gear and where leaders shoulder fees for printing materials or occasional supplies for group activities. Organizations that accept dues or have outside funders are probably more susceptible to having their group character shaped by people or organizations that provide them with large influxes of cash.

Very large organizations may also attempt to enact hierarchical national structures with visible leaders (like Stewart Rhodes) who at least claim to set the agenda for Oath Keepers across the country. The reality is more complicated. Some units, for example, who have adopted the Oath Keepers moniker have certainly identified themselves exclusively as a branch of the national organization. Others using the name, however, sew Oath Keepers patches on their gear and pay dues to the national organization but only loosely follow any instructions from national Oath Keepers leadership. Several units I encountered in my original fieldwork had a name that reflected their community or geographical location and simultaneously identified as Oath Keepers or Three Percenters as a kind of double (or triple) affirmation of the principles they believed the names collectively reflected. In another example, members of the Ohio State Regular Militia did not include "Oath Keepers" as part of their formal name yet considered themselves dues-paying affiliates of that organization as they followed Rhodes' incitement to invade the US Capitol on January 6, 2021. Additionally, because so many militias and their members build their identity on individualism and defying formal authority, it is incredibly difficult for a unit of any size or affiliation to successfully maintain a single, consistent leader. Militias are, across the board, hallmarked by strong personalities that instigate infighting and stymie any real efforts at an effective national militia coalition.

Some militia units include women in their ranks, typically the wives or girlfriends of some of the members.[2] Women who do participate typically hold high status in their units. Male members tend to be frustrated that militia participation is not a greater priority to the women in their lives, and this amplifies their respect for the women who do participate. Their respect nonetheless exists alongside misogynistic endorsement of commonplace sexist stereotypes. For example, militia members usually believe most journalists will misrepresent their actions and are careful to vet members of the press before allowing them at unit functions. Most journalists who attend are male, but one attractive female journalist who had negatively covered some other conservative organizations in a different country was allowed to attend one training during my fieldwork with little pushback, with one unit leader commenting, "I don't care what comes out of her mouth as long as she looks like that." From my own perspective, interacting long term with male militia members, the sexism I experience from them is no greater than what I also regularly experience from male academics and substantially less than what I experienced growing up in an evangelical community.

Some majority-white militias include members of color but well below their demographic representation in the overall population. Most units have zero members of color. Some have one or two, usually Black but sometimes Latino members, who are frequently made highly visible whenever the unit appears publicly or posts public photos of their gatherings. Units that highlight non-white membership are engaging in tokenism, whereby a non-white member is essentially being asked to carry out a large symbolic duty. They are supposed to represent how the unit must logically not be racist if they

14 *The Modern US Militia Movement*

include a member of color while often simultaneously visually implying that the group is more diverse than it is. These tokenistic efforts are, in my observations, often well intentioned on the part of white members, who hope to attract more members of color to the unit, yet tokenism still otherizes, or marks as fundamentally different, that member and others like him. It signals, whether consciously or not, that members of color may be valued more for their perceived race than for their skills, ideas, or individual identity. This superficial focus is especially evident in units that regularly make their members of color visible to the media or in promotional materials without also giving them leadership positions, as is almost always the case in the mixed-race units I have observed.

Militias that are not majority-white do exist, including and perhaps most notably the Not Fucking Around Coalition (NFAC) that emerged, largely in the South, after two white male vigilantes murdered a Black jogger named Ahmaud Arbery (Wright, 2020). Black militias feel different than predominantly white militias, in no small part because they have tended to muster specifically in response to Black civilians being murdered by police or in defiance of local efforts to defend Confederate monuments. Much more robust research is needed on Black militias, but based largely on news and social media reports, it currently appears that, relative to their white counterparts,

Figure 1.2 A view inside one of the COVID-19 protests at the Michigan State Capitol building. It features Paul Bellar, who was later among those accused of plotting to kidnap Governor Gretchen Whitmer.

Source: Photo courtesy of Daniel Hud.

Black militias more typically rely primarily on open calls for support at protests and marches rather than on ongoing pre-event training and organizing.

Some NFAC members and supporters distance themselves from the legacy of the Black Panthers (Tripathi, 2020) and yet echo the Panthers' statements that Black folks must arm and protect themselves against growing white supremacist elements because the police will not extend them the same protections afforded to white people (Chavez et al., 2020). Law enforcement agents, in turn, certainly respond to Black militia members with substantially more fear and aggression than they direct toward white militia members. Agents aggressively monitor or shut down Black militias' activities and seem quick to arrest their members (Carless & Stephens, 2021). While white militias do sometimes receive police attention, it is often only after situations dramatically escalate and violence occurs. Reports indicate, for example, that the Federal Bureau of Investigation (FBI) actually asked Michigan State Police to allow armed, mostly white protestors, including militia members, to enter the state capitol building during the now-infamous lockdown protests of 2020 (Schakohl, 2022), something that would have been inconceivable had the angry mob been predominately Black. Another notable example is how police told Kyle Rittenhouse that they "appreciate[d]" him and other armed civilians, giving him a water bottle shortly before he fatally shot two people and injured another in Kenosha, Wisconsin, during the protest over Jacob Blake's death at the hands of other officers (Williams, 2020).

Even when they are *un*armed, Black protestors may face more forceful police presences than armed, white mobs. One such contrast is how US Capitol police responded aggressively in May 2020 to peaceful Black Lives Matter activists who were protesting George Floyd's murder, then responded relatively complacently to mostly white insurrectionists less than a year later during the January 6, 2021, coup attempt (Chavez, 2021). Various law enforcement agencies downplayed the threat of that insurrection, even though its emerging plans had been discussed in public online forums. Some agencies were reticent to respond even as those threats came to fruition. This insurrectionist mob, which included militia members, was more than 90% white, based on people charged for crimes due to their involvement (Katz, 2022). The close connection between whiteness and the militia movement is not new, but the racial skew of January 6th participants underscores how analyzing whiteness is crucial for understanding armed collective action.

What Do Members Believe?

Racism

Militias are, in my experience, rarely racist at the organizational level, meaning that racism, overt embrace of white supremacy, or explicit efforts to exclude people of color from full civic participation are not unit-level goals. Individual militia members similarly express overt racism or racial resentment only rarely. Members are, in my estimation, no more racist or otherwise exclusionary than any other group composed of the same conglomeration of white, middle-aged men, and most of their racism consists of belief in still-pervasive racial stereotypes that are falsely endorsed across the political spectrum (Hughey, 2012).

My characterization of militia members contrasts the recent tendency to refer to militias as equal partners in a broader "white power movement" (Belew, 2018), and this is not simply a linguistic point of disagreement or pedantic academic debate. Social movements have different actors with different tactics, but all share the same core goal. A white power movement does exist across various neo-Nazi and similar groups whose shared goal is, explicitly, the maintenance of white supremacy, and different groups within that movement vary in their endorsements of violence and other tactics to achieve this end. There is a separate militia movement. Their core goals, in contrast, are about stopping potential government tyranny. They do not intentionally center whiteness or its preservation. Showing up armed to monitor ballot boxes with the intention of protecting election integrity may nonetheless and reasonably be intimidating to voters who are not white and thus, in practice, further one of white supremacy's aims to nullify the civic participation of people of color. Asserting that such actions make militias part of a coordinated and concerted white power movement, however, confuses the distinction between white supremacy and white supremacists.

White supremacists are people who seek the primacy of whiteness. It is an active and often proactively violent identity. White supremacy is a much broader system that has been created and maintained over time through ingrained social patterning and practices (Bonilla-Silva, 1997, 2006). Many who benefit from white supremacy are passive recipients who do not intentionally contribute to ongoing racial disparities but who also do nothing to ameliorate those disparities. White supremacy is why there are enormous racial gaps in our educational, health, and criminal justice systems. People of color have higher risk factors for negative outcomes in these systems that have been shaped by ongoing social practices: factors like redlining, higher mortgage rates, and other barriers to intergenerational wealth attainment and transmission (Conley, 1999); factors like greater exposure to pollution and environmental stressors combined with lower access to quality medical care (Morello-Frosch & Lopez, 2006); and factors like over policing and criminalization of Black communities combined with more limited access to effective legal advice (Pager, 2009). As author Nels Abbey (2023) notes:

> White supremacy is not just a klansman burning a cross. . . . White supremacy is not just 14 words,[3] it shapes what is seen as worthy history and what is dismissed as 'wokery': who is viewed as worthy of respect and empathy, and who are dismissed as grifters with a 'victimhood mentality.'

White people can perpetuate white supremacy without that being an intentional, or even conscious, goal. They may, for example, make decisions that are objectively in their own best interest about where to purchase a house while inadvertently and perhaps even unknowingly contributing to practices like gentrification that undermine Black communities and economic prospects. White people making such decisions in their individual best interests are likely not doing so with the goal of displacing or harming their Black neighbors, thus not qualifying as white suprema*cists*. Yet they still contribute to white suprema*cy* as an aggregate and patterned practice that has very real negative consequences for people of color. It is worth reiterating that this outcome can occur even if the white people in question do not intend this outcome and even if they are unaware of gentrification and their role in it. In the same way, militia members and others may genuinely believe, for example, that undocumented migrants unilaterally pose legitimate national security threats without being aware of complex immigration and refugee policies that, in practice, have clearly contributed to perpetuating white supremacy.

Contrary to proclamations of some self-described "anti-woke activists," recognition that social structures and practices impact different racial groups differently does not mean that all white people are under attack. It likewise does not mean they are all white suprema*cists* or part of an intentional white power movement. Practically speaking, if our goal is to promote inclusion and equality and to remove white supremacy's impediments to success, there is a very different logical starting point for interventions with people who are overt, happy supremacists versus people who, to varying degrees, unwittingly support and perpetuate white suprema*cy* as a structure.

Equating white supremacy and white supremacists downplays the potential extraordinary harms from supremacist actors who want to commit violence and disruption in non-white communities and on non-white bodies. The popularity of this conflation makes even the words "race" and "racism" anathema in some circles, eliminating the possibility of addressing racist structures. Fallaciously categorizing militias as intentional white supremacists also facilitated dismissing them and their ideas as being social outliers, rather than understanding how they represent much deeper social currents about government trust and political anxieties. Not wanting to believe the vast pervasiveness of nativist nationalism among US citizens was a major reason that many people were shocked to see a Trump Presidency and, later, the January 6th Capitol incursion.

Conflating suprema*cy* and suprema*cists* in other words helps us ignore how "normal" white Americans, including white liberals (Hughey, 2012), fall far short of the overt and violent racism promulgated by white supremacists but share racial stereotypes and privileges that contribute to ongoing oppression today. Discounting racism that is less visible than the old-fashioned Jim Crow variety leads to inaction to stop it, on both interpersonal and more systemic social dimensions. This is a similar process to how people from US states outside the South sometimes claim racism does not exist in their region and that the South is an outlier that is behind the social progress already accomplished in the rest of the nation. We know racism exists everywhere, as recent high-profile examples of police brutality, among others, painfully show, but the South becomes a specter, an easy scapegoat because of its history that allows deflection from very real problems of racism in other places. The possibility of mass, and in many ways, mundane, radicalization of broad segments of citizens is precisely why it is necessary to have a more nuanced understanding of how seemingly rare ideas and practices are often much more pervasive than they may seem.

Our public educational system bears much of the responsibility for limiting white people's understanding of the full scope of racism and its effects. History lessons typically fail to provide full explorations of our national origin that delve into how our collective missteps inform the present day, instead focusing only on our perceived accomplishments. We do not have robust national data on precisely how many classrooms continue to omit lessons that would help our populace better understand ongoing racism and other social problems, but as journalist Nikita Stewart notes (2019), "Unlike math and reading, states are not required to meet academic content standards for teaching social studies and United States history." Stewart argues that "slavery illiteracy" is a systematic problem in our educational system and cites an earlier study that found that, among other issues, only 8% of 1,000 surveyed high school students identified slavery as the Civil War's main cause (SPLC, 2018). Education about Indigenous genocide is similarly minimal and glossed over in favor of stories that highlight the accomplishments of the nascent nation and its founders (Diamond, 2019).

Even when curricula do include some of the more negative elements of our national history, they seem to rarely explain those elements' ongoing consequences, including how different economies and social conditions continue to exist for different demographic groups due to this discriminatory legacy. This omission was highlighted, for example, when Tim, a 39-year-old delivery driver, insisted during my interview:

> There are very few mistakes in the Constitution and the Declaration of Independence. The one about three-fifths people is one of them. It was a compromise because the thinking of the day was, you know, the slaves are property. So it was a compromise they made at the time. The majority of the founders, if not all of them, believed that it was a mistake. But it was, you know, it was a mistake that was made to get our country started.

At the time of my interview with him, Tim minimized slavery in the interest of a supposedly greater good without recognizing how many people were excluded from this ostensibly utilitarian calculus. He also still attempted to affirm the moral superiority of the Founding Fathers as they made this "compromise." I've continued to watch Tim's interactions on various social media channels in recent years, and he is still one of the loudest voices opposing Affirmative Action policies or, alternatively, supporting legislation requiring voters have official government identification. From his perspective, his policy support or lack thereof is rooted in fairness, in ideas of holding everyone to the same standard for striving toward the American Dream. But his analyses miss how both historical and ongoing discrimination impact people of color today, leading to hampered odds of success in ways that are not as visible or visceral to people who are not on the receiving end of discrimination. It is easy for men like Tim to misunderstand both the intent and outcome of such policies, given not only those policies' absence from formal education but also the pervasive misinformation about them that is intended to make people like this delivery driver feel like he is being unfairly treated.

States have further limited formal instruction about ongoing social oppression and possible solutions in the past few years, a trend amplified by protests and outright intimidation of school boards and other entities involved in curriculum adoption. Seven states have banned "critical race theory," and another 16 states have bills to do so in their legislative process (*States That Have Banned*, 2023). Most legislation in question does not actually address the social-legal theory formally titled "Critical Race Theory" (CRT) but instead effectively limits very broad and important discussions of racial equity (Kahn, 2021). Twenty-four states have proposed at least one version of a "don't say gay" bill that prohibits classroom discussions about LGBTQ+ issues (Pendharkar, 2023), targeting education about other oppressed groups and their experiences. Schools that continue to teach only a selective history thus serve as a key pillar of the foundational ignorance that makes it very easy for relatively privileged people to overlook others' ongoing experiences of oppression. This is true even for people who may be very well-meaning, who do not openly deny continuing racism or other oppression, and who, during their own pursuit of the American Dream, genuinely want to believe social and economic conditions are better than they truly are. This is not to excuse people from seeking out more accurate understandings of both history and the social world around them but rather to say that white militia members are not outliers in terms of their limited understanding of racial dynamics or partial views of history. Their partial and often unnuanced view of the racist and other oppressive barriers that still exist today is shared well beyond their unit rosters and serves as a microcosm of much broader trends.

Citizenship and Politics

The Dream-informed desire to believe in a superior and equitable society where any person's possible achievements are limited only by their individual efforts is central to the militia mindset. Militia members see themselves both individually and collectively as super citizens who are the last line of defense preventing cultural slippage away from a promised land of opportunity and rely on a literal interpretation of the Constitution to support this framework. One long-time leader, for example, told me he believed the biggest problem facing the country was:

> The bending of words and the loss of meaning and the philosophy that there is no truth. You know? They would teach the Constitution as a living document that changes its mind and is affected by feelings. It's like, no, there's truths that are self-evident. Those words mean something, they're *self-evident* . . . it's not open to a lot of interpretation.

Militias have traditionally seen their role as opposing the development of an overly strong government that defies their understanding of the founders' intent. There have nonetheless been times when some units have primarily viewed themselves as a civilian extension of the government, supposedly working to instill law and order at the southern national border or to prevent general anarchy during times of mass protests or social unrest. This apparent contradiction in attitudes, where members fundamentally outwardly oppose the government while sometimes working to defend it, has been especially noticeable in recent years as more militias have openly shifted to a pro-law enforcement framework that pervades their statements and public actions.

Within militia members' worldview, this perspective is not so much a contradiction as it is an extension of their understanding of the "proper" role of government. They believe that the government, especially at the federal level, should be highly limited. They also believe that one of the few legitimate functions of the federal government is to protect the nation through military force. They cite the Constitution's granting of congressional power to maintain armies and a navy to protect against invasion. Police become an extension of that protectionist stance. Even as members maintain a distrust for policing as an institution that could enforce government overreach, militia members nonetheless tend to believe that most individual police officers are fundamentally good people working to defend law-abiding citizens against criminals and other threats. Local police, especially sheriffs, tend to have the greatest trust and respect among militia members because they see these officers as part of the local community and therefore as more loyal to it than other levels of law enforcement (Cooter, 2022a; Jackson, 2020).

Militia members do not believe, however, that having "good" police as protectors absolves them of their own imperative for self- and community defense. This is because they tend to believe that crime is always growing in both frequency and severity and that police ability to respond to these threats is limited by resources that were maliciously decreased by liberal politicians even before discussions of defunding garnered public attention in recent years. Carl, a 56-year-old IT professional, personalized this inability to rely on police as he related an interaction with anti-gun coworkers who said they would simply call the police if someone broke down their door at three in the morning:

> Okay, the police get there, what, in 10 minutes, 15 minutes? And if they only got there in three minutes, you're dead if he's—if he's armed and you're not. You know. Yeah, you would call the police, but that's not the only thing you would do if you want to live.

Political and social events of the last several years have amplified militia members' feelings of being under threat and needing to bolster possible avenues of self-defense. The sources of members' perceived threat are not new but have been amplified through COVID-19, economic uncertainty, and social unrest regarding these and other issues. The primary catalyst for these fears has been former President Donald Trump, who told the country that such fears were both urgent and well-founded. As political scientists Phillip Gorski and Samuel Perry observe, "Trump exchanged the dog whistles for a bullhorn" (2022, p. 77).

Many, but certainly not all, militia members I observed have supported Trump from the early days of his campaign, even while identifying as long-term Libertarians. Even before Trump, the vast majority of these members told me they "settled" for Republican candidates, at least in national contests, because they believed that supporting their preferred Libertarian or other third-party candidates would simply be "throwing away" their vote given those candidates' improbability of winning in our two-party system. Republicans, relative to Democrats, more closely represent militia members' values of small government, lower taxes, lenient gun laws, and stringent immigration policies. Yet militia members are typically hesitant to trust Republicans, too. Members often frame their support for Republicans as the lesser of two evils or as a vote *against* Democrats rather than as an unhindered endorsement for Republicans—an oppositional and polarized attitude that seemed to become substantially more prevalent in the US overall during and after Trump's campaign.

Nationalism and Nostalgia

Trump exacerbated the perceived differences between the Republican and Democratic parties by making repeated verbal and political attacks against a variety of targets. He did so in a way that echoed concerns that have long been sources of fear and motivation in militias and broader conservative circles. These attacks were not only rife with racism, xenophobia, and sexism but also gave listeners who see themselves as egalitarian some degree of plausible deniability of those exclusionary principles. Perhaps one of the better-known examples is Trump's reference to "bad hombres" during a 2016 debate. Although many commentators quickly called him out for implying that all undocumented migrants have nefarious intentions, many of his supporters nonetheless insisted that Trump was not referring to all migrants but only to the migrants who wanted to import drugs or otherwise harm productive citizens. Trump's various attacks included appeals to nationalism and rejections of the supposed Socialism or Communism that have become synonymous with conservative descriptions of the Democratic Party. People hearing Trump's attacks could then identify with those ostensibly patriotic principles (or at least claim to do so) while downplaying the messages' overt exclusions.

Trump's version of nationalism is nonetheless inherently exclusionary. It is not a mere love for country, what some scholars distinguish as "patriotism," but rather the stance that the US is fundamentally superior on every metric than any other nation and must be protected at all costs. This framework is a national version of otherization, where Americans are considered both inherently and unquestionably superior to citizens of other countries, even as questions remain about who is truly considered "American." White men are most easily accepted as "real" Americans because the myth of our national founding centers them as the ultimate models of citizenship (Gibson, 1994). Militias and related groups that host trainings and other events that regularly rehash this mythologized history further experience a deepening of their belief that people who spend time memorializing these stories are special and morally set apart from typical citizens who are, in members' view, oblivious to the need to protect their nation.

This is how nostalgia and self-described patriotism become weaponized against other people who have different priorities or ideas about how the country should be. People who look or sound different from this ideal may face near-constant challenges to their belonging, irrespective of their legal citizenship status. More easily seeing people who look different than this white ideal as less patriotic or as less committed to a unified country helps explain, for example, why we've seen more legal challenges to votes and voters in disproportionately Black and Latino districts (Phillips, 2020). Black people's contributions to the nation remain glaringly omitted from much of our official history, making them seem even further away from this patriotic American ideal, at least to those who do not seek out supplemental stories.

Even people who think about themselves as being welcoming, non-racist, or egalitarian can slip into an exclusionary mentality under the right circumstances. With encouragement from a President or another strong authority figure, it can be easy to start to believe that anyone with different ideas or practices could be a threat to one's supposed national supremacy, then to gradually move into a strong protectionism that rests on distrust of others. People attempting to hold onto the idea of national superiority and of their own relative power in that nation often act as gatekeepers. They think of themselves as the only true patriots and the only arbiters of whether other people sufficiently prove their Americanness. Another way of thinking of this mentality is how, rather ironically, many of the same people who oppose the spread of so-called wokeness—a term usually meant to disparage efforts to improve racial and gender inclusion—actually see themselves as the only truly "woke" citizens; they believe they are uniquely aware of the meaningful currents in society to which the masses are oblivious and that they alone are heroically fighting to preserve a nation under threat. When people who do not look like you or who have different values than you become so easily and frequently painted as some nefarious enemy, there is a real potential not only for polarization but also for possible violence that can flow from and be justified by that polarization.

Boy Scouts or Extremists? A Militia Typology

Militias receive enhanced attention after their alleged involvement in some violent plot or after their armed presence in public visually insinuates a threat of violence. Yet most militia members themselves say that the militia units that end up in the news are outliers who are unrepresentative of the overall movement. Historian Robert Churchill developed a typology that helps resolve this dispute while accurately categorizing militias and assessing their threat. This typology divides militias into two kinds: constitutionalist militias and millenarian militias.

Constitutionalist militias see themselves as representative of the movement while discounting other militias that do not follow their standards. They focus on camaraderie and a relatively open approach to sharing information by, for example, having public websites or social media pages that advertise and share pictures or videos from events that are open to the public. They insist that their actions are not only legal but in reverence of the Constitution, and they hope to encourage others to participate through their visibility. They do allow some members who are worried about career or other repercussions of militia participation to conceal their identities but assert that most members should not hide and instead should normalize their actions.

Constitutionalist militias typically revile conspiracy theories. One longtime leader even created some stylized YouTube videos to mock the usual cadence and content of conspiracists. In one, for example, he attempted to use absurdist humor to highlight conspiracists' logical fallacies by using visual styling common in other conspiratorial videos and pretending to encourage people to "wake up" to the conspiracy that powerful elites expect people to believe vanilla extract is cream colored even though vanilla beans are brown. Constitutionalist units are wary of the government but not necessarily hostile toward it. They have a large focus on history and incorporate lessons from the mythologized version of the Revolutionary War or other historical battles into their trainings. World War II maintains a special focus in these groups, both as a cautionary tale about oppressive governments and as an example of the heroism of the US military and its veterans, whom militia members frame as saving the free world from dictatorial collapse. These inspirational history lessons are selective and focus only on the triumphs of early patriots, with little acknowledgment and less discussion of any missteps or murky ethical territory in our collective past.

Many constitutionalist members are themselves former service members who remember their time in the military with more than a hint of wistfulness and nostalgia. They openly share stories about their time in the service, recalling even their negative experiences with a degree of fondness for the bonds they created during those times. Constitutionalist units tend to have veteran members in leadership positions because members without military experience revere veterans' knowledge and service and frequently say they are grateful for opportunities to learn military tactics and survival skills from them. Larry, a 42-year-old man who worked in IT, told me he and his wife both wanted to train with a militia unit while they increasingly transitioned into homesteading,

> because I had never served in the military, and since we are always trying to get more skills with, you know, putting solar up in the barn, doin' the animals or wood heating or all of the things that we like to do to kind of self-sustain, [be] self-reliant, that's one of the things that there's really no other place to go and get that. . . . How do you get some of those times to shoot—shoot and with people that really know the stuff with the larger guns? Or, you know, patrols or communication, things like that. You have to either be in the military or something or have someone that's been there and they're willing to teach you.

Veterans-as-leaders do plan events like brief land navigation courses in addition to lessons on firearm usage and safety, or teaching people how to best use maps and compasses, or how to use the length of their own stride to measure distances while traversing terrain. These leaders also typically take primary responsibility for keeping up with local and national political events of interest so that they can give advice to the entire unit about possible threats and suggested mitigations, including occasional protests or political actions. They, for example, encourage members to contact their congressional representatives to express their disapproval any time potential legislation that restricts gun rights is in the news and usually share a website where people may easily identify their representatives if they need help doing so.

Millenarian militias, in contrast, more closely match the stereotypical image of militias. They are comparatively much more secretive and typically do not openly advertise on public websites or public social media pages. Instead, potential members must find out about these groups through word-of-mouth from an already-connected member or request access to join closed online groups. Millenarian militias typically go through the motions of superficially vetting interested individuals before allowing them into their spaces, but this vetting has proven to be ineffective in cases where law enforcement agents or informants have successfully infiltrated and built criminal cases against such groups after initially doing nothing more than vaguely echoing the unit's appeals for violence against government tyranny (Lehr, 2021).

Loathing for the government tends to be substantially greater and almost palpable in millenarian versus constitutionalist groups, with millenarian members often wanting to actively attack the government or its agents rather than taking the constitutionalists' defensive posture toward them. One of the most extreme millenarian militia members I encountered during my fieldwork, for example, described his motivation for joining a militia unit as not being about serving his country or maintaining his military skills, the way constitutionalist members usually did, but rather simply "for revenge." He believed he and his fellow service members had been deployed to the Middle East under false pretenses and that the government had no interest in fighting terrorism, establishing peace, or even protecting oil pipelines but rather solely intended to experiment on soldiers by forcibly exposing them to untested vaccines, chemical agents, and other unknown substances. He was not sure why the government would engage in these actions, other than what he called a fundamental "hatred" for citizens with individual liberties but was convinced of the truth of his claims because, he said, almost everyone in his unit had since experienced devastating health conditions, namely various cancers and children with severe birth defects.

As was true for this man, veterans involved in millenarian militias have a different on-average outlook toward the government than veterans involved in constitutionalist groups. They view their service from a fundamentally negative perspective and the government and its representatives as something to be actively fought or even attacked in retribution either for their treatment while enlisted or for supposed nefarious truths revealed during their service about government actions and intentions. Veterans in millenarian groups also tend to remain in relatively subservient positions within the group. They do not frequently act as unit leaders but rather follow other men who lack military experience and instead attempt to capitalize on veterans' expertise and negative emotions to hone the skills and hostility of the entire unit for potentially violent action. These non-veteran millenarian leaders frequently appropriate military titles like "commander" or "captain" and impose a strict hierarchical rank structure on their units that is uncommon in constitutionalist groups. Constitutionalist units often disparage this approach, comparing it to stolen valor, and suggest that most veterans are put off by militia units that use rank model. As Billy, a widower in his thirties, snarkily remarked:

> I think the veterans . . . when they get into a group that has a whole rank structure, it's like, they haven't seen them earn it. And [the veteran] served and maybe they made it to sergeant or some higher rank and, it's like, they *earned* it. [In contrast,] I've seen this guy come along and what, because he has four-wheel drive he's the colonel? You know, it's his property so he's the colonel?

Conspiracy theories further feed millenarians' fear, suspicion, and anger about the government and other social forces. Long-standing conspiracy theories insist, for example, that government actors were the true perpetrators of the 9/11 terror attacks and of mass shooting events like Sandy Hook for various speculated aims such as promoting gun control or somehow generally controlling citizens. Newer theories include claims about COVID-19's origin and impacts or QAnon-driven ideas about global pedophile rings headed by Democrats and other social elites (Cooter et al., 2023). All these theories connect by offering "proof" of the purported tyranny of the government. This linchpin of government nefariousness can also serve as a route through which millenarian and constitutionalist units can find common ground. Social media's influence in recent years has amplified this effect, making it easier to share not only the content of various conspiracy fantasies but also their perceived urgency across group lines. Intentional sharing of conspiracy allegations alongside social media algorithms that amplify content that a given user is believed to enjoy helped to create online echo chambers (Cinelli et al., 2022) that, in my observations, became one major ingredient in the blurring of boundaries between formerly opposed constitutionalist and millenarian groups in recent years.

Typological Blurring

The typology that separated these two types of units had remained remarkably stable within the militia movement from the early 2000s through approximately 2015. Dr. Churchill and I have spoken several times about this divide and agreed that, in our observations, constitutionalist groups historically comprised roughly 90% of the militia movement. Millenarian groups, while a small portion of the movement, nonetheless shaped the general public's perception of the entire movement when affiliates were arrested and accused of various violent plots in the 1990s and beyond. This negative publicity often incentivized constitutionalist groups to attempt to normalize their image and actions through advertising events that were open to the public or through successfully inviting local media coverage when their units participated in things like search and rescue missions that they could frame as community service.

Millenarian groups that received negative public attention also further incentivized constitutionalist groups to watch for signals of extremism from possible new members beyond their baseline vetting. I personally witnessed some prospective members who first attended one or two constitutionalist events but did not find support for their anger or their hints at desiring violence. They effectively tested the waters at their first meeting by, most commonly, talking about their past experiences, life circumstances, and vaguely implied or joked about possible desires to seek retributive violence. Constitutionalist members would typically first attempt to talk the person down from this stance by, first, expressing empathy for whatever the person was experiencing and, second, patiently explaining the values and goals of the unit, suggesting the person talk to other members and "stick around to see who we are."

I also witnessed a few cases where prospective members were handled with less openness and patience. In one case, a man displaying swastika and iron cross tattoos on his forearms was asked to leave immediately when one constitutionalist member who moonlighted as a bouncer and had a physical type that matched that job description bluntly informed him, "we don't tolerate any of that Nazi shit." In other cases, constitutionalist members reported calling law enforcement, usually an FBI contact whose business card several unit leaders kept in their wallets, after a prospective member suggested violence during private conversations.

In some cases, I saw the prospective members who had been rejected from constitutionalist units later participating in events hosted by millenarian groups, indicating that these men were not discouraged from seeking out more radical groups that fit their goals after their initial rejection. In one case, a man from a millenarian unit who joined the militia before I started my fieldwork told me that he had a similar trajectory. He had first tried to connect with a large, well-known constitutionalist group in his area but told me he found them to be too "soft" and called them "keyboard warriors," meaning they were unwilling to take definitive, preemptive actions against the government as he believed was necessary.

This man provides one example that shows how the cultural rejection across the boundary of this typology usually worked both ways: it was not only constitutionalist units who rejected millenarian aggression but also millenarians who rejected the perceived complacency of constitutionalist members. This mutual rejection is important because it solidifies the boundaries between unit types while undermining some traditional academic claims about how less extreme militia units must function as above-ground, approachable factions that are intended to provide cover for more extreme, underground elements. While prospective members could indeed slide from constitutionalist to millenarian groups, this slippage happened because of a lack of ideological or personality fit, rather than because constitutionalist groups were intentionally funneling select members to extreme units while maintaining a public facade that was strategically intended to allow for more covert, violent operations from millenarians.

From what I observe, these disparate groups genuinely do not like each other or their contrasting approaches, with open ridicule extending both ways across the divide. Units in a given area nonetheless maintain awareness of each other and of each unit's key members. This happens in part because militia members comprise relatively small social circles with similar interests and in part because the groups want to keep an eye on each other due to mutual distrust, framing this monitoring as a form of operational security. Mutual awareness also occurs because—despite their differences—these oppositional units sometimes share goals. After, for example, natural disasters like a tornado that occurred during my fieldwork, members from multiple units regularly participated in first aid and cleanup efforts. Cooperation across events like this previewed what was to happen on a much larger scale when a variety of nostalgic groups coalesced around perceived common and urgent political interests in the Trump era, leading to protests and an attempted coup that were jointly conducted by groups that had traditionally rejected each other.

In short, then, it is not the case that militias as a whole can be so clearly identified as either innocuous Boy Scouts or dangerous extremists, though constitutionalists are closer to the former end of that spectrum and millenarians are closer to the latter. Militia behavior and risk should be thought of as a continuum, where individuals and units alike can shift depending on their reaction to social-political events. These shifts, especially when happening en masse, then have the potential to reshape the character of the movement as a whole and to push militia units into cooperation with more extreme and exclusionary organizations.

Distinctions and Overlaps With Other Nostalgic Groups

There are other groups that, at least at first glance, strongly resemble militias but are distinct organizations. Defining firearms and firearms training as the central focus of militias means that groups that exist exclusively in online spaces without having in-person interactions are not militias. Groups like this may eventually evolve into a militia if, for example, a subset of members begins offline training, but such groups are generally more like social clubs, interest groups, or, in some cases, political action organizations that may be dominated by lurkers or casual members who would be unlikely, even in emergencies, to provide the kind of in-person network that militias attempt to foster.

There are other in-person groups organized around the Second Amendment that are not necessarily militias. Various shooting clubs, the National Rifle Association (NRA), and another group called Project Appleseed, for example, all prioritize firearms as simultaneously a recreational practice, a self-defense mechanism, and a way to honor national heritage. However, groups like this often take great pains to separate themselves both publicly and privately from militia units, even as they repeat the same stories of national origin and supposed cultural decline. Project Appleseed offers one comparative example. This organization includes many homeschoolers and homesteaders and borrows from an evangelical model of outreach saying they want to spread certain values and history lessons in the same way that folk hero Johnny Appleseed planted apple trees across much of the country. In their own words, Appleseed wants to

> 'ensure that future generations of Americans will learn and benefit from the lessons of our colonial past' by using 'rifle marksmanship instruction as a gateway to help bring our nation's history to life and to show

that many of the values that our forefathers relied on to win our independence are still very much in demand today.'

At the end of their multiple-day events, instructors encourage attendees to keep spreading their metaphorical apple seeds by taking what they hope is "a renewed sense of civic responsibility" back to their own communities.[4]

The focus of their lengthy historical lessons during their training weekends is Paul Revere. Although instructors also present other Revolutionary War figures, including some women, as colonial heroes whose ethos should be emulated, Revere's ride as told in historian David Hackett Fisher's 1995 book is held up as the quintessential patriot parable that embodies character traits necessary for maintaining a free nation. Instructors lament how most Americans are losing their history and how values like integrity and personal responsibility are not as important to younger generations as they should be. Appleseed especially attempts to incentivize women's participation in their target shoots by hosting women-only events and giving them free admission to co-ed events. This group is not a militia, however, because they see firearm proficiency as instrumental for reasons largely limited to self-discipline and other individual traits, rather than as a tool for community defense. Appleseed also does not have organized units that regularly meet and train together; instead, participants may travel long distances from their home communities to engage in one-off weekend events.

There are four other groups that, because of their size, notoriety, or frequent conflation in common usage, should also be distinguished from militias. First are neo-Nazis, who are overtly racist and seek either separation from or outright violence against people of color; they sometimes have members who are visibly armed at certain protests or other gatherings. However, firearms are typically more of an individual preference, rather than a requirement or central focus within such groups. As one example of this, I conducted a survey in 2008 (the same year I first started fieldwork with militias) and solicited responses from various, large, overtly neo-Nazi internet forums. Among other issues, I asked respondents about other groups they supported or activities in which they engaged. Only 3 of the 162 respondents mentioned firearms in any capacity across any of their answers. Other respondents to my survey may have trained with guns or carried them without mentioning them in their responses, and the number of neo-Nazis prioritizing firearms may have increased in the intervening years. Nonetheless, firearms' relative absence from the survey's responses exemplifies how firearms are not at the forefront of neo-Nazi identity or group organizational focus in the same way they are for militia groups.

The Proud Boys are the second group sometimes equated to militias. This group is perhaps best succinctly described as a street-fighting gang with an overtly misogynist, anti-democratic agenda. Some individual members may carry firearms and even wear military-style vests or other gear in public that visually resembles or even duplicates items that militia members wear. But, just as with neo-Nazis, firearm proficiency is not a requirement or a central focus of group membership. Proud Boys have instead been known to prefer physical brawls at protests as a tool to assert their authority. They follow a long legacy of men's groups that fault women or, specifically, feminism for "softening" men, claiming that modern men are unable to protect themselves or are too reliant on modern technology and conveniences while advocating a return to traditional gender roles (Kutner, 2020). Street fights where one's body is the only available weapon best allows claims of this kind of reasserted traditional masculinity.

The third group to distinguish from modern militias are the so-called Minutemen, the people who patrol the southern US border, claiming to guard it from migrants crossing into the country illegally, people whom the Minutemen claim are almost uniformly drug dealers or human traffickers. As sociologist Harel Shapira wrote in *Waiting for José: The Minutemen's Pursuit of America* (2013), and as he and I have privately discussed, Minutemen rarely accomplish any protection that they claim to do. Instead, they generally camp and surveille the desert but make reports to Border Patrol agents, who often ignore these vigilante efforts. Shapira reported to me that although some Minutemen carry personal firearms for use during possible self-defense scenarios, the groups he studied never had target or tactical practice in preparation for their excursions. Some Minutemen groups go so far as to forbid carry during night patrols to avoid accidents, in part due to their distrust in some participants' firearm competence. Guns are thus once again more of an individual accoutrement than an organizational fixture, though it is important to note that Minutemen have committed murder and other violence using firearms.

The fourth and final point of comparison is a group I collectively call "off-gridders" because of their general desire to exist independently, off the grid. This group encompasses survivalists, preppers, and homesteaders, all of which have distinct but heavily overlapping characteristics.[5] Militias argue that they are serving their communities through their actions, but off-gridders instead focus exclusively on their and their family's own survival and preparation. They typically believe that some apocalyptic event is more imminent than not, even though they differ on what they believe is the best approach to this perceived inevitability. For the off-gridder community, firearms are typically seen as just another tool, often one less important than tools related to gathering or preparing food, rather than a core identifying feature. Guns within these communities are, in other words, for protecting yourself and the goods you have stored for emergency use, not for protecting a nation already seen as a likely lost cause.

Nostalgic Group Interconnections

Distinct organizations can, despite their differences, have overlapping ideologies, and the extent of this overlap ebbs and flows over time in response to the broader social environment. A metaphor I use to help explain the interconnected nature of groups that are typically labeled "right-wing" is that of different trees sharing a plot of land (Cooter, 2022b). These trees are different entities yet grow in the same soil, and sometimes—when the wind blows just right—their branches may intermingle and become indistinguishable.

In the same way, different groups that we have traditionally labeled "right-wing" have their own trajectories, ideologies, motives, and tactics. At the same time, they also have much in common, particularly regarding the "soil" from which they emerge. That soil is a shared, nostalgic vision of the past, one that insists the ideal US is halcyon: achieved but long-lost to cultural degradation or corruption. This common thread of looking to an imagined past to construct an idealized future is the lowest common denominator across distinct groups, which is why I prefer the adjective "nostalgic" over either "right-wing" or "patriot" to capture the shared essence of these organizations. Nostalgia as the shared reference point also avoids conceptual complications. Although militia members do nearly uniformly support conservative values regarding anti-immigration, anti-taxation, and small-government policies, many of them, perhaps surprisingly, have traditionally supported or at least been ambivalent about both abortion and LGBTQ+ rights, which defies the usual implications of the "right-wing" label.[6] It also avoids reifying notions of false or self-defined patriotism that risk providing an overly rosy gloss to such groups.

Nostalgic groups vary in terms of their precise definitions of "ideal," of what they aspire to fight to restore (or guard against further slippage) in their imagined, pristine nation. Some groups, especially neo-Nazis, openly work to achieve their ideal of an all-white nation, exacting violence against those who challenge their vision. Militias' ideal national vision focuses on a small government with lower taxation and regulation. However, militia members who advocate for a return to "simpler times," as many wistfully framed it during my conversations with them, nonetheless ignore how those earlier eras were far from ideal for anyone, but especially people who were not white and male.

Nostalgia, even with its slightly different content across group lines, also supports verdant opportunities for shared goals and actions across these divides under the right circumstances. Militias already overlap with Minutemen, for example, because some militia members (usually men who are past retirement age, in my experience) may sojourn to the border once or twice to contribute what they think of as volunteer service to defend the country. Taking a cross-country pilgrimage at their own expense, they temporarily join up with a Minuteman organization to participate in border excursions that result more in bragging rights back home than in success spotting undocumented migrants. Militia members who believe good citizens should be prepared for any disaster also already borrow principles and practices shared with off-gridders, including having stores of nonperishable goods and potential action plans for various disasters. While most militia members do not consider themselves as being equivalently invested in stockpiling or similar activities as much of the off-gridder community, others simultaneously identify as militia members and homesteaders and encourage people in those respective communities to learn more from each other.

These preexisting ideological connections, rooted in a shared vision of what constitutes patriotic action, can be activated and amplified by social and political currents that threaten members' vision of a nostalgically informed future.[7] These currents are my metaphor's wind that sometimes indistinguishably pushes groups together and creates opportunities for collective action that span usual ideological divides. When different groups (branches, in the metaphor) intermingle in this way, we see the potential for them to draw more from one another and, therefore, the potential for both members and groups to slip further into extremism. The more forceful the wind—the urgency and volume of the social-political currents—the more opportunities for slippage and metastasization of action and core ideology into paranoia and violence.

This kind of slippage across nostalgic group lines has happened before, with the outcome being virulent anti-government sentiment and civilian deaths. There were several important events, which the next chapter of this book discusses in much more detail, in the early 1990s that led not only to the formation of the modern militia movement but also fostered greater communication and cooperation between white supremacist groups and other organizations (PBS, n.d.). These groups perceived common interests resulting from government actions and banded together to fight what they believed to be infringements on individual liberties, including both Second Amendment and religious liberties. Groups put aside their differences as they highlighted and amplified their common interest, eventually culminating in the deaths of nearly 200 people in the Oklahoma City bombing.

Political Winds

The contemporary potential for group boundary dissolution, or at least weakening, became startlingly clear in recent years when the long-standing constitutionalist-millenarian typology started to fracture. Both Dr. Churchill and I estimate that Millenarian units are likely at least a quarter of the militia movement today and note that militias generally have fuzzier boundaries with more extreme groups like Proud Boys and overt neo-Nazis than had been true in the past. The already-permeable boundary between unit types became even more fluid in 2015 when Donald Trump started his campaign for President. Groups who had previously disdained each other instead worked together at a variety of events leading up to and during Trump's administration; they literally rubbed shoulders with each other as they opposed Black Lives Matter at racial justice protests, as they intimidated school boards they believed to be corrupting children through liberal curriculums or enforcing COVID-19 mitigation efforts, and as they coordinated to "stop the steal" at the January 6, 2021, insurrection. Trump's direct influence on this group boundary slippage cannot be overstated. His direct appeals to long-standing fears of issues like encroaching Marxism or government tyranny that extended beyond militia movement rosters increased their perceived need to act definitively to protect an idealized national character and culture.

Perceived threats from immigrants and, in particular, from immigrant Muslims took center stage in this narrative early in the Trump administration and were shared widely in social media echo chambers. One image in the style of a political cartoon became a frequently shared image in the online militia communities I was researching in the lead-up to the 2018 midterm elections, for example. It depicted mostly white Republicans holding American flags standing opposite racially diverse Democrats who were holding several other countries' flags and burning an American flag. The image was a visual representation of Trump's recent comments about Democrats supposedly supporting dangerous migrants at the expense of citizens' interests as he insisted:

> Democrats want to spend your money and give away your resources for the benefit of anyone but American citizens. . . . If you don't want America to be overrun by masses of illegal immigrants and massive caravans, you better vote Republican.
> (Shear & Hirschfeld Davis, 2022)

Another major factor in blurring the boundaries of the constitutionalist-millenarian typology has been the emergence of Boogaloo, a nebulous group of people who believe that a second Civil War is inevitable. Boogaloo has what social movement scholars call a low barrier to entry, meaning that Boogaloo has no membership dues and no need to sign a group roster. Interested individuals can simply join social media communities or show up to in-person events wearing affiliates' unofficial uniform: a Hawaiian shirt often paired with dark sunglasses, a military-style vest, and an AR-15 or other semi-automatic rifle. Extremism expert J.J. Macnab suggests that Boogaloo is "a dress code" rather than a social movement because of this noticeable visual marker (Johnson, 2020). Other analysts do use the movement classification, while yet others think of it more as an overarching ideology (Kriner & Cooter, 2023).

The major reason there is disagreement about how Boogaloo should be classified is because its adherents differ in terms of how they conceptualize their own relationship to their fantasized Civil War. Some affiliates believe they must simply prepare for some unknown but inevitable violent confrontation and be ready to defend themselves and their communities. Others believe it is their duty to initiate the War through an approach known as accelerationism that seeks to use social disruption to more quickly bring about conflict, and some develop specific plans for doing so. Boogaloo accelerationists have been charged with a variety of crimes, including inciting riots and attacking and murdering police officers (Newhouse & Gunesch, 2020).

For them, police are not only the enforcement officers of a tyrannical government but also represent a high-profile target that is certain to invite a reciprocal violent response that would, they hope, catalyze other people into mass violent action and mark the beginning of a Civil War against the government.

Boogaloo affiliates who are not militant accelerationists often have a different view of police, further complicating their dynamic. This divide was especially evident in May 2020, in the wake of George Floyd's murder at the hands of police, when racial justice protests occurred all across the country and even abroad. When media coverage of these protests turned to relatively rare acts of violence (Chenoweth & Pressman, 2022) that were, in some cases, instigated by white supremacist actors attempting to discredit Black Lives Matter (Allen, 2020), some nostalgic groups, including some Boogaloo affiliates, embraced a positive perspective of police. They understood police as protectors against violence and anarchy that they imagined was threatening to spread to their own neighborhoods. These affiliates who wanted to "back the blue" often argued openly during this time on Facebook pages with other members who wanted to "back the boog" and use the protests as an opportunity to discredit police powers more broadly (Cooter, 2020).

Such internal divides and contradictions increase Boogaloo's potential to blur disparate group boundaries—to help those metaphorical branches intermingle and create opportunities for increased radicalization. Members from some units claim they are attending a protest only to defend property from rioters and wear Hawaiian shirts or otherwise visually identify with Boogaloo because they perceive protestors' actions signal a dangerous escalation in social disruption. Visually identifying with Boogaloo, they believe, is an indication they are ready to defend against harm from that disruption. Members from other groups with more extreme goals, such as initiating riots or harming either protestors or police, might also wear Boogaloo gear as a signal of their intention to *commit* social disruptions. Although the underlying motives for Boogaloo affiliation are different across these cases, the core potential for militancy encapsulated within the Boogaloo approach is what appeals across nostalgic group lines. The Hawaiian shirts and other gear visually signal this core interest, creating at least temporary allies in this protest space and potentially contributing to members of these groups either overlooking or discounting fundamental differences between them in the name of longer-term shared interests. Similar processes happened online, with Boogaloo memes proliferating across a range of anti-government spaces, entangling the metaphorical branches of different groups even further. While this effect is impossible to accurately quantify, we know that Boogaloo has likely permanently pushed the militia movement more into the extreme millenarian end of the spectrum (Kriner & Cooter, 2023).

This radicalization of certain elements has happened even while the militia movement as a whole has reembraced police officers. While the wariness of policing as a tool of tyranny remains, the "back the blue" discourse has largely won out, at least for now. Most militia affiliates oppose efforts to

Figure 1.3 A militia unit engaging in a training exercise that used a red smoke bomb.
Source: Photo courtesy of Daniel Hud.

defund the police or reduce spending on police budgets, citing their perceptions of growing crime and threats to their idealized way of life. Members frame discussions about shifting funding or removing police power as efforts by Democrats or "brainless libs" to weaken our social structures and our collective ability to resist what they believe to be growing threats from "radical minorities." The militia communities I currently observe most refer to "radical minorities" when influenced by anti-LGBTQ+ propaganda, buying into notions that drag queens or transgender people are pedophiles or are otherwise attempting to corrupt children through unregulated school curricula.

Boogaloo's impact is also likely emblematic of what we should be watching for within the militia movement headed into the 2024 Presidential election and beyond regarding these cultural and media-driven focuses. Any force that facilitates the militias and their members crossing over more radical boundaries within their own movement and cross-pollinating with other, already more extreme groups during times of strife and duress need only capitalize on these groups' shared metaphorical soil of a "lost" national character. Media trends that falsely present oppressed groups—whether transgender people, immigrants, or others—as threats can be a strong source of this facilitation. Figures like Trump, who openly appeal to fear and notions of cultural degradation that these issues supposedly represent, can then inflame a virulent supporting base whose ire can be directed toward a variety of targets.

It is, unfortunately, easier to understand and forecast the likely sources of the proverbial wind in this metaphor than it is to untangle different groups' branches after they have become intermingled. The remainder of this book is nonetheless my effort to elucidate the inner workings of militia units in a way that routes for intervention in the process of radicalization might eventually be possible. For the initial step in that process, I first look back to outline the history of militia activity in the US, starting during the Revolutionary War period. Exploring militia history leading to the formation of the modern militia movement contextualizes their lineage and likely trajectory as explored through the remainder of the book.

Notes

1. "American" and related terms are increasingly falling out of favor among scholars who are discussing people who live in the United States of America because it is imprecise and often negates people who live in other South and North American countries. I maintain the term in this manuscript because of its heavy linguistic and ideological presence within militia groups.
2. See my earlier work (Cooter, 2013) for more information about race and gender dynamics in militia units.
3. This is a reference to an infamous white supremacist mantra.
4. https://web.archive.org/web/20220905040224/https://appleseedinfo.org/about/
5. My goal here is not to distinguish among these groups in fine detail but instead to focus on what they have in common for the purpose of delineating them from militia groups. For some of the important distinguishing features among these groups, see Bounds (2020), Mills (2019, 2021), and Mitchell (2002).
6. Militia support for LGBTQ+ rights has dramatically declined in recent years as various anti-trans talking points have become common in media and political circles (Kishi, 2022).
7. Firearms and their accessories, tactical gear, radios meant for security professionals, and other "toys" (Cooter, 2013) can also facilitate this intermingling. Gun shows, courses that focus on survivalism or similar skills, and other events where such gear is displayed and sold can foster intermingling and connection across people with a variety of motives for investigating these tools. Some companies are adept at catering to mixed motives for their products' use and exist completely within this liminal space.

References

Abbey, N. (2023, May 20). It's easy to see white supremacy as the thinking of extremists. We know that's not true. *The Guardian.* www.theguardian.com/commentisfree/2023/may/20/white-supremacy-extremists-joe-biden

Allen, K. (2020, July 29). Man who helped ignite George Floyd riots identified as white supremacist: Police. *ABC News.* https://abcnews.go.com/US/man-helped-ignite-george-floyd-riots-identified-white/story?id=72051536

Belew, K. (2018). *Bring the war home: The White power movement and paramilitary America.* Harvard University Press.

Bonilla-Silva, E. (1997). Rethinking racism: Toward a structural interpretation. *American Sociological Review*, 62(3), 465–480. https://doi.org/10.2307/2657316

Bonilla-Silva, E. (2006). *Racism without racists: Color-blind racism and the persistence of racial inequality in the United States* (2nd ed.). Rowman & Littlefield.
Bounds, A. M. (2020). *Bracing for the apocalypse: An ethnographic study of New York's 'prepper' subculture*. Routledge.
Carless, W., & Stephens, A. (2021, October 8). Black people formed one of the largest militias in the U.S. now its leader is in prosecutors' crosshairs. *The Trace*. www.thetrace.org/2021/10/nfac-black-militia-grandmaster-jay-prosecution/
Chavez, N. (2021, January 10). *BLM vs Capitol protests: This was the police response when it was Black protesters on DC streets last year*. www.cnn.com/2021/01/07/us/police-response-black-lives-matter-protest-us-capitol/index.html
Chavez, N., Young, R., & Barajas, A. (2020, October 25). An all-Black group is arming itself and demanding change. They are the NFAC. *CNN*. www.cnn.com/2020/10/25/us/nfac-black-armed-group/index.html
Chenoweth, E., & Pressman, J. (2022, October 16). Black Lives Matter protests were overwhelming peaceful, research finds. *Washington Post*. www.washingtonpost.com/politics/2020/10/16/this-summers-black-lives-matter-protesters-were-overwhelming-peaceful-our-research-finds/
Cinelli, M., Etta, G., Avalle, M., Quattrociocchi, A., Di Marco, N., Valensise, C., Galeazzi, A., & Quattrociocchi, W. (2022). Conspiracy theories and social media platforms. *Current Opinion in Psychology*, 47, 101407.
Conley, D. (1999). *Being Black, living in the red*. University of California Press.
Cooter, A. (2013). *Americanness, masculinity, and whiteness: How Michigan militia men navigate evolving social norms* [Thesis]. http://deepblue.lib.umich.edu/handle/2027.42/98077
Cooter, A. (2020, June 9). Militias evaluate beliefs, action as president threatens soldiers in the streets. *The Conversation*. http://theconversation.com/militias-evaluate-beliefs-action-as-president-threatens-soldiers-in-the-streets-140123
Cooter, A. (2022a). US Domestic Militias' intersections with government and authority: How a sociology of individualism informs their praxis. In D. Neubert, H. J. Lauth, & C. Mohamad-Klotzbach (Eds.), *Local self-governance and varieties of statehood: Tensions and cooperation* (pp. 31–49). Springer International Publishing.
Cooter, A. (2022b, January 1). Citizen militias in the U.S. are moving toward more violent extremism. *Scientific American*. www.scientificamerican.com/article/citizen-militias-in-the-u-s-are-moving-toward-more-violent-extremism/
Cooter, A., Taylor, M., & Hansen, T. J. (2023). Cultural change and conspiracism: How conspiracy theory trends reflect threat and anxiety. In M. A. Argentino & A. Amarasingam (Eds.), *Far-right culture: The art, music, and everyday practices of violent extremists*. Routledge.
Diamond, A. (2019, September 18). Inside a new effort to change what schools teach about Native American history. *Smithsonian Magazine*. www.smithsonianmag.com/smithsonian-institution/inside-new-effort-change-what-schools-teach-about-native-american-history-180973166/
Gibson, J. W. (1994). *Warrior dreams: Violence and manhood in post-Vietnam America* (Reprint ed.). Hill & Wang.
Gorski, P. S., & Perry, S. L. (2022). *The flag and the cross: White Christian nationalism and the threat to American democracy*. Oxford University Press.
Hughey, M. (2012). *White bound: Nationalists, antiracists, and the shared meanings of race* (1st ed.). Stanford University Press.

Jackson, S. (2020). *Oath Keepers: Patriotism and the edge of violence in a right-wing antigovernment group*. Columbia University Press.

Johnson, B. (2020, July 21). Accelerationists including Boogaloo gain strength online, pose mass-casualty threat—HS today. *Homeland Security Today*. www.hstoday.us/subject-matter-areas/counterterrorism/accelerationists-gain-strength-online-pose-mass-casualty-threat-lawmakers-warned/

Kahn, C. (2021, July 15). Many Americans embrace falsehoods about critical race theory. *Reuters*. www.reuters.com/world/us/many-americans-embrace-falsehoods-about-critical-race-theory-2021-07-15/

Katz, J. (2022, January 5). White masculinity and the January 6 insurrection. *Ms. Magazine*. https://msmagazine.com/2022/01/05/white-men-insurrection-january-6-masculinity-trump/

Kishi, R. (2022, December 6). From the Capitol Riot to the midterms: Shifts in American far-right mobilization between 2021 and 2022. *ACLED*. https://acleddata.com/2022/12/06/from-the-capitol-riot-to-the-midterms-shifts-in-american-far-right-mobilization-between-2021-and-2022/

Kriner, M., & Cooter, A. (2023). America's militant nostalgia: The role of accelerationism in the contemporary militia-patriot movement. In M.-A. Argentino & A. Amarasingam (Eds.), *Far-right culture: The art, music, and everyday practices of violent extremists*. Routledge.

Kutner, S. (2020, May 26). Swiping right: The allure of hyper masculinity and cryptofascism for men who join the proud boys. *International Centre for Counter-Terrorism*. www.icct.nl/publication/swiping-right-allure-hyper-masculinity-and-cryptofascism-men-who-join-proud-boys

Lehr, D. (2021). *White hot hate: A true story of domestic terrorism in America's heartland*. Mariner Books.

Marder, M. (2013). *Plant-thinking: A philosophy of vegetal life*. Columbia University Press.

Mills, M. F. (2019). Preparing for the unknown . . . unknowns: 'Doomsday' prepping and disaster risk anxiety in the United States. *Journal of Risk Research*, 22(10), 1267–1279. https://doi.org/10.1080/13669877.2018.1466825

Mills, M. F. (2021). Obamageddon: Fear, the far right, and the rise of "doomsday" prepping in Obama's America. *Journal of American Studies*, 55(2), 336–365.

Mitchell, R. G. (2002). *Dancing at Armageddon: Survivalism and chaos in modern times*. University of Chicago Press.

Morello-Frosch, R., & Lopez, R. (2006). The riskscape and the color line: Examining the role of segregation in environmental health disparities. *Environmental Research*, 102(2), 181–196. https://doi.org/10.1016/j.envres.2006.05.007

Newhouse, A., & Gunesch, N. (2020, June 22). Boogaloo movement update: Violence, schisms, and bans. *Center on Terrorism, Extremism, and Counterterrorism*. www.middlebury.edu/institute/academics/centers-initiatives/ctec/ctec-publications/boogaloo-movement-update-violence-schisms-and

Pager, D. (2009). *Marked: Race, crime, and finding work in an era of mass incarceration* (Illustrated ed.). University of Chicago Press.

PBS. (n.d.). Timothy McVeigh at Waco. *PBS*. Retrieved July 17, 2023, from www.pbs.org/wgbh/americanexperience/features/oklahoma-city-timothy-mcveigh-waco/

Pendharkar, E. (2023, February 28). Which states are considering "don't say gay" Bills and where they stand. *Education Week*. www.edweek.org/policy-politics/which-states-are-considering-dont-say-gay-bills-and-where-they-stand/2023/02

Phillips, K. (2020, December 1). "Damaging to our democracy": Trump election lawsuits targeted areas with large Black, Latino populations. *USA Today*. www.usatoday.com/story/news/politics/2020/12/01/trump-voter-fraud-claims-target-counties-more-black-latino-votes/6391908002/

Schakohl, T. (2022, August 16). *FBI asked cops to let protesters into Michigan State Capitol building, informant says*. https://dailycaller.com/2022/08/16/informant-fbi-armed-protesters-michigan-capitol/

Shapira, H. (2013). *Waiting for José the Minutemen's pursuit of America*. Princeton University Press.

Shear, M. D., & Hirschfeld Davis, J. (2022, April 22). As midterm vote nears, Trump reprises a favorite message: Fear immigrants. *The New York Times*. www.nytimes.com/2018/11/01/us/politics/trump-immigration.html

SPLC. (2018, January 31). Teaching hard history. *Southern Poverty Law Center*. www.splcenter.org/20180131/teaching-hard-history

States that Have Banned Critical Race Theory 2023. (2023). *World population review*. https://worldpopulationreview.com/state-rankings/states-that-have-banned-critical-race-theory

Stewart, N. (2019, August 19). 'We are committing educational malpractice': Why slavery is mistaught—and worse—in American schools. *The New York Times*. www.nytimes.com/interactive/2019/08/19/magazine/slavery-american-schools.html

Tripathi, N. (2020, July 5). #BlackPanthers trends as White Twitter users mix NFAC up with socialist group after armed march clip goes viral. *MEAWW*. https://meaww.com/black-panthers-trends-as-white-twitter-users-mix-nfac-up-nightmare-racist-slam-bpp-doesnt-exist-guns

Williams, K. (2020, September 17). US cops are treating White militias as "heavily armed friendlies." *Truthout*. https://truthout.org/articles/us-cops-are-treating-white-militias-as-heavily-armed-friendlies/

Wright, B. C. T. (2020, May 12). Legally armed Black citizens patrol white neighborhood where Ahmaud Arbery was killed. *NewsOne*. https://newsone.com/3940390/ahmaud-arbery-armed-black-protesters-patrol-georgia-neighborhood/

2 Militia History in the United States

Contextualizing the Modern Movement

> I am an American, my Founding Fathers and my heritage of being an American have tasked me with protecting my Constitution, my Bill of Rights and our heritage and our way of life. And I'm sorry, that's just the way it is. If them people up there in DC can't understand that, well, then they got a problem. Don't make it mine.
> —64-year-old interviewee Oscar, retired phone company worker

Colonial Roots and Catalysts

Although many people in the US only recently became aware of civilian militias as a social and political phenomenon, militias have a long global history. Outside the US, we frequently assume that militias appear alongside relatively weak governments that cannot effectively control opposing privatized fighting forces, or, in some cases, weak governments that rely on supplemental support from such civilian, military-style units to maintain fragile power.[1] Inside the US, militias have typically been portrayed in popular lore as a response to *strong* governments: first, to the British monarchy and, later, to various overly restrictive instantiations of the US federal government. Most popular historical analyses of domestic militias center the Revolutionary War as a cornerstone to their history. From the perspective of the contemporary militia members whom I have spoken with, the relevant militia lineage starts and ends with Revolutionary militias, excluding accounts of other historical militias whose activity is substantially more morally ambiguous than what is represented in mythologized Revolutionary War stories. As scholar Alex Trimble Young (2020) remarks:

> Militias . . . proudly imagine themselves as the inheritors of the revolutionary violence of the militias at Lexington and Concord, but they are inheritors of a tradition of paramilitary organizing that just as surely has its roots in the slave patrols and colonial militias whose violence was aimed not at the imperial state, but the racialized other.

Understanding a more complete trajectory of militias is essential for fully capturing their potential today as political forces that may either challenge

DOI: 10.4324/9781003361657-3

or support existing power structures. Historian Zachary Schrag traces US domestic militias' ideological origins back across the pond to the British Whig party, well before the first whispers of revolution began on colonized soil. The Whigs, defined by their resistance to unlimited monarchial power, were wary of professional armies that owed their salary and loyalty to the king. They believed that a volunteer force would serve as "liberty's guarantors" by ensuring those soldiers' loyalty to their community, rather than to a king (2021, p. 26). Militia members echo this sentiment still today, insisting that both they and US military members would never take up arms against citizens.[2] Schrag suggests it is natural that early colonists who wanted to escape the control of the monarchy would carry forward this framework as they formalized authority structures needed for successful organization and defense in the US territories.

Activist and historian Roxanne Dunbar-Ortiz reports, however, that these early colonists did not only use militias for self-defense but also to proactively terrorize Indigenous communities to steal their territory (2018). She notes that several colonies both in the South and in New England instituted laws as early as 1632 requiring that families or at least male colonists possess functioning firearms to defend emerging white settlements. Although these laws largely created individual imperatives, the resulting armed communities also facilitated the formation of larger forces when settlements were under duress from real or perceived threats.

Dunbar-Ortiz suggests a direct logical and legal lineage from these laws to the Second Amendment's ratification more than a century later in 1791, a lineage she argues is essential for understanding how nostalgic groups continue to implicate whiteness today. She argues that the Second Amendment formalized settlers' "*right* to form volunteer militias to attack Indians [sic] and take their land" (*ibid.*, p. 18) (emphasis added). Because of this lineage, she thus rejects legal interpretations of the Second Amendment as being inconsistent either with individual firearm ownership or with volunteer citizen militias today. Other scholars similarly argue that the Second Amendment effectively codified colonists' obligation to help defend the early states (Cornell, 2008), highlighting the importance of firearms to the identities of these early male settlers and of the emerging nation alike. Irrespective of legal interpretations about the original intent of that Amendment, colonial firearms were unquestionably an essential ingredient in the genocide of native peoples, even while they today maintain a revered and romanticized role in the stories of the Revolutionary War and the founding of the US.

The legendary heroism that Revolutionary War soldiers themselves embody in these accounts is also not as clear-cut as our narratives usually suggest. Militia units of this era were often substantially less organized and disciplined than their retrospective portrayals indicate, and different colonies had different rules for their creation or organizational structures. Some colonies had legal requirements for men from their teens through their sixties to be armed, while others merely encouraged it; some would-be militias waited for the legal authorization of their state's Provincial Congress prior to organizing, while some did not (Churchill, 2009).

There was also an important regional difference between militias that complicates their retrospectively positive representations. Historian John Shy (1990) notes that the higher population density of town-based communities in the North facilitated mustering relative to the plantation-based territory of the South. At the same time, smaller southern militias were more internally organized than those in the North because they adopted the model of preexisting slave patrols that had been formed there to forestall threats of slave runaways or rebellions and that could be quickly mobilized for the protection of white supremacy (Churchill, 2009; Mahon, 1983; Shy, 1990). The British, for their part, recruited enslaved men to their ranks in some southern colonies and, in other cases, encouraged them to flee plantations to further destabilize the southern economy, further underscoring the raced and racist delineations of early militia ranks (Shy, 1990).

On the whole and in contrast to our overly positive historical imagination, Shy notes that revolutionary militias were "poorly trained and badly led, often without bayonets, seldom comprised of the deadly marksmen dear to American legend" (1990, p. 236). His book generally describes a division between official militias as recognized by emerging colonial governments and purely volunteer associations of militia members who acted independently with little oversight or formal organization. This split makes for confusing distinctions while reading historical accounts and apparently also made for confusing distinctions of authority structures across these organizations at the time of the Revolutionary War. Historian John Mahon emphasizes this complexity, saying that in the lead-up to the war, "there were *at least* 13 different militia systems" (1983, p. 31) (emphasis added), meaning that each colony at best had its own, distinct organizational structure, while some colonies relied on local organization that may have differed even across neighboring towns. Historian Darren Mulloy suggests that it is easiest in this context to think of militias as being "adjuncts" to the Continental Army's efforts for most of the war effort, helping to supplement more official and organized forces (2008, p. 62).

In some places, militias were also responsible for finding men to effectively be drafted into the official Continental Army. But they did not draw soldiers from their own ranks, preferring to leave those men behind to protect their local communities. Militia towns would instead pool resources to pay other men, usually the most severely economically marginalized ones, to be conscripted in militia members' place. Most colonial soldiers did not serve in the war because of a sense of duty or loyalty to an emerging national ideal, but rather "because they were the ones least able to resist a crass economic appeal" (Shy, 1990, p. 128). Many Revolutionary War soldiers were effectively mercenaries, men whose loyalty was to a paycheck rather than to a higher calling or to their community, a notion that belies our usual storytelling of these soldiers' character. Shy even goes so far as to say that while pre-war militias were focused on ideas of defense and territorial acquisition, Revolutionary militias were "a police force and an instrument of political surveillance" (*ibid.*, p. 176) against other colonists that forced men to publicly take a side regarding the conflict during conscription efforts. Iconic stories of men like Paul Revere and Samuel Adams are thus not representations of a typical Revolutionary War militia man but are rather outliers, in other words, and their actions and symbolic power should not be seen as representative of the war's full fighting force.

Historian Charles Royster (1996) says that the early colonists had nonetheless already valorized the idea of citizen-soldiers, framing them as stalwart individuals ready to fight against a tyrannical monarchy. The shared mythos of a militia and its members was already symbolically important for creating an idealized United States of America for which these Revolutionaries were fighting, an idea that modern militia members internalize still today. Some colonial actors, especially in the North, were also already beginning to think of militias as important for maintaining state military control relative to an untested and emerging federal government (Shy, 1990).

This complicated and, frankly, messy and disorganized framework for early militias may help explain why even George Washington, who is often depicted as fighting alongside scrappy militiamen in our modern retellings of his endeavors, believed them to be "worse than useless" (*ibid.*, p. 126). At the same time, the war's opening battles of Lexington and Concord, now synonymous in our national mythos with an independent settler spirit, heavily relied on militias, as did other battles before the Continental Army was created in June 1775. Mulloy says these iconic battles "represent the high point of the militias' military contribution to the war" (2008, p. 58) and says it is thus "unsurprising" that modern militias put such a heavy emphasis on their importance in accounts of the nation's founding. Shy, who throughout his book highlights the disorganization and unprofessional nature of the colonial militia, nonetheless credits them for much of the war's success following the momentum of these battles because their unpredictability and sheer numbers proved endlessly vexsome for the British (1990).

At the close of the war in 1783, the early colonial government needed to bring together what had previously been largely separate colonies with disparate governmental structures. Churchill says that "control over the militia [became] a central issue" in this process (2009, p. 40). Some early leaders saw utility in keeping a militia organized under official governmental structures to try to temper their potential for insurrectionary mobilization directed toward these emerging governments. Other leaders, fresh from their victory over the British monarchy, worried about lending too much power to an untested federal government and wanted to avoid leaving civilians without access to an organized defense against possible internal tyranny (*ibid.*, pp. 41, 47). Despite his skepticism of their effectiveness, George Washington himself believed the militia should be somewhat maintained and best conceptualized as a kind of national reserve (Mahon, 1983). Ultimately, there was not one single national resolution to the debate over how to organize and oversee militias. This lack of effective compromise has left a legacy of lingering questions today about how to conceptualize militias, regulate them, and interpret them relative to the Second Amendment.

Nineteenth-Century Militias

Militias continued to evolve as the eighteenth century came to an end. Congress enacted several Militia Acts in part as a response to attempted rebellions against the early colonial governments. One rebellion attempted to overtake the Massachusetts state government but was foiled by the state militia and a privately funded militia. Another rebellion was in response to perceptions of harsh taxation, especially in the state of Pennsylvania, and militias were involved in both sides of that conflict (Kerby, 1977; Vladeck, 2004). Notable versions of the Militia Acts included two separate pieces of legislation in 1792 that, respectively, gave the President limited authority to call out state militias to defend against insurrection or invasion and allowed state militias to conscript free, adult men to their ranks (Vladeck, 2004). These acts were intended to be temporary, but a 1795 version of the act reinstated these provisions while making the President's power to rely on state militias permanent.

Other acts in the early 1800s, usually titled not after militias but instead with regard to their focus on the requisition or detachment of forces, required governors to keep state militias in a condition of readiness for any potential federal action (Kerby, 1977). Contrary to the mythology that all colonial boys grew up with an almost inherent proficiency for firearms, many militia members of this era echoed their Revolutionary War predecessors and did not possess basic weapon competencies, including the essential knowledge of how to insert flint into the rifle (*ibid.*). Historian C. Edward Skeen (2021) reports that less than one-third of militiamen at this time were likely armed as the law required. In an effort to address militias' lack of preparedness, Congress gave $200,000 (nearly $5 million in today's currency) to states via another Militia Act in 1808 to fund their militias. Kerby notes that, despite this investment, "both the states and the national government avoided responsibility for the militia" (1977, p. 110), thus producing insufficient cooperation to create an effective national militia structure.

Historians believe that the US's fate in the War of 1812 suffered because of this lack of cooperation and because many people, including Thomas Jefferson, had started to conceptualize the militia as a purely defensive, rather than offensive, force, further contributing to a lack of investment in their preparedness for combat (Mahon, 1983). Militia members continued to have little training or discipline, and some still lacked weapons. Kerby (1977) notes that perhaps the militia system as envisioned by the previous Militia Acts could have succeeded had militias been properly funded and trained, but instead, the federal government shifted to a regularly maintained, professional army while pointing at the failures of the unsupported militia system as the primary justification for doing so.

By 1820, compulsory militia membership was regarded with disdain in many places and as an unnecessary historical leftover from earlier wars. Some men chose to be fined rather than participate, and the entire endeavor was so unpopular that Schrag (2021) cites a Philadelphia newspaper of the time insisting compulsory militias had nearly irreparably degraded military pride as a whole. Desertions and resignations were so common that "sunshine soldiers" became a common moniker for the men who would join during easy, proverbially sunny moments, only to leave and be quickly replaced by equally short-lived participants as soon as they faced any real requirements of membership (*ibid.*, p. 29).

Volunteer militias maintained a different tenor, however. They persisted, often remaining part of official state militias, such that membership in them was one route for exemption from their compulsory counterparts. Schrag says volunteer militias also saw a resurgence in 1825 for the 50th anniversary of the Revolution's start. Although seemingly brought together for symbolic and celebratory purposes, these volunteers expressed sentiments of true patriotism and of being the real line of defense against foreign invasion, which are ideas repeated by today's militia members. Schrag says this mentality was likely facilitated by perceptions of invasion being culturally heightened by veterans from prior British skirmishes and by ongoing and contentious boundary disputes in the western states. Skeen (2021) suggests that these volunteers were also more likely to possess better military training and discipline compared to those who were drafted.

Volunteer units also served other purposes beyond symbolism and escaping compulsory duty. The role that militias played in suppressing various riots during the 1820s–1840s, often supplementing law enforcement efforts, is usually completely excluded from modern militia lore. Most contemporary militia members may never have learned these stories because this era's militias were less entwined with the narrative of the nation's founding, but this exclusion may also happen because it is much harder to paint militias of this era as moral authorities or freedom fighters striving for the common good.

Schrag's account tends to frame militia actions during these decades rather positively, saying in the early pages of his book, for instance, that militias "proved themselves ready to fight, to kill, and to die in defense of the rights of a minority" (2021, p. 9). He presents evidence consistent with this claim, showing that militias helped quell some rioters who were opposing immigrants or certain minority religious groups. And yet, many riots during this time protested factory owners and industrialization's dangers to workers, and Schrag also acknowledges that slavery's abolition was the single most common impetus of riots that militias helped suppress. He thus glosses over how, in most cases, militias were actually functioning to protect the status quo, the interests of industry, financial elites, and white supremacy rather than the interests of those fighting for freedom and greater protections for citizens as a whole.

Similarly, Schrag only mentions in passing how militias engaged as "expeditionary forces" and how units from Philadelphia "fought the Seminoles in Florida" in 1837 and 1838 (*ibid.*, p. 29). He does not connect these ostensibly isolated events to the Trail of Tears or the 1830 Indian Removal Act. In fact, he does not mention those events at all. Historian Heather Cox Richardson (2008), in contrast, details militias' active role in the genocide of Indigenous groups during the 1850s, recounting instances of their involvement in slaughtering women and children and highlighting how militias once more weaponized themselves as agents of white supremacy in the name of safety and territorial expansion.

Schrag also does not mention militias' ongoing role in actively maintaining slavery during the late 1800s. Dunbar-Ortiz, however, writes that new militias were formed during this time "under the guise of private rifle clubs" (2018, p. 241) for the explicit purpose of having ready-made slave patrols, repeating the pattern from before the Revolutionary War. Slavery's centrality to the southern economy likely made it inevitable that such militias would continue to play a military role both leading up to and during the Civil War.

Three days after Confederate troops forced a Union surrender of Fort Sumter in South Carolina on April 12, 1861, President Lincoln called for 75,000 militia troops from across the states in what historian J.G. Randall calls the "beginning of the war without a declaration" (1961, p. 275). Randall suggests that Lincoln believed the early signs of war would turn out to only be a small insurrection, one quickly handled, similarly to the uprisings that happened shortly after the Revolutionary War. However, as is profoundly unsurprising in retrospect, some southern states like Virginia instead took this Presidential order to muster militia forces as further confirmation of an out-of-touch federal government. These states responded by amplifying their support for the Confederacy, hastening, in some cases, their announcements of secession and their amassing of militias to support Confederate troops, rather than Union fighters (*ibid.*).

When the war did not come to a rapid conclusion, Congress once more relied on a Militia Act in 1862 to strengthen the Union Army by instituting an unpopular draft. Although men selected could, as in earlier battles, pay for someone else to go in their stead, federal militia members were needed at some draft selection sites to avoid violence due to the draft's divisiveness (*ibid.*). This Act also nominally freed soldiers who were enslaved and forced to fight by Confederates and, in contrast to the 1792 version of the Act that specified only white men would be considered militia members, formally allowed Black men to serve as soldiers to the obvious benefit of the Union (Randall, 1961; Smith, 2004).

Once the war finally ended in 1865, militias continued to be entangled with bigger ongoing social debates, particularly related to race and racism. Mahon says that in the South "The militia was virtually the old Confederate Army down to the worn gray uniforms left over from the Civil War" (1983, p. 108), even though some southern states were explicitly prohibited from maintaining militias as terms of the war's conclusion. This period also saw the development of Black militias in some southern states, units that undoubtedly arose out of the necessity to protect emerging free communities and to prevent hostile white efforts to reenslave or otherwise harm Black people and their property. Some historians who mention these Black militias nonetheless use dramatically different framing when talking about these units, previewing our differential treatment of contemporary Black versus white armed groups. Randall, for example, refers to them as "murderous mobs" (1961, p. 852), while Mahon insists they were "obnoxious" at election polls and suggests that it was the behavior of Black militias, not the preexisting racism they were opposing, that drove racial hatred and lethal attacks on Black leaders during this era (1983, p. 109).

Randall (1961), at least, nonetheless acknowledges how the first wave of the Ku Klux Klan (KKK) emerged in 1865 as a way to combat Black militia units (and other Black activists), echoing Dunbar-Ortiz's assertion that the KKK grew directly from the lineage of early slave patrols and further underscoring militias' role in the preservation of these oppressive and genocidal power structures. The KKK, whose first-wave members were often armed Confederate veterans, cannot be ignored in the history of US domestic militias, even though contemporary militia members insist that they and various other armed, racist, or otherwise exclusionary organizations are not part of their ancestry. Even when militia members openly reject the Klan and similar groups, the Klan's racist and oppressive actions, at the bare minimum, contributed to the social and political context that eventually gave rise to modern militias and their interest in firearms.

KKK members used a variety of terror tactics to attempt to enforce or regain white supremacy in contravention of Black people's new-found legal freedoms (SPLC, 2011). They, just as many militia members today, often saw themselves as working not only in their own best interests but also in the interest of their nation, which they believed was strongest when exclusively politically and economically controlled by white men. The early Klan's efforts were facilitated by the 1878 Posse Comitatus Act, which was designed to prohibit federal military interference in southern Reconstruction's efforts to continue oppressing and controlling Black people via Jim Crow and other measures (Nunn, 2021). This Act continues to maintain relevance in some militias' interpretations of their role through present day.

After the war and during the period of rapid industrialization known as the Gilded Age, militias also became barriers to workers who challenged the power of growing coal, rail, and other industries. There were cases where employers formed and trained militias to oppose early union efforts (Fogelson, 1989; MacCabe, 1971), others where militias were used to protect the exploited labor of Chinese rail workers (Lew-Williams, 2018), and yet others where wealthy businessmen or high-society families formed private militias. These private armies, some armed with Gatling guns, were paid to protect financial elites' interests, including not only their businesses but also their private homes and neighborhoods where their broader networks of family and friends lived. Sociologist Larry Isaac (2002) reports that militias tended to be ineffective in these roles, in part because they often sided with workers during the spreading strikes around the coal industry in particular. Yet, it is notable that those with property and means who wanted to limit the power and wages of the working class viewed militias as a potential tool for quelling class conflict.

Militias of the 1900s

As the Gilded Age came to a close, Congress passed one more notable Militia Act, also known as the Dick Act, in 1903. This Act created and provisioned the first, formalized version of the National Guard by repealing the 1792 and 1795 Militia Acts and redefining the militia as two different branches: the reserve militia and the organized militia. The latter referred to the Guard and was intended to more decisively give federal and Presidential (rather than state) control over militia actions as needed while still, in practice, allowing for an unorganized volunteer force. The 1903 Act was amended several times, but it remained largely intact and shifted focus in future wars from as-needed volunteer militias to longer-standing forces (Mahon, 1983; Stentiford, 2002). The nature of US domestic militias thus shifted further away from formal military ties into formations that relied more on local leadership and control, in some ways returning their general structure to what had existed in early colonial days.

The second wave of the Klan, which emerged around 1915, followed this model. Although a widespread and hierarchically structured organization, Klan chapters were largely able to establish their own localized agenda for both the terror they enacted and the political efforts they supported in their pursuit of white supremacy's maintenance. KKK members of this wave found Black people and increasing numbers of Catholic migrants to be near-equal threats to what they called "100 percent Americanism" (McVeigh, 2009, p. 21), which they believed to be white, Protestant, and male-controlled. This second Klan wave declined in the early 1920s, in large part because they had national political successes that institutionalized their desired social outcomes and lessened the need for extra-institutional actions like protest and terrorism.

Private militias remained relatively quiet for the next several decades, while mainstream movements continued to represent their idealized national values on a more public stage. The 1930s, for example, brought the Great

Depression and a widespread resurgence of anxieties about a changing cultural landscape. Despite the continued social disdain for Catholics during this time, a priest named Father Charles Coughlin from Michigan harnessed the mass economic fear and resentment and directed it toward Communists,[3] who remained an acceptable target of open nationalist ire through the McCarthyism of the 1950s.

Advances from the Civil Rights Movement and specifically the desegregation resulting from *Brown v. Board of Education* in 1954 spurred the KKK's third wave as well as the formation of new groups, like the John Birch Society, that were ostensibly less violent and more politically oriented than the Klan but still aimed to maintain white supremacy. Despite claiming to be a non-racist organization, John Birchers regularly spewed both anti-Black ideas and anti-Jewish conspiracy theories, thus promoting the same, racially, and culturally exclusive version of nationalism espoused by the Klan and earlier racist movements (Diamond, 1995; Lipset & Raab, 1978). While Birchers were rarely accused of violence or organized, armed efforts that would qualify them as a militia group, their support of unrestricted gun rights[4] and their overarching message were complementary with the KKK's and helped contribute to a general legitimation of racist threats from the more violent organizations during the era.

Hard-fought social progress resulting from the Civil Rights Movement and second-wave feminism through the 1960s and 1970s ensured that white men who were uncertain about their continued social power remained on edge and eager for ways to oppose cultural changes brought about by expanded rights for people of color and increased workplace participation and economic freedom for women. A group called the Posse Comitatus, named for the 1878 Act that limited the federal government's ability to enforce the law, emerged during this time and is one of the more recognizable and impactful factors that led directly to today's domestic militia structure. Posse's founder, William Potter Gale, had open affiliations with numerous racist organizations and relied on a relatively obscure—and British—piece of legislation called the Sheriffs Act 1887 to claim that local sheriffs have more power than other law enforcement officials or even the President.

Sheriffs, according to Gale's logic, could effectively deputize "posses" of local citizens to enforce their understanding of the law, and modern Posse affiliates continue to justify their ideology by citing the US Constitution even though the word "sheriff" never appears in that document. This justification nonetheless has superficial appeal and may create the most significant element of the Posse's continuing legacy on the modern militia movement. As extremism researcher Mark Pitcavage (2001) notes:

> Gale appropriated the term *unorganized militia* from federal law; by so doing, he hoped to link his group to the militia mentioned in the constitution and federal and state law. This claim of legitimacy and authority distinguishes both Gale's group and the subsequent militia movement

from other paramilitary groups, including some that even use the term militia in a more generic sense.

Referencing the historical split between the official National Guard and the volunteer militia, Gale succeeds (at least in his supporters' view) in giving an air of Constitutional credence to volunteer militia organizations that have no federal or state oversight. Militias through present day use this same logic to insist that their units are legal, patriotic, and, in some cases, constitutionally *required* for men of a certain age, even when state or other statutes seem to prohibit their formation. In a May 1995, letter to the editor of the *Petoskey News-Review*, for example, Michigan militia founder Norm Olson cites a 1973 court case from Arkansas[5] where a judge relied on the Posse Comitatus Act to rule that civilians are required to assist law enforcement when requested. Olson equates the militia with the Posse and says:

> Since the sheriff is the servant of the citizens who are inhabitants of the county, it is not his choice as whether or not the Posse is organized and brought into being, it is only his choice as to whether or not he wishes to use it.

Posse affiliates who made similar claims regarding the inherent righteousness or legitimacy of their actions and whose beliefs were, in many cases, amplified by longer-standing tax protestor ideology also fostered another group known as Sovereign Citizens. Sovereign Citizens adhere to an incredibly strict and idiosyncratic reading of the Constitution that is informed by obscure interpretations of legalities and outright conspiracy theories. They directly borrow from Posse Comitatus's core principles and reject the legitimacy of the federal government. They believe they are using highly technical legal interpretations to justify ignoring most, if not all, laws, including refusing in some cases to obey even basic traffic regulations like red lights or stop signs (Sarteschi, 2020). They are known to refuse to obtain birth certificates, driver's licenses, and license plates, claiming those documents are artifacts of an illegitimate government. One such man I encountered during my fieldwork referred to official government documents as "slave papers," insisting that compliance with the illegitimate system was willfully giving up inherent rights and inviting other unnecessary, tyrannical control over individual autonomy. Sovereign Citizens are sometimes known as "paper terrorists" because of their proclivity for filing false liens and other lawsuits to drag out various court proceedings. When facing legal action themselves, they often insist the court is illegitimate by citing trivial "evidence," such as claiming that the courtroom flag being trimmed with gold fringe is a violation of the flag code and nullifies any proceedings within it, all in an effort to avoid consequences for any charges they face. Their behavior often leads to confrontations with law enforcement officers (LEOs), dozens of whom have been wounded or killed during hostile interactions with Sovereign Citizens since the group's emergence (Sarteschi, 2021).

Despite this general hostility toward law enforcement as agents of an illegitimate government, most Sovereign Citizens claim that "real," or so-called Constitutional, sheriffs will support their efforts to resist governmental tyranny. They circularly define Constitutional sheriffs as those who endorse claims of federal illegitimacy and who see their primary responsibility as protecting the perceived interests of the local people who elected them, even if those interests contravene the law. Strongly echoing Posse Comitatus influence, they believe that such sheriffs are the last line of defense for the Constitution and for the patriotic Americans the document represents a belief often shared by contemporary militia members (Cooter, 2022).

Both Posse and Sovereign Citizen groups received a boost in support from veterans who returned from Vietnam disaffected both with the war and with how their government and fellow citizens treated them once they returned home. Perceptions of Vietnam and of domestic social change surrounding race, gender, and economy led to a surging extremism among veterans who believed this conflict to be a failed effort that undermined the legitimacy of US policy and military strategy alike (Belew, 2018; Gibson, 1994). Although we do not know how many veterans may have joined these or other groups as an expression of their anger, we do know that some notable figures within these groups, including some who had clear connections to openly racist organizations, talked about their experiences in Vietnam as further evidence of the federal government's illegitimacy and ineptitude (Pitcavage, 2001). The influx of military veterans also likely amplified preexisting interest both the Posse and Sovereign Citizens had in firearms and gun rights preservation, creating yet another logical connection from these groups to the formation of modern militias.

The theme of uncertainty regarding social change in the 1960s and 1970s once more took an institutionalized turn headed into the 1980s. Anxiety certainly continued among white people who were frustrated by continued cultural changes they believed deprived them of power, as in part evidenced by a return of notable violence perpetrated by neo-Nazi and other overtly racist groups during this decade. However, President Ronald Reagan's election also offered many of these people an archetype of a cowboy patriot who could return the country to what they saw as the correct path. While distrust of the federal government did not disappear from these communities, many of them saw a spark of hope—one that Donald Trump would later similarly fan into a conflagration—for a return to supposedly simpler and purer times. Reagan's presence coincided with the emergence of the Christian Right as a political force that capitalized on the uncertainty of the previous decade to attempt a "return to traditional values" (Diamond, 1995; Hardisty, 2000).

Reagan's legacy continued briefly under one-term President George H. W. Bush, who similarly cultivated a self-image of a down-to-earth Texan military veteran to appeal to nativist and originalist sentiments. He, like Reagan, intentionally and successfully tapped into the allure of cowboy masculinity and its promise of maintaining a traditional national culture. Some conservatives believed the formal efforts to return the country to its supposedly proper path came to an abrupt end, however, when Bush lost his second election in 1992 to Democrat Bill Clinton. Despite Clinton's blue-collar southern bona fides, conservatives viewed him as an outsider and a threat to their ideal national identity due to his supposedly socialist or immoral policies surrounding health care, including abortion, and gay rights. Clinton largely failed to deliver on these minimal promises once in office, but his detractors' uncertainty regarding his influence on a national landscape that they believed to have been course-corrected under the prior administrations created conditions ripe for the resurgence of groups opposed to policies that are typically considered socially progressive. The next chapter examines specific events in the early 1990s under Clinton's administration that led directly to the formation of the modern militia movement.

Notes

1. The dynamics of militias including what factors create them, their degree of popular support, and what variables can limit their power vary enormously across national contexts. This book's focus is exclusively on US domestic militias, but Day et al. (2020), Grandin (2000), Febalb-Brown (2016a, 2016b), Raleigh (2014), and Thorning (2005) are an excellent starting point for information about militias in other countries.
2. Some militia units take oaths to this effect, echoing similar oaths taken by military and law enforcement officers. The most notable example are militias who affiliate with the Oath Keepers, which was originally formed around the premise of reminding military and law enforcement veterans of their duty to the populace (Jackson, 2020).
3. He also targeted Jewish people until forced to stop by Catholic leadership during WWII (Lipset & Raab, 1978).
4. See, for example, https://web.archive.org/web/20220705053138/https://jbs.org/tag/gun-control/
5. https://web.archive.org/save/https://casetext.com/case/williams-v-state-6868

References

Belew, K. (2018). *Bring the war home: The White power movement and paramilitary America*. Harvard University Press.

Churchill, R. H. (2009). *To shake their guns in the Tyrant's face: Libertarian political violence and the origins of the militia movement*. The University of Michigan Press.

Cooter, A. (2022). US Domestic Militias' intersections with government and authority: How a sociology of individualism informs their praxis. In D. Neubert, H. J. Lauth, & C. Mohamad-Klotzbach (Eds.), *Local self-governance and varieties of statehood: Tensions and cooperation* (pp. 31–49). Springer International Publishing.

Cornell, S. (2008). *A well-regulated militia: The founding fathers and the origins of gun control in America*. Oxford University Press.

Day, A., Felbab-Brown, V., & Haddad, F. (2020). Hybrid conflict, hybrid peace: How militias and paramilitary groups shape post-conflict transitions. *United Nations University Centre for Policy Research*. https://cpr.unu.edu/research/projects/hybrid-conflict.html#outline

Diamond, S. (1995). *Roads to dominion: Right-wing movements and political power in the United States.* The Guilford Press.

Dunbar-Ortiz, R. (2018). *Loaded: A disarming history of the second amendment.* City Lights Publishers.

Felbab-Brown, V. (2016a). Hurray for militias? Not so fast: Lessons from the Afghan local police experience. *Small Wars & Insurgencies, 27*(2), 258–281.

Felbab-Brown, V. (2016b). The rise of militias in Mexico: Citizens' security or further conflict escalation? *PRISM, 5*(4), 172–187.

Fogelson, R. M. (1989). *America's armories: Architecture, society, and public order.* Harvard University Press.

Gibson, J. W. (1994). *Warrior dreams: Violence and manhood in post-Vietnam America* (Reprint ed.). Hill & Wang.

Grandin, G. (2000). *The blood of Guatemala: A history of race and nation* (Illustrated ed.). Duke University Press.

Hardisty, J. (2000). *Mobilizing resentment: Conservative resurgence from the John Birch society to the promise keepers.* Beacon Press.

Isaac, L. (2002). To counter "the very devil" and more: The making of independent capitalist militia in the gilded age. *American Journal of Sociology, 108*(2), 353–405.

Jackson, S. (2020). *Oath Keepers: Patriotism and the edge of violence in a right-wing antigovernment group.* Columbia University Press.

Kerby, R. L. (1977). The militia system and the state militias in the war of 1812. *Indiana Magazine of History, 73*(2), 102–124.

Lew-Williams, B. (2018). *The Chinese must go: Violence, exclusion, and the making of the alien in America.* Harvard University Press.

Lipset, S. M., & Raab, E. (1978). *The politics of unreason: Right wing extremism in America, 1790–1977* (2nd ed.). University of Chicago Press.

MacCabe, J. D. (1971). *The history of the great riots, together with a full history of the Molly Maguires* (Reprint ed.). Augustus M. Kelley.

Mahon, J. K. (1983). *History of the militia and the national guard.* Free Press.

McVeigh, R. (2009). *The rise of the Ku Klux Klan: Right-wing movements and national politics* (Vol. 32). University of Minnesota Press.

Mulloy, D. (2008). *American extremism: History, politics and the militia movement.* Routledge.

Nunn, J. (2021, October 14). The Posse Comitatus act explained. *Brennan Center for Justice*. www.brennancenter.org/our-work/research-reports/posse-comitatus-act-explained

Pitcavage, M. (2001). Camouflage and conspiracy: The militia movement from ruby ridge to Y2K. *American Behavioral Scientist, 44*(6), 957–981.

Raleigh, C. (2014). Political hierarchies and landscapes of conflict across Africa. *Political Geography, 42*, 92–103.

Randall, J. G. (1961). *The civil war and reconstruction* (2nd ed.). Heath.

Richardson, H. C. (2008). *West from Appomattox: The reconstruction of America after the civil war* (Illustrated ed.). Yale University Press.

Royster, C. (1996). *A revolutionary people at war: The continental army and American character, 1775–1783*. Omohundro Institute and University of North Carolina Press.

Sarteschi, C. M. (2020). *Sovereign citizens: A psychological and criminological analysis*. Springer.

Sarteschi, C. M. (2021). Sovereign citizens: A narrative review with implications of violence towards law enforcement. *Aggression and Violent Behavior, 60*. www.ncbi.nlm.nih.gov/pmc/articles/PMC7513757/

Schrag, Z. M. (2021). *The fires of Philadelphia: Citizen-soldiers, nativists, and the 1844 riots over the soul of a nation*. Pegasus Books.

Shy, J. (1990). *A people numerous and armed: Reflections on the military struggle for American independence* (Revised ed.). University of Michigan Press.

Skeen, C. E. (2021). *Citizen soldiers in the war of 1812*. The University Press of Kentucky.

Smith, J. D. (2004). Let us all be grateful that we have colored troops that will fight. In J. Smith (Ed.), *Black soldiers in blue* (pp. 1–77). The University of North Carolina Press.

SPLC. (2011, March 1). Ku Klux Klan: A history of racism. *Southern Poverty Law Center*. www.splcenter.org/20110228/ku-klux-klan-history-racism

Stentiford, B. M. (2002). *The American home guard: The state militia in the twentieth century* (Vol. 78). Texas A&M University Press.

Thorning, R. (2005). Civil militias: Indonesia and Nigeria in comparative perspective. In *Civil militia*. Routledge.

Vladeck, S. I. (2004). Emergency power and the militia acts. *The Yale Law Journal, 114*(1), 149–194.

Young, A. T. (2020). The necropolitics of liberty: Sovereignty, fantasy, and United States gun culture. *Lateral, 9*(1). https://csalateral.org/forum/gun-culture/necropolitics-of-liberty-sovereignty-fantasy-us-gun-culture-young/

3 Militia Origins
The Gospel According to Norm Olson

"You might say I'm the founding father of the militia movement," Norm Olson told me unnecessarily during my first phone conversation with him in late August 2010. By this point, I had been attending meetings, trainings, and other events with different militia units in Michigan for nearly two and a half years. I had formally interviewed 40 militia members and informally interviewed many more. I was well acquainted with Mr. Olson's history and reputation.

He continued, "I've been waiting for someone to come along that I could pass along my legacy to." I was less sure about this second part of his statement. By "someone," he meant me. He had first emailed me a few days earlier after seeing some news coverage that included my commentary on the Hutaree "Christian" militia whose members had been arrested in Michigan for alleged plots to murder police officers. Olson told me that he thought I gave a "fair" description of the movement as a whole and was calling to discuss the logistics of shipping seven boxes from his home in Alaska to my apartment in Ann Arbor. Each box weighed approximately 40 pounds, and they were collectively filled with his personal archive of the movement's founding. While I was excited about the opportunity to be the first researcher to see many of these materials, I saw my job not as preserving a legacy and instead as interrogating the complicated dynamics of a movement 16 years after its birth.

Olson's claim to founding father status was not an overstatement. He and another Michigander, Ray Southwell, started the Michigan Militia Corps of Wolverines (MMCW) whose name unironically referenced Patrick Swayze's band of patriots heroically resisting Russian invasion in the 1984 film *Red Dawn*.[1] Michigan's organizational structure quickly became a model for nascent militia groups all across the country, and Olson and Southwell maintain a special place in national militia lore. This lore sees militia adherents as following directly in the footsteps of the country's Founding Fathers: White men, who, in a mythologized telling, bravely charted a new and dangerous path against all odds to set the foundation for a tenuous experiment in liberty. Olson told me in our 2010 phone chat that he believed the militia movement

DOI: 10.4324/9781003361657-4

was a reflection of "how the people of America—'we the people'—started to reflect ideas, aspirations, and the spirit of Founding Fathers; [it was] a reemergence of 1776, of Jefferson Payne and Patrick Henry and all those heroes." Olson's claim was as much a symbolic reference to this perceived lineage as it was a factual statement about his role in the militia's origin.

Olson was retired with limited income. He asked me to cover shipping costs for his archive, so I mailed him a check for about $200 and anxiously awaited the boxes' arrival several weeks later.[2] Upon receipt, there was a daunting trove of information: several VHS cassettes, handwritten letters that supporters had sent to him (a few of which had never been opened), and approximately 3,000 pages of assorted papers. Those musty pages were mostly old faxes to and from others in the so-called patriot network and copies of MMCW press releases. That tally does not include many duplicates of materials that had clearly been made in overly optimistic anticipation of attendance at various events before being added to a pile of other memorabilia. Most of the documents were clearly legible; a few were at least partially discernable; but another 30 or so that were on slick, old fax paper had been lost to UV rays and the passage of time. After I sorted and digitized the material with the enormous help of then-undergraduate Mark Suchyta, I delivered the papers to the Bentley Historical Library in Ann Arbor, Michigan, per Mr. Olson's request, where they may be found in the collection titled "Norm Olson Papers."

Olson was not quite ready to let go of a few materials in 2010. He reached out to me again in fall 2020, saying he "had a few more things to add to the archive." I again paid for shipping, this time just $50, and asked him to send the materials to me first, promising I would eventually add them to the Bentley after I was finished with them. I received one box very similar

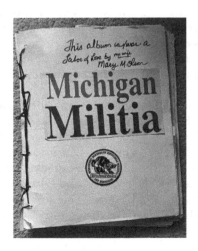

Figure 3.1 Cover of Norm Olson's album.
Source: Photo by the author.

to those from the earlier shipment and, just four days before Trump failed to win reelection, a large, flat scrapbook. Made of 73 sheets of 19-inch by 25-inch white poster board and held together by an intricately tied bootlace, the album, as Olson called it, weighs 18 pounds. It is filled mostly with newspaper clippings and various writings from Olson himself that all capture the early days of the movement. Other bits of memorabilia are sprinkled through the pages—things like identification badges Olson received for some of his media or other official visits, and stubs from airplane tickets to important events like his eventual testimony before the US Congress about the goals and intentions of the militia movement.

Some of the news articles in the scrapbook cultivate a positive impression of the militia, implying that such an organization might be an innovative solution to real problems or including upcoming meeting times and locations, thus effectively acting as advertisements for the early movement. Other articles are reasonably neutral, with quotations from both militia leaders and local officials or law enforcement who are assessing militia activities. Many articles (perhaps a surprising number given the scrapbook's purpose) are negative, criticizing the militia's actions if not their intent, or some even outright ridiculing Olson and other members by name. One example of these negative portrayals is a political cartoon by David Simpson depicting militia men as a literal regression in human evolution. These men are shown in a spin on the usual visual rendering of evolutionary stages as being more atavistic than Neanderthals and more even than an ape-like creature labeled "Canthrop Man."

By the time I received it, the scrapbook had visible wear. The bootstring was tearing through some of the poster board's hole punches. Some documents were falling off their pages where their glue had given out, but all entries were legible and, with a few exceptions, in chronological order. A small number of materials, largely from the later stages of Olson's militia trajectory, were unmounted and instead arrived seemingly randomly sandwiched between the album's pages: embroidered patches intended for placement on militia uniforms, an entire newspaper issue devoted to coverage of the Oklahoma City bombing, and a few other articles or documents perhaps once intended to be attached to the very few still-empty spots at the end of the scrapbook. The care imbued in the book's compilation was obvious even with these signs of age and shifting attention.

Meticulously compiled by Olson's wife, Mary, as memorialized in sharpie on the front cover, the scrapbook entered the public spotlight when *VICE* media filmed a television special in 2009 (VICE Staff, 2009), where Olson showcased some of its contents. Some long-time militia members knew of its existence well before the show's airing and had already mentioned it as something that I should seek out for my research. The scrapbook, like Olson himself, held a good deal of symbolic importance to these militia members. It was effectively a sacred text, representative of not only their origin story but, from their perspective, also a representation of the labor, risk, and ingenuity that went into building the modern militia movement in the spirit of the nation's founders.

Some members of the contemporary movement went so far as to say that they believe the militia as a national phenomenon would never have existed were it not for Norm Olson's vision and influence. I do not agree with that assessment. The national landscape was such a tinderbox in the early 1990s that someone else could have started a similar mass response that embodied the fear and anger that many Americans were feeling about the government. Similar efforts were indeed underway in other states at the time, most notably Montana. It is, however, undeniable that Olson played a pivotal role in the early days of the movement as it developed. Instead of speculating about what hypothetical similarities and differences may have existed under different leadership, it is valuable to understand his influence and to use his perspective and presence as a lens for understanding the movement as a whole.

Olson's materials confirm the known timeline of the militia's birth but yield greater insights into his thought processes and tactics than are present in existing accounts of this history. Olson and Southwell[3] had a formal planning meeting in March 1994 to finalize details but had already started sussing out interest in such a group and thinking about their desired organizational structure. Olson wrote letters to the editor in local papers and hosted a "Patriot Meeting" in early March to encourage others to recognize the dangers that they believed the federal government posed.

They said they feared the government was turning increasingly tyrannical and that it could, if unopposed, expand in size and power such that individual liberties would effectively cease to exist altogether. This fear was rooted in three specific and snowballing events that each stoked concerns about the limits of federal authority. These events individually (and especially collectively) served as what social movement scholars call "moral shocks," worldview shattering events that make people reassess the world around them and make them feel an urgent need for action.

Sowing the Seeds: Crucial Events in the Militia Movement's Formation

The Weaver Family in Ruby Ridge, Idaho

The cascade of moral shocks began in 1992 when US Marshals surveilled a homestead owned by Randy and Vicki Weaver. Randy Weaver was a military veteran who seemed increasingly drawn both into racism and into conspiracy theories that caused him to distrust the government.[4] The Weavers had lived a secluded lifestyle for some time and would reportedly travel with their children to socialize with members of the overtly racist group Aryan Nations 60 miles away. Weaver's daughter, interviewed as an adult for a documentary about the events that forever changed her family, remembers being taken to the Aryan Nations compound as a child. She says her experiences there felt like a "family vacation," seeming to focus not on the racism but rather on the social development that she was otherwise denied on the isolated homestead. Part of what drew the Weavers to this particular location, she says, was the way the racists at the compound advocated living outside of a mainstream society that they believed to be incompatible with their values (Goodman, 2020).

The Bureau of Alcohol, Tobacco, and Firearms (ATF) had asked Randy Weaver in 1990 to act as an informant against Aryan Nations, and he declined. Seven months later and in what some saw as retaliation for this refusal, Weaver was charged with selling illegal weapons to an undercover agent. Weaver did not appear for the trial on these charges, reportedly due to a probation office incorrectly communicating the trial date information, and a judge issued a warrant for his arrest. Weaver's anti-government sentiments and commentary about intending to use violence to resist arrest were so well known by this time that Marshals continued to warily monitor him for 18 months rather than carry through with the warrant (DOJ, 1994). Weaver's cold-war style standoff against the government earned him local media attention and support during this time, even—and perhaps especially—as the Weavers became aware that Marshals and ATF agents had placed surveillance cameras on their property and were conducting foot patrols there (Crothers, 2019).

It was during one such patrol in August 1992 that the impasse ended. While the initial sequence of events on this day is disputed, the outcome was clear. The Weaver's 14-year-old son Sammy was shot in the back and died while he was out with the family dog. A federal agent was also shot dead, and a Weaver family friend named Kevin Harris was wounded by gun fire. An FBI hostage team responded to the site after the agent's death, but instead of cooling tensions, the situation escalated further. Randy Weaver was himself shot on the second day of the siege as he was going to tend to his deceased son (*ibid.*).

In retrospect, it seems that agents likely did not know that Sammy had been killed the previous day. The firefight happened in a wooded area with agents returning fire uphill in the general direction of whoever (likely Harris) had shot a Marshal. Agents, in short, panicked after the initial confrontation. Some agents improperly left their surveillance posts, resulting in misinformation about what was happening on the property. This lack of accurate information enhanced the agency's perceptions of Weaver's threat and ultimately led to the use of a modified version of the FBI's usual rules of engagement. Agents on site began operating on an order to shoot to kill armed men on the property (*ibid.*). This order led to the bullet that hit Randy Weaver's arm and, moments after, another bullet that went through a partially open door and through Vicki Weaver's head, killing her instantly. Sara Weaver reports that her mother was killed as she was standing inside their home and holding Sara's 10-month-old sister (Goodman, 2020).

Speculation about the events unfolding on the Weaver property was rife among a group of protestors and observers stationed round-the-clock at a road near the property. As the situation escalated, these observers grew to include national news media, which shared rumors and updates from the homestead. Some of those updates were from federal agents, but others came from a man named Bo Gritz, a former Army ranger, one-time Populist Party Vice Presidential nominee, and known conspiracy theorist (SPLC, n.d.), whom the FBI brought in to act as a mediator.

People across the country watched as the drama unfolded on their TV screens, unsure, perhaps, of what was happening out of view of the news cameras but certain they did not want government agents similarly accosting them on their own land. Concerned viewers included my parents and their rural Baptist pastor, who, from 2,400 miles away in East Tennessee, asked a prayer for the Weaver family's surviving children the day after Vicki Weaver's death. It may now be difficult to fully appreciate how frightening this news was to a variety of people, Republicans and Democrats alike, given what has transpired both politically and technologically in the intervening years. Today, we all too often see global tragedies on our phones, even as they are still unfolding.[5] In 1992, it was chilling to hear from your own living room Gritz's announcement of Vicki Weaver's death, an announcement underscored by the protesters' collective and instantaneous gasp of horror that transformed into a cacophony of individual wails of grief.

Ten days after the first shots were fired, Randy Weaver surrendered himself to custody, a move that Gritz helped facilitate. Weaver and Harris both ended up facing several charges related to the siege. Defense attorneys for the high-profile case successfully kept the focus on the missteps of government actors, vigorously portraying them as having engaged both in a conspiracy against Weaver and in a cover-up of their actions. As professor of politics and government Lane Crothers notes, "the way [defense attorneys] kept the intensity of Weaver's racist religious beliefs out of the trial informed the myth that the Weavers were [completely] innocent people brutalized by a rampaging government. They became Everyman" (2019, p. 43). Becoming "Everyman" meant that people who watched fearfully during the siege saw themselves as future possible victims of government tyranny.

Harris was acquitted of all charges, while Weaver was convicted of only one—failure to appear. The acquittals notably included the original weapons charges that led to the homestead surveillance and eventual deaths. Weaver's punishment was a $10,000 fine (paid by a supporter) and 18 months in prison, of which he had already served 14 by the time of conviction (*ibid.*). The federal government eventually paid the surviving Weavers a substantial wrongful death settlement and paid Harris a civil rights settlement (The Associated Press, 2000). Several federal agents were professionally disciplined but faced no criminal charges after the Department of Justice and US Senate both investigated the events at Ruby Ridge.

David Koresh and the Branch Davidians in Waco, Texas

The second event crucial to the militia's founding began in February 1993, just six months after the Weaver standoff. This time, federal agents raided a compound occupied by Branch Davidians—a radical religious sect—in Waco, Texas. The Davidians' leader, David Koresh, had been under investigation for allegations of child abuse and illegal firearms modifications. When an Australian television show drew increased attention to Koresh's polygamous marriages with teenage girls, several of whom bore children, officials escalated their actions. Agents planned an elaborate operation to secure the compound and Koresh without violence. This was a smart tactic given the vast quantity of firearms and ammunition known to be on the grounds, but the plan as designed never came to fruition. Instead, agents had a too-visible presence to go unnoticed. Reporters caught wind of the raid and came to town to cover it before it began. One inadvertently asked a Davidian postal worker for directions to the compound while mentioning the raid. The tipped-off sect member passed on this information, and Koresh and others inside the compound were able to arm themselves and prepare for the incursion. As Lane Crothers (2019, p. 49) once again eloquently observes:

> Thus a raid premised on secrecy, speed, and surprise was allowed to take place even after its targets announced their knowledge of the coming assault. The ATF force was simply ordered to get to the Davidian compound faster. For conspiracy theorists, this served as proof that the raid was deadly in its intent.

There is still disagreement over who fired first—Davidians or a federal agent (possibly even via an accidental discharge)—but bursts of gunfire and return volleys went on for hours, this time in full view of grainy news cameras that again broadcasted these images nationwide to an anxious audience. Memorable scenes included a black helicopter flying low over the property and several agents using a ladder to try to access a building through a second-story window before one was shot, the bullet hitting him after being fired through a wall.[6] Agents and Koresh agreed to a ceasefire at noon, by which point two dozen people were injured, most of them ATF agents, with an additional four agents dead. The FBI then took over the site and managed what metastasized into a 51-day siege.

Koresh, who was among those injured during the raid, used the many weeks of the siege to preach his personal gospel. Curious bystanders and supporters—both independent individuals and members of various nostalgic groups—continued to travel to Waco to bear witness, driven by their common worry of an increasingly tyrannical government. One of those supporters was Timothy McVeigh, whose actions would make him a household name two years later (PBS, n.d.). The FBI managed to negotiate the release of 21 children from the compound during this siege (DOJ, 1993), but little else changed. The agency tired of waiting and received approval to use a gas similar to tear gas to try to force remaining sect members, including other children, out of the compound. Several fires started nearly simultaneously across the compound shortly after the introduction of this CS gas, with brown smoke quickly erupting into enormous blazes that were fueled by the plywood construction.[7] Only nine sect members survived this day, with at least 75 members believed to have been killed across both raids (Crothers, 2019). The government maintains the fires were deliberately set by the Davidians to avoid arrest (DOJ, 1993), but others believe the fires were caused, or at least made inescapable, by the flammable CS gas (Crothers, 2019). Some of those who died in the compound died by gunshots or other causes in what some believe to have been mercy killings to avoid the flames.

This second deadly raid began on April 19, 1993, just seven days after the opening arguments for Randy Weaver's criminal trial. It was impossible for a national audience that was still invested in Weaver's trajectory to ignore the similarities between his firefight with the government and that with the Branch Davidians. Eventual Senate hearings into the Waco siege concluded that the FBI had once more acted improperly, this time losing (or perhaps even intentionally hiding) evidence and violating typical procedures for hostage scenarios (Kopel & Blackman, 1997). Rather than coming across as proof of a system slowly but surely working toward justice, concerned observers saw these findings as confirmation that their fears of government overreach were justified. Many people who did not know the specific allegations against either Weaver or Koresh ultimately perceived both events as the government persecuting people who were little more than social outcasts. Especially for these Americans, Ruby Ridge and Waco together became emblematic of a nation under threat from the inside, from a federal government that was seemingly turning against its own people.

Those Americans who believed themselves to be true patriots were inspired to stand up and challenge this development. Norm Olson was among those Americans, as is reflected in his personal archive. For example, his letter to the editor of the *Petoskey News-Review* published March 29, 1994, references the "BATF and FBI [executing] their deadly campaign against the Branch Davidians." Later in the letter, he pleads for his audience to "Remember that it was not a mob of angry torch-bearing citizens that attacked Mount Carmel [the name of the Davidian compound], but the government sworn to protect their rights." A month later, on April 23, 1994, the day after the first official MMCW meeting, he signed a homemade press release and flier that aimed to recruit more "Patriot[s] willing to defend the Constitution." It reads:

> As was apparent in the case of Randy Weaver and the events in Waco, Texas, the Federal Military and the National Guard have conspired to deny US Citizens their right to due process of law. The time has come for the formation of a citizen militia unit in our area to prevent another Waco from happening.

Militia Origins 63

That Olson sees the government's intervention in these events as intentional, nefarious acts (exactly as Weaver's lawyers had argued regarding his case) is underscored by a hymn that Olson composed titled "Sammy's Dog."[8] With instructions to be "sung prayerfully," two of the five versus read:

But Lord, I think of Striker, the Weaver's faithful hound
Standing between young Sammy and the man who gunned him down.
And when I think of that old dog who stood its ground that day
I know that love kept Striker there to let Sammy get away

Striker's just a dog, dear Lord, and perhaps it's strange to hear
My prayer is that I might have the love, that kept that old dog there;
And if I must die, Dear Lord I ask, let me die like Sammy's friend.
An old hound dog who stood his ground, faithful till the end.

Love and dogged loyalty to his vision of the country make Olson not eager to die, according to this representation, yet willing to do so to defend this vision. At the same time, the metaphor is perhaps revealing about Olson's understanding of his odds of success. Striker, whether a heroic family pet as portrayed in this homage or, as some believe, a hapless casualty of federal agents attempting to remain hidden, died in vain moments before Sammy was also killed. Olson is unsure of the fate of his country or of the utility of his hypothetical sacrifice, even as he remains willing to offer it.

The Brady Bill

Ruby Ridge and Waco undeniably induced fear about the federal government and were instrumental in the formation of the militia movement, but what explains the year-long lag between the second Waco raid and the first militia events? This is where the third necessary event—the passage of the Brady Bill (formally, the Brady Handgun Violence Prevention Act)—aids our understanding of the movement's trajectory. This bill was intended to set some limits on handgun sales, with the major changes being the introduction of certain background checks for purchasers and a five-day waiting period before the purchaser could take possession of a new handgun.

The Brady Bill was, after an earlier failure, reintroduced in February 1993, the same month as the first Waco raid, and it was covered fairly heavily in the national news as it made its way through committee and Congressional debate in subsequent months. The bill was signed in November 1993 but did not go into effect until February 1994, the same month the first modern militia met in Montana and the same month that Olson and Southwell held early meetings about their plans for a Michigan militia.

The Brady Bill's passage became the proverbial last straw in the creation of the movement. Many conservatives who had no interest in joining a militia were angry about this bill's perceived infringements on their Constitutional right to bear arms. But people who had been frightened by the events of Ruby Ridge and Waco saw something even more sinister happening with this bill's passage: a federal government actively trying to inhibit people's ability to defend themselves from violence initiated by that very government. Their fear was heightened by the Federal Assault Weapons ban, which took advantage of the Brady Bill's momentum. This ban was a subsection of the Violent Crime Control and Law Enforcement Act of 1994. It was introduced in November 1993 and went into effect in September of the following year. A reporter who covered the MMCW's response to this Act quotes Southwell as saying it was "the latest step in a plot to disarm the public. . . . We need to take a stand before all our liberties are gone" (Flesher, 1994).

This quote exemplifies an important point that is often overlooked in coverage of the militia movement's affinity for the Second Amendment. Although there is indeed stand-alone symbolic power in their relationship to firearms, many members also genuinely believe that private gun ownership actively prevents the government from infringing on other "inherent" rights. As one member told me, echoing language used by the NRA since at least 1958 (Lacombe, 2021), "The Second Amendment is what *allows* us to have the First." This member, just like Southwell, believed that without the perpetual threat of force from citizens, the government would wantonly trample citizens' rights. Members who espouse this perspective invoke comparisons to dictatorships or other regimes where dissidents "are disappeared," meaning killed or incarcerated without recourse by their governments. In using these comparisons, members are emphasizing their belief that the Second Amendment is thus crucial for maintaining the US as a nation that promotes life, liberty, and the pursuit of happiness better than any other. They then interpret any federal efforts to restrict gun ownership of citizens described as "law abiding" as a sign that the government is shifting away from that valued national identity by actively engaging in tyranny in what is supposed to be the land of the free.

Tending the Flock: From Fear to Action

On the phone, it is difficult to ignore Norm Olson's charisma and cadence, which make him sound very much like an old-style Baptist preacher. Olson is, in fact, a pastor, one whose sermons continued to be on Facebook until Fall 2023, even after most other militia-connected Facebook pages were deplatformed in late 2020. He easily slips into religious metaphors during our conversations about militia history and social events. Sometimes his responses feel like miniature sermons that do not quite deliver concrete answers to my questions yet still provide insights into his broader thoughts and worldview.

Olson's beliefs about patriotism, national identity, and God are intimately connected to each other. According to handwritten notes on a 1993 wall calendar that was among the second set of materials he mailed me, Olson gave his first sermon at Calvary Baptist Church in Brutus, Michigan, in July of 1990 before being voted in there as pastor ten months later. The archive includes a few materials with Calvary Church's name and address, including a lengthy lesson on Lexington and Concord (battle sites considered crucial in the American Revolutionary War) with no clear religious allegory.

Olson's ability to draw strong connections between US mythology and scripture rapidly developed, however, and is showcased in materials connected to a different church, which he founded in May 1994, the month after MMCW's birth. It was named Freedom Church, and it was eventually located[9] in a former gun shop that Olson and some friends converted for this purpose in Wolverine, Michigan. Olson, of course, served as pastor, and Ray Southwell was a deacon. The apparent church motto on some undated fliers reads "Standing Where Our Forefathers stood," almost-too-obviously alongside the church's name, harkening ideas of morally upright forebearers and attempts to preserve individual liberty as described in American mythos.

The church's nationalistic implications are even clearer in a recruitment pamphlet for the new congregation. Its opening passage includes:

> Freedom Church is not a typical or ordinary church. . . . We believe that God had, and still has, a purpose for America. We are not ready to surrender to corruption, oppression, or tyranny while believing that God will miraculously intervene. We blend our spiritual beliefs with patriotism, recognizing that God who gives us life also gives us liberty. We do not *worship* America, its government, or its Constitution, but we believe that as faithful stewards, we must protect what God has given to us [emphasis in original].

Olson takes care to separate his aims from those of most churches, centering the perceived connections between God's will and patriotic actions, including a duty to protect America from tyranny. Emphasizing this theme in a September 1995 press release, Olson writes that it is to be "a church of those who felt outcast by other churches, and for those who felt alienated and disenfranchised by their government." Several contemporary militia members told me that men or at least deacons in Olson's church were required to be armed during service. Nothing to that effect is present in the church's bylaws in the archive. Olson told me that "most" of the congregation was armed, "especially the ladies," and that being armed was highly encouraged but not required for church membership. Collective misremembering of the requirement for male church members to be armed is another indicator of the fuzzy boundary between his church and his militia, however, one made even more blurry by Olson's recollections that, more often than not, he and several other members would target shoot at the range behind the former gun shop immediately after church services.

Olson's archive includes several back-and-forth communications with local and state officials regarding his efforts to avoid registering this so-called Militia Church in order to qualify for tax-exempt status as provided in the Michigan State Constitution. Olson says in these exchanges that the act of registering is a violation of the congregation's religious beliefs. This, plus a general appeal to the separation of church and state, meant, according to him, that the church was not required to register to have tax-exempt status. Within this framing, Olson appears to believe that tax exemption is an unqualified constitutional provision, but that registering the church would then make the church susceptible to other legal provisions—specifically the requirement for churches to avoid making political endorsements to maintain that tax-exempt status. In other words, and in a move sure to be dizzying for those in the legal profession, Olson was arguing that the church could have whatever political involvement it wanted and maintain tax exemption as long as it did not complete the registration process in the state constitutional provision.[10]

The pastor's intent to forefront political discussion was clear later in the same pamphlet I draw from above. There, Olson notes, "We discuss political issues and bring into focus the behavior of elected officials and government agencies." He echoes that a refusal to register as an officially recognized church put them "under no constraint by the state to remain quiet. As John the Baptist spoke out against Herod,[11] so we speak out against the injustice, and righteousness, abuses and corruption of government. We mark those who stand opposed to God." Olson thus creates a parity between God and patriots who organize to oppose perceived governmental tyranny even while accepting the possibility of mortal risk to do so. This parity, which functions as a divine directive, is made even more overt in the pamphlet's closing lines, which read, "if in your heart there beats the passion of the Founders and Patriots who held the vision that God has blessed America for a purpose, then you will discover that Freedom Church is the place where your patriotism will find company."

Fellowship in the Militia Church is based simultaneously on religious and nationalistic doctrine. In essence, being a patriot *is* worshiping God, and vice versa. It is then a *moral* duty to oppose tyranny and its perceived symptoms like gun control. This duty took on increased urgency after the cascading social and political events of the early 1990s, and—for Olson and other church members—God was unquestionably on the side of these patriots' efforts to defend themselves and their country.

Someone who equates their actions with God's divine intentions can easily move into thinking that anyone who opposes their efforts is similarly opposed to God's will. Such a mental move makes it easier to engage in dehumanization and possibly even violence toward those who disagree, especially when considering people perceived to be actively working against God's will (Berger, 2018; Juergensmeyer, 2003). That is, governmental officials and LEOs who are seen as creating or enforcing immoral or even "evil" laws can become conceptually easy targets in efforts to prevent further slippage away from a nationalistic ideal.

Olson, to my knowledge, never advocated such proactive violence from the pulpit or otherwise even as he discussed the moral duty to stand against tyranny. Instead, he, like many other militia members, sees his advocacy as defensive, as stepping up in response to violence initiated by the government. He retrospectively describes his role in the Militia Church as helping people manage their growing anxiety. In a 1999 interview with historian Robert Churchill, a transcript of which Olson kept in his archive, Olson noted that his congregation was comprised of people who were on edge about a variety of "unseen" and "nebulous" threats, comparing their fears to imaginary, "snakes under the bed when we were children. You know, [things like] the UN [United Nations] was going to attack, . . . black helicopters, cryptic stickers on the back of road signs and all of this nonsense."

His choice of examples here is interesting. Despite dismissing them as "nonsense," all these conspiracy theories became a lingering part of militia lore. Olson himself believed the US was in danger of ceding sovereignty to the UN and, according to an article in the *Lansing State Journal*, headed a 300-person protest in October 1994 to oppose a UN flag being raised over the Lansing City Hall for UN Day. Militia members were instructed to be in uniform but unarmed in a message that Olson sent prior to the event, saying, "The only weapons shall be the [American] flag and our loyalty to it," alongside a suggestion to purchase "affordable" flags at places like K-Mart. Olson's militia repeated this protest the following year; the number of those in attendance is not listed in news coverage, but a picture accompanying the *Petoskey News-Review* article shows several dozen people watching two unidentified militia members dressed in camouflage set fire to a UN flag—an activity that Olson had expressly prohibited the previous year.

The UN is at the center of a variety of sovereignty-related conspiracy theories, most of which at least hint at the idea that powerful non-US actors want to use the UN to enact gun control or outright gun confiscation from citizens. Olson's mention of stickers on the back of the road signs references rumors that government agents subtly placed stickers on the back of some signs to give directions to secret Federal Emergency Management Agency (FEMA) camps ostensibly used to "disappear" or re-educate patriots opposing the government. One of the more extreme members I met during my fieldwork referenced these stickers as an ongoing worry in 2009. Conspiracy theorists have also referenced the possibility of similar camps being used in response to COVID-19 (Hagerty, 2021). Ideas about black helicopters—the same kind that flew over Waco—running vague but nefarious military operations on US soil were so common that they became synonymous with the militia movement during Olson's tenure. It seems his comments here can only be read as an in-hindsight distancing from his earlier beliefs.

He goes on in his interview with Churchill to explain:

> We [as a community] were talking more about the problems than we were doing about the solutions, and I knew [the church] couldn't do that, because what we were going to do is we were going to build more paranoia, we were gonna build more of these neuroses and these mental problems, and people are going to see bigger snakes and monsters under the bed. *Someone's got to turn the light on* [emphasis added].

Despite evidence that he had in fact imagined some monsters himself, Olson retrospectively asserts responsibility for showing his parishioners that they had nothing to fear. His language about turning on a light is not just completing the comparison to childhood nighttime fears. It also references common metaphors in Christianity about lightness versus darkness. Light represents goodness, truthfulness, and even God himself, while darkness represents evil, despair, and Satan. Christians are supposed to walk in the light, pursue righteousness and truth, and avoid darkness.[12] In his use of the metaphor and in the context of his theological connections between God and patriotism, Olson wants his congregation to know the truth of their power to engage in collective action. He wants to present a solution and stop the federal government from turning into an even bigger monster by empowering the militia movement.

Olson clearly saw not only his church ministry but also his militia leadership as a kind of higher calling. Most members that I have encountered do, including most of those among the 30% of my formal interview sample who said they consider themselves Atheists or Agnostics. The idea of a holy calling comes out of a Calvinist tradition where adherents believe that God has a special vocation for everyone; failure to identify and wholeheartedly participate in one's calling leads to sadness and separation from God's plan (Weber, 2002). It is not God alone that ultimately calls many militia members, however, but rather a different higher power: a sense of duty to the nation and to a nostalgic vision of what once was and what might be.

Olson alluded to his sense of being called by both heavenly and patriotic forces in my January 2022 conversation with him when he said that he hoped the movement "had made a mark," that he "always wanted to establish a legacy, to have someone to remember that we tried. That's really all that's expected of us on Earth, try your hardest to do what's right." Looking back on his legacy during our conversation, he sounded wistful and expressed that he felt the militia had not accomplished nearly enough to preserve the vision of America as he thought it should be. I asked him what he would change now, if he could, with the benefit of hindsight, looking back over the history of the militia. His response, though perhaps unsurprising, nonetheless reflects another pivotal moment for the militia movement. In the next chapter, I examine how the Oklahoma City bombing and Olson's response to it altered the course of US militias.

Notes

1. The original name Olson & Southwell picked was the Northern Michigan Regional Militia because their intention had been to focus the militia's development in only four counties in the northern part of the mitten. Within two months, however, their membership and aspirations had grown substantially. They quickly changed their name, and the short-lived original moniker is all-but forgotten.
2. I remain grateful to both the National Foundation Graduate Research Fellowship that gave my graduate student bank account the spare cash for this unexpected expense and to the beleaguered UPS deliveryman who helped me haul the boxes up three flights of stairs.
3. The archive makes clear that Southwell is just as important to the militia movement's formation and character as is Olson. From these materials, one easily receives the impression that several important decisions Olson makes were strongly guided by Southwell's less public opinion and the platonic affection between the men. I nonetheless focus here on Olson's voice because he did take the more public-forward role, because Olson cultivated and sent me the archive, and because I have never had direct contact with Southwell, meaning I have not had the opportunity to follow-up with Southwell about pieces of his perspective that are missing from the documentation.
4. Readers interested in even more details of the Ruby Ridge standoff will find Lane Crothers's *Rage on the Right* (either the 2003 or 2019 edition) an invaluable resource for understanding the origin of the movement, and I draw heavily from his work in this chapter.
5. While writing my first draft of this chapter, a hostage situation at a Texas synagogue was being broadcast over Facebook live, rather underscoring this point.
6. A compilation of some such footage is here: https://web.archive.org/web/20220617171214/www.youtube.com/watch?v=r-dcZaPTKdQ
7. Some footage of the fires can be seen here https://web.archive.org/web/20220617171232/www.youtube.com/watch?v=TYSJJCwkY0A
8. This document is undated, but the font and styling are consistent with other documents in the archive that are dated in 1994 or 1995.
9. The original location was Vanderbilt, Michigan, but the congregation relocated to the renovated gun shop in October 1995.
10. This is not to say that Olson was misrepresenting his religious beliefs. As I discuss here and elsewhere, his understanding of the nation and of individual liberties are intimately connected to his understanding of God. Many other militia members I have met make various philosophical arguments against the need for permits or other forms of registration for what they believe to be fundamental rights. My point here is that, sincere belief or not, Olson's framing was instrumental in his effort to be openly political from the pulpit without facing financial repercussions.
11. King Herod is described in some Christian traditions as a despot who mass murdered infants. When John the Baptist publicly decried some of his misdeeds, Herod had him beheaded.
12. For example, see Luke 12:2–3 or John 1:5–7.

References

The Associated Press. (2000, September 23). U.S. settles final civil lawsuit stemming from ruby ridge siege. *The New York Times*. www.nytimes.com/2000/09/23/us/us-settles-final-civil-lawsuit-stemming-from-ruby-ridge-siege.html

Berger, J. M. (2018). *Extremism*. The MIT Press.

Crothers, L. (2019). *Rage on the right: The American militia movement from ruby ridge to the Trump presidency* (2nd ed.). Rowman & Littlefield.

DOJ. (1993). *Report to the deputy attorney general on the events at Waco, Texas: The aftermath of the April 19 fire*. U.S. Department of Justice. www.justice.gov/archives/publications/waco/report-deputy-attorney-general-events-waco-texas-aftermath-april-19-fire

DOJ. (1994, June 10). *Department of Justice report on internal review regarding the ruby ridge hostage situation and shootings by law enforcement personnel*. U.S. Department of Justice. www.justice.gov/sites/default/files/opr/legacy/2006/11/09/rubyreportcover_39.p

Flesher, J. (1994, September 5). Militias aim wrath at crime bill. Oakland Press.

Goodman, B. (Director). (2020). Ruby ridge (6). In *American experience*. PBS. www.youtube.com/watch?v=vsjUqXWv-zI

Hagerty, C. (2021, February 11). COVID-19 is helping revive a conspiracy about FEMA camps. *Daily Dot*. www.dailydot.com/debug/fema-camps-covid-19-florida/

Juergensmeyer, M. (2003). *Terror in the mind of god: The global rise of religious violence* (3rd ed.). University of California Press.

Kopel, D. B., & Blackman, P. H. (1997). *No more Wacos: What's wrong with Federal Law enforcement and how to fix it*. Prometheus Books.

Lacombe, M. J. (2021). *Firepower: How the NRA turned gun owners into a political force*. Princeton University Press.

PBS. (n.d.). Timothy McVeigh at Waco. *PBS*. Retrieved July 17, 2023, from www.pbs.org/wgbh/americanexperience/features/oklahoma-city-timothy-mcveigh-waco/

SPLC. (n.d.). Bo Gritz. *Southern Poverty Law Center*. Retrieved March 20, 2023, from www.splcenter.org/fighting-hate/extremist-files/individual/bo-gritz

VICE Staff. (2009, November 10). Norm's militia scrapbook. *Vice*. www.vice.com/en/article/ppk45b/norm-s-militia-scrapbook

Weber, M. (2002). *The protestant ethic and the spirit of capitalism: And other writings*. Penguin Classics.

4 The Oklahoma City Bombing and Militia Decline

A Floundering Father

In early April 1995, the militia movement seemed to have unstoppable momentum. According to notes from Norm Olson's archive, the movement boasted ten thousand members in Michigan alone, and there was at least one unit in all 50 states, with a touted national membership of three million members who had tentative plans for a national organizational structure. Olson and his model had become widely recognized, and people in different countries were asking for his advice and for training materials to help start their own militias.[1]

On April 11, 1995, Olson sent a fax to four Michigan State Representatives (Allen Lowe, David Jaye, Deborah Whyman, and John Jamian) inviting them to an event to celebrate the first anniversary of the MMCW's founding. He followed up with another fax three days later, indicating that a crew from the television show *60 Minutes* had confirmed they would be present to film the event, which promised a lineup of unidentified speakers and a ceremony to thank all state sheriffs. It is unclear if any of the Representatives responded to these requests, but four days after this second request, Olson again wrote Rep Whyman, asking her to sponsor a bill titled "No More Wacos." Olson had been promoting a draft of this bill for at least a couple of months and, according to press releases and news articles in the archive, was aiming to require federal law enforcement agencies to receive—with some exceptions—permission from local sheriffs before conducting searches or seizures in Michigan, clearly drawing from the Posse Comitatus efforts to limit federal reach and authority. Federal officers who did not comply with this rule would, according to the bill, face possible prosecution.

Oklahoma City and a Nation's Tribulation

On the morning of April 19, 1995, and just two days after Olson's appeal for legislative assistance, a homegrown terrorist murdered 168 people. The terrorist initially appeared to have connections to the Michigan Militia, and the federal government was his target. The site of the bomb, the Alfred P. Murrah Federal Building, housed offices for several federal agencies, including

DOI: 10.4324/9781003361657-5

the ATF. The Oklahoma City bombing became known as the deadliest terror attack on US soil up to that time, and once more left Americans feeling uncertain about the violence they saw being broadcast over the news. For many viewers, time seemed to stop as they watched surreal footage of injured and disoriented people. They listened attentively to news commentators making comparisons between the carnage and scenes from Beirut[2] or other cities where Americans clearly felt like violence was supposed to happen instead of so close to home in a country they had imagined to be insulated from such pain. This sentiment was echoed by my middle school teacher, whom I vividly remember wheeling a TV into our classroom to watch the live coverage. This was a questionable decision, but one originating from a sense of uncertainty, of not knowing what to do under such circumstances, yet still feeling some need to bear witness, and that was a reaction shared by many across the country. Uncertainty and fear pervaded the coverage in the days and weeks that followed, even as law enforcement assured the public that the terrorist had been apprehended shortly after the attack.

One of the reasons this story was so frightening was not merely the visible destruction of a symbol of the government's strength, nor even the overall fatalities. The Murrah building housed an employee daycare, and 19 babies and toddlers were among the dead, their broken bodies providing some of the most lasting images of the bombing. This terrorist act was almost four years to the day before the first mass school shooting that would capture the public's attention at Columbine High School, and at this time it was almost incomprehensible to many Americans that children, let alone ones so young, could be targets of this kind of destruction. The terrorist later claimed he had not known there was a daycare inside the building in response to this outcry, but analysts and others connected to the case remain dubious of that claim given the preparation and motive behind the bombing (Michel & Herbeck, 2001).

The terrorist's name was Timothy McVeigh. He was a racist, disaffected Gulf War Army veteran who later confirmed that the bombing's date on the second anniversary of the second Waco raid was no accident: it was intended as retaliation against the government for their perceived sins of Waco, Ruby Ridge, and other unspecified raids (Fox News, 2015; The Associated Press, 2001). Shortly before the bombing, McVeigh had been living in Michigan with a man named Terry Nichols who was eventually convicted as a coconspirator for helping plan the attack. McVeigh and Nichols were familiar with both the militia milieu and with overtly racist groups, reportedly drawing most of their social connections exclusively from those circles (Crothers, 2019).

McVeigh had a strong and obvious hatred of the federal government, a focus on events that, at least in his mind, were similar to Waco, and a general interest in firearms, all of which were familiar themes in the growing militia movement. It was reasonable for law enforcement to examine his connection to the militia and to assess whether other people from the militia movement were involved in the attack.

Official findings indicated that McVeigh was never a member of the militia despite the clear overlap in ideology (Crothers, 2019; Duffy & Brantley, 1997).[3] But how did militia members themselves see possible connections? During my fieldwork, two different long-term members told me they had firsthand knowledge that McVeigh had attended one or two meetings before being asked to leave because he was attempting to hand out racist materials. Olson and Southwell are quoted in several news articles from the time saying something similar though they allude to McVeigh pushing general violence or an agenda "incompatible with [their] aims," rather than directly referencing racism. An email in Olson's archive from a man named James Caldwell to a militia listserv says that the Nichols brothers[4] "attended a couple of meetings. . . , but were asked not to come back because of their anarchist views on tax protests." It is unclear what exactly "anarchist" views were translated to in this context beyond vague hints of violence. What is clear is that the militia's narrative at the time of the bombing has remained fairly consistent through present day. They maintain that neither McVeigh nor Nichols had been a part of the militia, and this assertion continues to be members' primary route for distancing themselves from the bombing, something they felt pressure to start doing almost immediately after news of the attack broke.

McVeigh was arrested less than two hours after the explosion when he was pulled over for not having a license plate, and the officer arrested him for having an illegally concealed handgun. Authorities quickly linked him to the attack, and information about his military background and general beliefs soon leaked to the media and other commentators. These commentators had already been speculating about the likely symbolic connection to Waco and the possibility of militia involvement in the plot.

That same day, according to a handwritten "4/19/95" at the top of the page, Olson released a "Michigan Militia Corps National Statement" about the terrorism. In that note, Olson chastises the media for suggesting Waco had been a precipitating event for the bombing, saying such claims were "irresponsible action" designed "to cause further strife and suspicion among Americans."[5] He also suggests that the bombing was precisely the kind of violence the militia had tried to help other civilians prepare for and defend against.

Three days later, after public allegations about McVeigh's connection to his militia, Olson underscored the message of the bombing being incompatible with his aims through a "Statement from the Commander." This response said the bombing was "not the work of patriots, for patriots do not attack their countrymen. . . . Nor was this the work of the citizen militia." Instead, he says, the "perpetrators of the bombing" had been "turned away" from the militia "because of their unmanageable hatred for their government."

In this framing, militia members and other patriots are indeed angry at (and fearful of) their government, but what separates them from dangerous actors is that their emotions are "managed." Olson alludes to how anger and fear can be intimately connected when he shifts to the latter emotion at the end of his statement, saying, "perhaps one day, fear of government will be replaced with liberty and love [for] each other; that leaders will lead by example; and that government will be truly vested in the people once again."

Although not specified in this particular document, Olson as well as other members that I have talked with have discussed how militia membership can play a role in their emotion management. Some find their membership cathartic as being a space where they can experience a church-like fellowship as they share concerns with like-minded people and relive glory days from military service. Feeling as though other people share their concerns about the direction of the country can at least temporarily alleviate these fears; a weekend of training and camping outdoors with people they believe they could count on in the event of a real crisis makes them feel less alone. Other members instead have their negative emotions further legitimated and even stoked. They are made to feel an urgency to personally do something about the threats they believe they face. Rather than being brought into a community and developing a positive sense of self within their militia units, these members find evidence that they and their militia peers are unwillingly forced to the margins of society. That is, some people can find militia units as spaces to mitigate their anxieties, while others may find them to be catalysts for action. One of the biggest challenges militia analysts continue to face is identifying what personal, militia unit, and social-political variables push people toward a radicalized—and possibly violent—outcome rather than one that helps soothe negative emotions.

The Japan Allegation

One of Olson's fears as he released his dual statements was undoubtedly that the connections between McVeigh's ideology and his own would be used to undermine the militia movement. Another two days after Olson's second public statement on April 24, 1995, Olson received a series of faxes that gave him an alternate theory of the events in Oklahoma City. His response to this theory changed the fate of the militia movement and led to what he called his biggest regret.

A woman named Debra von Trapp claimed that Japan was responsible for the bombing. She insisted, with a handwritten note on a fax cover sheet, that "The FBI is using this opportunity as a 'witch hunt' to turn the public against organizations like yours . . . ." She sent copies of materials stamped in the upper left corner as being from the "Embassy of Japan." She said these had been sent to her in 1993 and supposedly constituted proof of a convoluted and nefarious relationship between US intelligence agencies, the copier company Xerox, and the Japanese government. These documents do not contain much discernable substance other than a claim that the Japanese government had been using software to spy inside the Clinton White House, but the paperwork nonetheless convinced Olson and Southwell of von Trapp's supposed insider knowledge.

In an escalating chain of proposed events, Von Trapp suggested that the FBI had been responsible for a deadly sarin gas attack in a Japanese subway one month before.[6] She argued that the subway attack was FBI-led retaliation for devaluing the US dollar relative to the Yen. The Oklahoma City bombing, then, was supposedly Japan's response to the subway attack, and von Trapp pointed to the date as purported proof of this claim. On another fax cover sheet, she scrawled "[US Attorney General Janet] Reno seized on the 19th" to justify the connection to Waco when discussing the case with the US public. However, von Trapp says Reno missed how, when the bomb detonated, the clock had just ticked past midnight and into the early moments of April 20 in Japan, "one month to the *day* of the subway attack" (emphasis in original). On yet another cover sheet, von Trapp pleaded, "help me distribute the truth of this situation."

Von Trapp's reference to Janet Reno was more meaningful here than might initially be obvious. Reno was indeed acting Attorney General under President Bill Clinton and, as a result, had a good deal of visibility in the aftermath of the Oklahoma City bombing. She led several news conferences to update the nation about the case and became the face of the justice system's response to the devastation.[7] Reno and President Clinton had both already captured the militia movement's attention years earlier, however. People attracted to militias or similar groups are generally more hostile toward Democratic than Republican administrations because they see Democrats as bigger threats to the values they hold. For some members, women Democrats, especially those in powerful and visible positions, are particularly threatening (Cooter, 2022). Militia disdain for Reno was much bigger than this standard politically based, antagonistic relationship, however. She and, to a similar extent, Clinton had in their view presided over the tyrannical interventions at Waco and represented the worst the federal government had to offer (Crothers, 2019). Von Trapp's implication that Reno was making a false and superficial analysis played into Olson's preexisting negative perceptions of her and into a broader anti-federal government framing, likely making von Trapp's attribution of Japanese culpability more tempting to believe and discouraging further critical investigations of the claim.

Olson and Southwell were quickly caught up in von Trapp's story. Within a few days, they had a lengthy phone conversation with her (the transcript and audio cassette of which are included in the archive) and met with the three other members of MMCW leadership about going public with the Japan story. Over the protests of those other leaders, Olson started talking with every media outlet that would listen. He also made a press release equating the bombing to Pearl Harbor, the implication being that the loss of life in Oklahoma would draw the government into even more violent action, resulting in the suffering of more citizens.

He and Southwell also resigned their leadership in the MMCW almost immediately. Olson told me in 2022 that he felt strongly enough about von Trapp's allegations that he wanted to share them but also wanted to respect the rules of his organization. Since he was outvoted and would be defying the leadership's collective will, he said he felt honor-bound to resign. He was quoted making similar remarks about honor and duty in newspapers at the time. Some local news articles in the archive covered Olson's formal departure by the beginning of May. He nonetheless remained visible in the national and Michigan militia landscapes as he prepared to testify to Congress about possible connections between militias and terrorism. On the 8th of May 1995, a woman named Linda Thompson who had been heavily involved in trying to start[8] the militia movement over a "patriot fax network" before the movement's formal inception sent Olson a scathing note. Thompson's blunt language reflects the derision that Olson faced publicly for espousing the Japan theory.

> You're being played like a violin and making us all look like a bunch of dolts. The cammos, the interviews where you all look like a bunch of illiterate goobers, and now this, is doing a lot of damage to the militia movement. People distancing themselves from you will cause even more dissension in the ranks. You're rapidly losing any and all credibility and I strongly advise you to reconsider your position and attempt to present a dignified, intelligent front.

Olson nonetheless persisted, though his stated reason for resigning shifted later that same month in an exchange with a self-proclaimed investigative reporter named Gary Hunt, whose "Outpost of Freedom" newsletters that began in response to Waco was popular in militias and other conservative circles. There, Olson reflects, "Were we set up? I don't think so. To insulate the militia from such a ploy, Ray [Southwell] and I immediately resigned and left. If anyone is discredited, it will be Ray and myself, which is no big thing [relative to the reputation and integrity of the movement]." Here, Olson had started to consider whether the story blaming the Japanese had been intended to undermine the militia movement. He rejects this claim, but with less than full certainty. Instead, he suggests that he had considered this possible plot before his action and resigned to separate and protect the movement from his words in the event he was wrong.

Impact on the Movement

The movement nonetheless suffered immensely in the next several months, regardless of any leadership efforts to protect it. According to both Olson and other long-term members with whom I have spoken, some militia members nationally did fall away from the movement immediately after the bombing itself. Some of those who resigned wanted to avoid negative attention from being associated with the movement during its period of public scrutiny. Others reportedly realized one logical conclusion of their ire toward the government and wanted to stop their progression on the trajectory toward possibly engaging in other violence. Their collective separation also disrupted meaningful efforts to have a true national militia coalition.

According to those long-term members, the real dissolution of the movement did not, however, happen until after Olson's assertions of Japan's culpability for the attack. His commentary was (and still is) generally considered embarrassing. Members still characterize his blame of Japan much as Linda Thompson did, as being a blight on the reputation of the whole movement that Olson's resignation did nothing to soften. One member I met during my fieldwork told me that the public embarrassment reduced the public movement to "a shadow" of its former self nationally, as people did not want to be seen as endorsing such conspiracy theories. This man reported that such members worried that they would be perceived by friends and loved ones as unstable attention seekers, rather than as patriots.

It is worth noting that some scholars have made a different claim about the movement's trajectory in the years that followed the bombing (Crothers, 2019; Tharp & Holstein, 1997). Referencing the SPLC's *Intelligence Report* data, they suggest that the movement in fact *grew* nationally after the attack. This report, while drawing from a variety of sources, seems to most heavily rely on websites produced by groups the report investigates (Cooter, 2013). I am, frankly, skeptical of this growth claim. The SPLC does important work to combat violent extremism but has also faced a good deal of controversy and criticism (Chermak, 2002; Churchill, 2009; Freilich & Pridemore, 2005; Price, 2018; Satija et al., 2019; Silverstein, 2000). When I asked several members about their recollections of the movement during this time, one militia member cynically replied that he believed that the SPLC "realized that stoking fears of militias would be good for their pocketbook" in the aftermath of the Oklahoma City bomb. He was referencing how the SPLC runs on donations and would at least theoretically benefit from militias seeming to be a bigger threat than they were.

We don't have to be quite so cynical about the organization's motives to still recognize that monitoring would naturally increase in intensity and in detail after such a momentous event. Beyond potentially increased efforts from the SPLC itself, militia units that had little online presence in 1994 and 1995 would have been less likely to make it into any official counts. The closer in time to the militia's inception we are considering, the more likely it is that militia units were not yet using websites to advertise their existence because personal or organizational websites were not yet commonplace. Heavily relying on websites as a proxy for the number of active units risks undercounting groups during those early years while later counts are less

78 The Oklahoma City Bombing and Militia Decline

susceptible to this particular error. Even if there were no other concerns with these data, we could not be confident in the real size of the apparent increase in the movement across these time points; doing so essentially risks mistaking a proliferation in all websites with a proliferation of militia groups.

Table 4.1 shows exponential growth in website usage alongside SPLC counts of militia units by year.

There are, unfortunately, other concerns with the *Intelligence Report*. In 2010, I examined each website listed in the then-current count of active militias and found numerous errors that collectively exaggerated the size of the movement. At best, only 70 of the listed 109 websites were active, unique sites that met the report's definition of militias. At worst, only 36 sites seemed to reflect truly organized units with any meaningful membership or funding being used to maintain an internet presence that would, in turn, be suggestive of a functional group (Cooter, 2013).[10] Without clearer guidelines and descriptions of methodology going into these *Intelligence Report* counts, researchers relying on these numbers may inadvertently be comparing apples to oranges when trying to understand militia-specific growth and threats.

When trying to assess movement characteristics accurately, we should ideally be looking for other sources to verify the claims of size. Militia members and the group materials they have maintained are the only other systematic data source for that retrospective information. Members are obviously subject to a variety of possible biases and inaccuracies in their reporting, inadvertent or otherwise. For example, a May 6, 2001, *The Detroit News* article titled "McVeigh's bomb shattered the militia movement, too" says that "Since the Oklahoma City bombing, 3/4 of the nation's patriot groups have disbanded, and membership has dropped to 80%." The reporter does not identify the source for these claims, but it is presumably Olson who is quoted elsewhere in the article. The unnamed source goes on to say that "Thousands [of patriots] are in prison," a false claim that implied that a variety of people who had been outspoken against the government had been rounded up and incarcerated. This clear falsehood, which the journalist uncritically presents as fact, sharply calls the other numerical claims into question as well. A more circumspect article from March 26, 1997, in the *Petoskey News-Review* titled "Militias smaller and more secretive" reflects that basic fact of the headline

Table 4.1 SPLC Militia Counts and Website Counts by Year

	Number of Militias According to SPLC	Number of All Websites According to InternetLiveStats[9]
1994	no data	2,738
1995	224	23,500
1996	858	257,601
1997	523	1,117,255
1998	435	2,410,067

without claiming specific numbers. Another article in the same newspaper from December of that year is titled "Recruits march back to the militias," and cites Olson's successor as saying the movement finally has renewed interest from new members after several years of paucity.

The truth about the overall numerical impact on the national militia movement is likely somewhere in between Olson's version of events and the SPLC's. Even with disclarity about the movement as a whole, there is sufficient evidence to assert that militia ranks specifically in Michigan were indeed reduced in size both because of the bombing itself and because of Olson's assertions about Japan. A reduction in size also logically follows from this state's unique relationship to the bombing. Michigan's militia units received more scrutiny and negative attention than other states' militias because of their proximity to the terrorists; McVeigh and Nichols likely planned the bombing while in Michigan and reportedly included Michigan militia members in their social circles. Michigan members certainly faced greater-than average pressure to disassociate from the movement, at least publicly, especially after Olson's Japan commentary was perceived as bringing even more disrepute to his Michigan associates. Olson's and Southwell's resignation following their decision to endorse the Japan theory of the bombing also created a power vacuum that fostered infighting among remaining members and further fractured that state's movement.

Olson's Transformation

After formally quitting as state commander, Olson says that he intended to return to quietly leading units in a few counties in the northern part of the mitten where the movement first began. He continued attending leadership meetings of the state organization, at least for a time, and turned down an offer to be the MMCW's official chaplain. He told me that several members asked him to again run for the position of state commander when the organization was voting for a leader in the summer of 1995. He said that there were too many "factions" for him to win that effort. News coverage at the time records some of the core debates across these factions. Olson thought it was time for the movement to essentially double-down and become even more vocal in its anti-government stance. Other members, who ultimately prevailed, urged moderation and separation from the aggressive, angry, violent associations that had become commonplace in the fallout of Oklahoma City.

Olson fought for control over the essence of the movement he created even as he lost its headship. He disdainfully noted that, "Moderates ... [are] turning the militia into a political action group," in a July 95 *Petoskey News-Review* article. He also revamped the Militia emblem to make his point, sardonically altering it from being a fierce wolverine to a lamb, telling reporter Bob Burns at some later date[11] that he "made it very clear that [he] wouldn't be part of a 'politically correct, socially acceptable, and squeezably soft'

Michigan Militia." The image, included in the archive, is openly insulting to remaining militia members. It includes text saying the remaining members have lost their way and evokes a connection to the idea of "sheeple," a term long used in conservative circles to refer to people who supposedly mindlessly follow the government or other authority figures.

Olson continued searching for new footing after the militia moved forward without him. Materials in the archive starting the summer of 1995 and extending over the next several years give the impression of someone who did not quite know where he belonged and of someone who would rather be at the center of decision making, rather than lingering at the periphery. His first effort to revive the militia was an effort to ally with Detroit's Black Panthers.

On July 31, 1995, just 11 days after Olson announced his rejection of the militia's new, more moderate focus, headlines started covering Olson's effort to connect with the Panthers. In the *Petoskey News-Review* on this date, Olson describes a parity between his vision of the militia and his understanding of the Panthers. He says both incorporate military references in their uniforms (camouflage for militia members and green berets for Panthers), that both are armed, and that both are "anti-fascist, anti-government abuse, and anti-tyranny." *The Detroit News* used this tentative allyship's announcement for the front page of their "The Metro" section on this same date. Their coverage is paired with another, less-flashy article titled, "Metro Detroiters vow to take back the night and fight against crime," seeming to suggest the militia could in fact have some positive influence in this fight.

In the *Detroit News* article about Olson and in some other news coverage that follows, a leader in Detroit's Black community named Clifford Brookins II is quoted as saying that he initiated contact with Olson, not the other way around. He cites the failure of structural solutions, saying that "dumping money downtown" has not alleviated the problems of Detroit. He continues, "look at the neighborhoods, at the drug dealers. If you say boo, a lot of people will be pulling out guns," and indicates his openness to work with anyone who "shows some concern." It is not clear how consulting a group fundamentally about firearms possession is supposed to improve drug or gun violence issues. Perhaps the implication was to give a "legitimate" or organized and disciplined purpose to firearm possession while encouraging law-abiding Detroiters to defend themselves and their property from perceived criminal threats.

Other Detroiters were not so sold on the potential coalition. Someone identified only as a "former Panther" is quoted in the same article as saying:

> These (Michigan Militia members) are the same kind of people who believe that the United Nations has a machine that makes tornadoes.[12] Very few black people would like to be affiliated with that. Besides, it's one thing for 1,000 white men to go out in the woods and train with rifles. If 20 [B]lack people go together like that here, the FBI would

come in and they'd all go to prison. It's a double standard. I can't see anyone, not even [B]lack Republicans, going along with that.

This person cynically observes that Black people have more practical concerns than the conspiracy theories that occupy many white militias before accurately noting the very different and serious perceptions law enforcement continue to have about armed Black versus white men. Similarly, Black Panthers' founder Bobby Seale is quoted in a *News-Review* article a few days later, on August 8, as saying he would "study" Olson's militia plan. He says he believes Olson's plan is free from racism and that he "cannot say that [Olson's] ideal is not in the right place" but nonetheless indicates he is "skeptical" of the plan's utility, seeming to imply that a cultural gap may prevent full allyship. News articles sporadically continued to cover the tentative conversations between Olson and the Black community through early 1996 even though nothing ultimately seemed to transpire from these talks.

In late March of 1996, Olson's attention shifted elsewhere. Another standoff began in Jordan, Montana, between the FBI and a group of self-described patriots known as the Montana Freemen. The Freemen were self-avowed Sovereign Citizens whose rejection of the federal government's authority had resulted in several members facing warrants and property foreclosure, with which they refused to comply. The day after the Freemen standoff began, Olson issued a press release calling it "a Waco-like situation." Another release the next day even more strongly alleged that the federal government "has the intent to murder." Olson may have genuinely believed that there was a high probability this conflict would turn deadly, but it also seems that he believed this was an opportunity to reinvigorate the movement. There are more than two hundred document pages in the archive related to this standoff. Many of them are communications from militias in several other states who are also monitoring the situation and contemplating traveling to Montana to apply pressure to the FBI and other federal officials on-site. The archive includes many fewer documents from other militias for similar past events where militias were concerned about government infringement on private land. It is impossible to know now whether this difference is because this particular standoff was sufficiently concerning to spur more communications from other states' militias or whether Olson himself made the choice to keep more communications from this incident than he had from other events; in either case, it is reasonable to assume their presence reflects the standoff's importance to him and, likely, to others in the movement who remained close to him.

The situation was momentous enough that Olson did travel to Montana, perhaps envisioning himself as imitating Bo Gritz's role in Ruby Ridge. Departing Michigan on April 15, he and Southwell timed their visit to overlap with the anniversaries of Waco and Oklahoma City because they perceived the risks of a deadly conflict to be highest on that date. The FBI refused to allow Olson to access the site, however, once more leading to ridicule. A political cartoon in *The Detroit News* on April 16, 1996, depicts Olson as a tiny, wind-up toy soldier attempting to capture the attention of FBI agents who are observing the Freemen property and seem, at best, indifferent to Olson's approach. Olson nonetheless sees his involvement as a success. In a lengthy email to a listserv with several militias across the country, Olson insinuated that his real purpose in Montana was intelligence gathering—to observe the FBI operation on the property and report back lessons that could be applied to other scenarios. He claimed they were asked by an unidentified party to gather this information "so that we will be prepared for similar actions of the federal government when they move against citizens elsewhere." Clearly anticipating future standoffs with the feds, he continues, "Don't pass up this opportunity to train against the people who think, repeat, *think* they are the best" (emphasis in original). This 81-day siege in fact ended with no bloodshed. Anxious militia members from across the country might have attributed this to their presence and attention, but experts have instead credited it to an enormous shift in federal agency tactics following the painful lessons of Ruby Ridge and Waco (Crothers, 2019).

Olson nonetheless tried to use the perceived success of the Montana standoff to reignite the movement. He called for a "Third Continental Congress" to meet and form a provisional government in purported anticipation of needing an alternate structure because of an imminent collapse of the "corrupt and out of control" federal government (Martindale, 1996). Olson said he was expecting dozens of people from numerous states to attend the event and contribute to the effort to "have a replacement government waiting in the wings." No sustained reinvestment happened with the militia movement after the siege's end, however, and a reprint of an Associated Press article in an October 31, 1996, issue of the *Petoskey News-Review* says that only 25 total people attended the "Congressional" meeting.

Olson involved himself in a few other events in 1996 and 1997 that he saw as having important parallels with the Freemen standoff. All involved people facing off with the government about what they were allowed to do with their own property. None of these stories received much coverage beyond local papers, and, despite some perceived successes with these incidents, Olson once more seemed to be left looking for a way to make his interests relevant to a broader audience.

His real opportunity happened in late 1998, when the public started to be aware of the impending disaster of "Y2K," which was short for "year 2000." Computing systems that had been designed decades earlier had not been intended to extend into the new millennium, and there were legitimate concerns about how global computer systems, especially those connected to power grids or to financial or travel systems, would manage the shift (Loeb,

2022; US House of Representatives, 1998). Computer programming and other information technology professionals around the world scrambled to design new software, patches, and other solutions to this problem, but, at the time, no one was entirely sure what systems might still contain errors (Uenuma, 2019).[13] National and local news shows ran numerous stories featuring families preparing for the worst with suggestions from various governmental agencies to stock up on basic supplies.[14] Some religious congregations even prepared for the rapture or some other version of the end of the world to happen when 11:59 p.m. on December 31 led into the new millennium (ADL, 2017). My parents' church was again among those taking part in this broader trend. Less extreme than some congregations, church leadership suggested that one should ensure their salvation "just in case" the apocalyptic predictions came true.

Olson started expressing concern about Y2K's possible chaos as early as winter 1998. On December 3 of that year, he wrote to Michigan Governor John Engler, whom Olson had previously seen as an ally before Engler's condemned the militia following Oklahoma City. Olson said that the best plans the federal government could construct

> will be far too inadequate to deal with the burning and rioting that may consume the major cities of this state. In an effort to escape, thousands will flee the cities as power, water, communication, and transportation structures collapse. Driven by fear, people will rush to the countryside only to find angry and defensive people who will protect their property with arms.

He goes on to say that the militia can help prevent this outcome and that Engler should call him so they can work together "before it's too late."

On December 5, 1998, Freedom Church hosted an event at North Central Michigan College, reportedly attended by 100 people who wanted to learn how to prepare for the aftermath of Y2K. Olson noted in a press release that he personally invited sheriffs and other officials from across 15 counties to attend the event, but none came. He remarked, "Their silence is deafening," and actively tried to stoke fears that the government had no plan for the potential emergency saying, "For the first time in fifty years, we will have to learn how to take care of ourselves without the government's help. The government's silence indicates that they have no answers." The militia had always included elements of preparedness in its training structure, so Olson was here suggesting the militia as an alternative source for disaster planning, preparedness education, general safety, and anxiety management.

Olson's rhetoric escalated further in two additional press releases later that month. No longer was the government merely absent and unprepared, it was, once again, actively threatening. He argued that the government would use Y2K's certain chaos to enact martial law, leading to a loss of liberty and other rights. On December 15, he wrote:

> We will not be easily enslaved if we are prepared to remain free. The government is preparing to control us in the midst of a crisis which they knew was coming yet about which they remained silent. It doesn't take a rocket scientist to conclude what is about to happen.

This insinuates that the government *was* knowledgeable and prepared for the crisis but unwilling to help civilians because of a bigger plan of control and "enslavement."

Freedom Church sponsored a few other preparedness meetings like this in 1999, and in May of that year, Olson continued to use worries about the so-called Millennium Bug to attempt the militia movement's resurrection once more. A press release in May of that year served as an open call inviting all militias across the state to "recall and reassemble." According to coverage in the *Herald Times*, Olson considered this meeting a success, touting the presence of 75 existing members and 13 new recruits.

Olson told me that his personal preparations for Y2K included purchasing large pallets of beans, corn, rice and lentils for his home as well as, alongside others in his congregation, "frantically buying" enough food to sustain all of Freedom Church for several months should the worst happen. Ultimately, computing and other preventative preparations were highly successful, and no major calamities occurred at the transition to the new millennium. Most people who had been concerned about a possible catastrophe were relieved. Olson, it seems, was disappointed. There are zero entries in his scrapbook for the entire year 2000.

There are some other materials from that time period elsewhere in the archive. On April 19, 2000, the 5th anniversary of the Oklahoma City bombing, Olson wrote a document whose audience is unstated but that is titled "OKC—Or How the Tyrants Avoided a Revolution." In it, Olson indicated that the bombing was what has now become known as a "false flag" event—an attack perpetuated by someone other than the apparent assailant, with the intent of manipulating perceptions and emotions around the event. Olson alleged the bomb was really a plot by the government to undermine the militia movement and that McVeigh was still a loyal soldier who took the fall as ordered. He wrote that it was designed

> to save the tyrant's own skin. . . . There can be little doubt that the corrupted federal government was frightened of a righteous rebellion. How many wicked judges, lawyers, and corrupted politicians would be dragged to the gallows if the militia movement were not stopped? . . . The federals devised a plan to put the brakes on the militia. . . . Direct attack on the militia would [have] only strengthen[ed] it.

It is worth noting that the false flag argument continues to have some support in the nostalgic group network and beyond. Even some notable liberal scholars and journalists (Belew, 2018; Weill, 2022) continue to argue that McVeigh could not have been a lone actor, and posit different possible motives for a lack of further arrests than those typical in nostalgic groups. This conspiracy theory is facilitated not only by a continued general desire to villainize the federal government, but also through two specific issues surrounding the case. First, in the aftermath of the bomb, it was believed McVeigh had not acted alone and that there instead had been a second terrorist on site in Oklahoma City. Multiple witnesses reported having seen a second person with McVeigh, including the employee who rented him the moving truck that housed the bomb. A rendering of "John Doe #2" was shared on nearly every news broadcast until the Justice Department announced that the moving truck employee had mistakenly thought another customer from a different transaction had been with McVeigh. Many people continue to find this explanation unpersuasive, and several assertions have been made about the "real" identity of a supposedly unconvicted second terrorist.

Second, after McVeigh's conviction, it was revealed that the FBI had withheld 3,500 pages of documents during his trial, news that delayed his original execution date that had been set in May 2001. The documents did not materially change the government's case or McVeigh's defense, and McVeigh waived his appeals, which meant his execution took place a short time later in June of that same year. Some people nonetheless continue to believe that the FBI engaged in intentional suppression of exculpatory evidence and that McVeigh waived his appeals to carry out his orders to be a "patsy" for the government's plot. Olson wrote his reflections alleging a false flag event in 1999, two years before this evidentiary revelation. His ideas were not extreme outliers among those with anti-government beliefs at when he wrote that and grew in popularity around the time of McVeigh's execution.

It is unclear exactly when Olson started to question his original belief that Japan perpetrated the terrorist attack. In January 2022, Olson told me that the one thing he would change in retrospect about his militia involvement was, "The whole Japanese connection thing. . . . I look back and ask how in the world was I taken in?" Perhaps he first began to change his mind in the aftermath of his testimony to Congress in the summer of 1995, which enhanced the public ridicule directed at both him and the movement. Regardless, it seems that his decision to go forward with the Japan allegations was sitting heavily in his mind at the turn of the millennium when the militia movement failed to rejuvenate following Y2K.

Entries in his scrapbook for 2001 are also very sparse. On April 30, 2001, just after the seventh anniversary of the MMCW's founding, Olson disbanded the militia, referencing a lack of interest (Bradsher, 2001). Having resigned as state commander six years earlier, this disbanding meant little, practically speaking, to the other operational units in the state or beyond, but it held enormous symbolic importance. This announcement was effectively the end of an era, the end of "the old guard," and a move into a "softer, gentler militia," as one modern leader who began his membership in the 1990s later told me. The disbanding was also Olson's seeming recognition that his vision of a more aggressive and active militia would not come to be. *The Detroit News* interviewed him, presumably in response to this announcement in an article published May 6, 2001. In it, his tone and perspective about Y2K had shifted. He told the reporter:

> All of a sudden, everyone has three generators sitting in their garage and tons of canned beans in the basement. People started thinking, boy, things aren't as bad as we thought. The Clinton-Reno regime is gone, the black helicopters are gone, there aren't Russian soldiers fighting in the mines below Detroit. There was no more fear to motivate people.

With this commentary, Olson was undoubtedly talking as much about himself and his own lack of fear and motivation as he was talking about other people. The movement saw Republican President George W. Bush as a leader who would largely uphold individual liberties, in contrast, they thought, to Clinton. Olson now had no tangible enemy to fight, no conspiracy theories for which he could find more mass support. He went on to say, in alarming contrast to his proposed "No More Wacos" bill in 1995, "What this country needs is a good old-fashioned Waco, with 50 people dead on each side. That would put fear back in society. You need fear to create a militia." My reading of this, given Olson's understanding of Waco as an intentional attack by the government on civilians, is not that Olson was urging proactive violence from militia members, but yearning for civilians and law enforcement deaths for the sake of fear and a reinvigorated militia growth is no less troubling.

Olson had indeed been considering the causal role of fear in his movement for quite a while. In the same 1999 interview with Dr. Churchill, where he insisted that he started his Freedom Church to alleviate fears, to "turn on a light" of truth and power, Olson also said that there had been four original motivators for starting the militia: "fear, vision, duty and love. Not hate." By this he meant that his motivations behind the movement were not hatred toward the federal government. Instead, he said, *fear* of government action and fear of patriot inaction, were motivations alongside more positive assessments: a vision of what he thought a government truly for the people could be, a duty to country and to God's will, and love for his country and neighbors. In that same interview he went on to say that with the militia movement, he was trying to dispel fear, but he "also knew that if we dispelled the fear then the militia [would] cease to exist." Rather than fully banishing the darkness as he had advocated to his parishioners, Olson needed at least some darkness to sustain the movement, and had, at times, perhaps intentionally exaggerated those specters for the movement's gain. Saying he "needed" another Waco was a reference to his lessened ability to tap into fears, which, for a time, were alleviated among his potential audience during the Bush administration.

Not even the terror attacks of September 11, 2001, were enough to bring Olson out of his seeming malaise. An entire issue of the *Petoskey News-Review* devoted to the attacks with the wreckage of the Twin Towers on the front page was folded and tucked into the scrapbook when I received it, but nothing about the terror attacks of that day was formally affixed to its pages. Any press releases or other commentary from Olson about them is missing from the archive. Americans across the political spectrum were indeed incredibly fearful after these attacks, uncertain about the attacker's motives and about the threat of more imminent carnage. This could have been a logical moment for Olson to again build on fear for potential militia growth, but he did not do that. I asked him in 2022 what he was doing in response to the terror attacks that was not present in the archive, and he claimed his recollections were as blank as that period of the scrapbook.

There is a small burst of activity reflected in the archive for 2002. In late March of that year, there is some news coverage about how the (presumably no-longer disbanded) militia would offer anti-terrorism training to civilians. There, Olson references the failures of the federal government in preventing the terror attacks and says he wants to empower citizens to "root out domestic terrorism." He noted that he had been "rebuffed" by the government in his efforts, likely referring to an unanswered letter to this effect that he sent to Governor Engler, but the article quotes Cheboygan County Sheriff Dale Clermont as being fairly supportive of this proposed initiative. It is unclear from the archive if any citizens ever took advantage of this training, but Olson told me that there had been a core group of 25–35 members who consistently attended for a time.

On August 26, 2001, *The Detroit Free Press* carried the headline "Founder ready to leave Michigan behind." Sheriff Clermont is again quoted here saying Olson's neighbors never complained about him, seeming to endorse him as an upstanding member of the community. Olson did leave the state, but not for another two years when he and Ray Southwell both moved their families to Alaska. Olson told me that he still had a large store of dried goods from his Y2K prepping days at the time of his move and laughed as he recounted giving the stale remainders to local farmers to use with their livestock. There are no real entries in the archive from the time of their move until September 2009 when the *Anchorage Daily News* reported that Olson was trying to start a militia in Alaska. He began with an informational meeting at a recreation center on the eighth anniversary of the 9/11 terror attacks, undoubtedly attempting, at last, to tap into the symbolic power of that date.

Though absent from the archive, there are a few news stories about Olson's activities in Alaska since then that one can find with a search of his name online. Most of the coverage concerns his support for another Alaska militia leader who was accused of various crimes. Another article asks for his perspective on the movement during the first half of President Obama's administration (D'Oro, 2009). The most recent coverage is a summary of a 2020 interview Olson did with a Michigan television station. In it, he renounced the alleged plot by militia members to kidnap Governor Gretchen Whitmer and put her on trial for tyranny even while he insisted that she is unfit for the office (Kolker, 2020).

His commentary on this case is a reminder of how Olson has always been implicated with the biggest news stories of the movement, often through his own actions, but also because others—researchers, reporters, and would-be imitators—continue to seek him out. His place in militia history has many unique elements, but he also poignantly exemplifies the movement's shared ideals and frustrations, including a distrust of the federal government that is common among many "normal" Americans who feel like that government has never done much for them. The next chapter analyzes how the themes that Olson references including a rural mentality and nostalgia for a lost but imagined settler colonial nation are crucial for understanding the movement and its members' motivations.

Notes

1. These estimations may not be strongly exaggerated as they seem at first glance. They are, in broad strokes, corroborated by letters from supporters and materials that are in the archive from other state militias. Long-term militia members whom I met during my fieldwork gave similar size estimates when I asked them their recollections of this time, and other scholars cite similar numbers (Churchill, 2009; Stern, 1996).
2. For example, https://web.archive.org/web/20220617171427/www.youtube.com/watch?v=Z53iTIBTdpk
3. Despite a lack of evidence that McVeigh was a militia member, Congressional investigations that ultimately enacted no sanctions on militias, and over the continued protestations of people who were present at events in the 90s, many journalists and some scholars today still insist otherwise. Part of this may be a continued desire to believe that one person, acting largely single-handedly, could not produce so much destruction. At its core, this perhaps reflects a desire to believe that none of us are as vulnerable as we truly are—a desire held in common with militia members.
4. The brothers were Terry, the coconspirator, and James, who was arrested after the bombing but never charged.
5. It is striking how similar this statement is to messages we hear today about it "is not the right time" to discuss possible gun control measures in the aftermath of a mass shooting incident.
6. In actuality, the attack was carried out by an antisemitic doomsday cult called Aym Shinrikyo (Weill, 2022).
7. For example, https://web.archive.org/web/20220617171643/www.youtube.com/watch?v=0QsgEn2vTX8
8. Some early accounts of the militia movement give Thompson a central place in its founding because she made a documentary about Waco, portraying it as a government hit job on a religious community. Archival materials, however, indicate that Olson and other leaders kept her at arm's length, perhaps in no small

part because of her directness and perhaps because she was a woman in a male-dominated space. Olson told me in 2011 that Thompson was never affiliated with any militia group, but instead had a practice of inserting herself into national debates of interest to militia members.
9. www.internetlivestats.com/total-number-of-websites/
10. Other scholars, including Berger (2013). have examined similar methodological issues with SPLC group counts.
11. The communication is undated but references events in early 2000, so it was written at least 5 years after the split.
12. There have been a number of conspiracy theories about weather or climate control, and this person is most likely referencing one referred to as "Agenda 21," where some people believed the UN's suggestions for voluntary programs to slow climate change would lead to a variety of nefarious outcomes. See Jackson (2017) for more information.
13. For examples of news coverage from this time, see https://web.archive.org/web/20220617172031/www.youtube.com/watch?v=SrqnF8ZdoKU; https://web.archive.org/web/20220617172015/www.youtube.com/watch?v=LaBjujpd9yo
14. For example, https://web.archive.org/web/20220617172116/www.youtube.com/watch?v=X_KoNZkf-2k

References

ADL. (2017, February 8). Y2K paranoia: Extremists confront the Millenium. *ADL*. www.adl.org/resources/report/y2k-paranoia-extremists-confront-millenium

The Associated Press. (2001, June 10). McVeigh offers little remorse in letters. *The Topeka Capital-Journal*. http://cjonline.com/stories/061001/new_mcveigh.shtml

Belew, K. (2018). *Bring the war home: The White power movement and paramilitary America*. Harvard University Press.

Berger, J. M. (2013, March 12). The hate list. *Foreign Policy*. https://foreignpolicy.com/2013/03/12/the-hate-list/

Bradsher, K. (2001, April 30). Citing declining membership, A leader disbands his militia. *The New York Times*. www.nytimes.com/2001/04/30/us/citing-declining-membership-a-leader-disbands-his-militia.html

Chermak, S. (2002). *Searching for a demon: The media construction of the militia movement*. Northeastern University Press.

Churchill, R. H. (2009). *To shake their guns in the Tyrant's face: Libertarian political violence and the origins of the militia movement*. The University of Michigan Press.

Cooter, A. (2013). *Americanness, Masculinity, and whiteness: How Michigan militia men navigate evolving social norms* [Thesis]. http://deepblue.lib.umich.edu/handle/2027.42/98077

Cooter, A. (2022, January 1). Citizen militias in the U.S. are moving toward more violent extremism. *Scientific American*. www.scientificamerican.com/article/citizen-militias-in-the-u-s-are-moving-toward-more-violent-extremism/

Crothers, L. (2019). *Rage on the right: The American militia movement from ruby ridge to the Trump presidency* (2nd ed.). Rowman & Littlefield.

D'Oro, R. (2009, November 20). Militia movement resurfaces across nation. *NBC News*. www.nbcnews.com/id/wbna34070149

Duffy, J. E., & Brantley, A. C. (1997). Militias: Initiating contact. www2.fbi.gov/publications/leb/1997/july975.htm

Fox News. (2015, January 13). Oklahoma City bombing timeline, 1994–2005. *Fox News*. www.foxnews.com/story/oklahoma-city-bombingtimeline-1994-2005

Freilich, J., & Pridemore, W. (2005). A reassessment of state-level covariates of militia groups. *Behavioral Sciences and the Law*, 23(4), 527–546.

Jackson, S. (2017). Conspiracy theories in the patriot/militia movement (Program on Extremism Occasional Papers). *The George Washington University*. https://extremism.gwu.edu/sites/g/files/zaxdzs5746/files/downloads/Jackson%2C%20Conspiracy%20Theories%20Final.pdf

Kolker, K. (2020, October 22). 'Father' of Michigan militia denounces 'rogue' plot. *Wood TV*. www.woodtv.com/news/target-8/father-of-michigan-militia-denounces-rogue-plot/

Loeb, Z. (2022). Waiting for midnight: Risk perception and the millennium bug. In J. Abbate & S. Dick (Eds.), *Abstractions and embodiments: New histories of computing and society*. Johns Hopkins University Press.

Martindale, M. (1996, October 27). Third continental congress is born out of distrust. *The Detroit Sunday Journal*.

Michel, L., & Herbeck, D. (2001). *American terrorist: Timothy McVeigh and the Oklahoma City bombing*. Harper.

Price, G. (2018, June 18). Southern Poverty Law Center settles lawsuit after falsely labeling "extremist" organization. *Newsweek*. www.newsweek.com/splc-nawaz-million-apologizes-981879

Satija, N., Lowery, W., & Reinhard, B. (2019, April 5). Years of turmoil and complaints led the Southern Poverty Law Center to fire its founder Morris Dees. *Washington Post*. www.washingtonpost.com/investigations/years-of-turmoil-and-complaints-led-the-southern-poverty-law-center-to-fire-its-founder-morris-dees/2019/04/05/58717bfc-50fa-11e9-8d28-f5149e5a2fda_story.html

Silverstein, K. (2000, November). The church of Morris Dees: How the Southern Poverty Law Center profits from intolerance. *Harper's Magazine*, 54–57.

Stern, K. (1996). *A force upon the plain*. Simon & Schuster.

Tharp, M., & Holstein, W. J. (1997, April 21). Mainstreaming the militia. *U.S. News and World Report*, 24–37.

Uenuma, F. (2019, December 30). 20 years later, the Y2K bug seems like a joke. That's because those behind the scenes then took it seriously. *Time*. https://time.com/5752129/y2k-bug-history/

US House of Representatives. (1998). *The year 2000 problem* (4). Committee on Government Reform and Oversight. www.congress.gov/congressional-report/105th-congress/house-report/827/1

Weill, K. (2022). *Off the edge: Flat earthers, conspiracy culture, and why people will believe anything*. Algonquin Books.

5 Settling for Nostalgia
How Nostalgia and a Rural Mentality Shape the Militia Movement

In his 1999 interview with Robert Churchill, Michigan militia founder Norm Olson opined, using his pastor's cadence, about the movement he helped start, saying:

> It's a rural movement because it's connected to the land. This is important. I believe truly that Americans are unique in all the world. People didn't come to America for religious freedom. They came here for political freedom. They came here so that they could own the land.... People came here so they could pick up the dirt and say 'it's mine'.... [R]ural people by their very nature are independent, suffer a lot, they do things for themselves. So when the Government starts to intrude, they feel that.

Others who have researched and written about the movement have likewise attributed rurality to the movement's essence. Some rely on contrasts between stereotypes of backwards or ignorant rural people relative to supposedly more sophisticated city dwellers to explain why people might be fearful of cultural change and join a nostalgic group as an expression of this fear. Others have referenced how open farmland has declined and imply that militia members are more likely to be farmers (or at least very closely connected to them) such that perceived threats to domestic farming trigger economic and cultural anxieties, thus explaining militia engagement.

A Rural Mentality

In my observations, however, the truth is much more nuanced. The vast majority of militia members I have spoken with are not rural dwellers, but rather suburbanites. The largest militia units with loyal, regular members tend to train and gather just outside of cities, and none of my 40 formal interviewees relied on farming for income, although three kept animals for their personal egg or milk production. Militia participation seems to be driven by how a *suburban* identity created a desire to be more in touch with nature

DOI: 10.4324/9781003361657-6

and to pursue more traditionally masculine activities than their lifestyles otherwise incorporate. David, a 52-year-old who worked in the auto industry before retiring early, for example, recounted his last militia excursion saying:

> It's nice to get out in the woods and sleep. I sleep better out there. You know, I've got a back injury that's bothered me for 5 years, and I'll go out and sleep in a tent on the ground, find just the right ground, and my back feels great. . . . [Last time] we went out, it was ten degrees. I had snow [half a foot] deep on my sleeping bag . . . I felt great! Fresh air! I mean I was curled up in a bag, I was underneath pine boughs, I just felt like 'Wow!' It's nicer out here, nobody's bothering us, we're out here in this wilderness. I really enjoy it, doin' that kind of stuff.

Some people do feel rejuvenated from sleeping in nature, but as I watched David massage his lower back even as he praised the merits of roughing it, I couldn't help but think it was a Shakespearean "he doth protest too much," trying too hard to convince me of his comfort. If this remark did reflect the near euphoria he describes, it is because of the sharp contrast it provides to his usual life. If, as is more likely, this was an overly favorable representation of his emotions waking in the elements, it indicates an even stronger effort to symbolically distance himself from his suburban identity.

Rurality's allure is neither new nor unique. Many organizations have openly encouraged men to remove themselves from cities and from the feminizing effects of women—the "sissification of society," as one of my militia contacts terms it. Organizations like this claim that men need to reinvigorate themselves and recapture a masculine ideal that becomes lost or at least muted when away from nature for too long. Some scholars think nature is less a source of power in this framework than it is something coded feminine (i.e., mother nature) and thus something to either be conquered or cared for in ways that rely on tropes of traditional masculinity (Belmont & Stroud, 2020). The Mythopoetic Movement is perhaps best known for this model. It encouraged men to seek personal growth through participating in appropriated Indigenous rituals, a practice that has been copied to some extent by neo-Nazis, mass shooters, and survivalists in recent years (Bounds, 2020; Miller-Idriss, 2020). Scholars Daniel HoSang and Joseph Lowndes (2019) call this "racialized cross-dressing that selectively incorporate[s] characteristics attributed to Indigenous people, such as incorruptibility, aversion to foreign rule, autonomy, ferocity, and a tie to the natural world," while others note that such practices have a long history, going back to the Boston Tea Party and other settler-era gatherings, and started, in part, as a way to distinguish emerging American masculinity from a supposedly softer British masculinity (Gorski & Perry, 2022).

Other organized efforts to reconnect men to nature have included the Promise Keepers, which asserts that Christian men must forcefully reclaim their proper place as heads of the household, and even the Boy Scouts before its substantial modernization in recent years. The Scouts' founder touted the explicit goal of "fostering manly strength [while countering] corrupting and debilitating effects of urbanization and social change" (MacLeod, 1982, p. 3). Remasculinization through ruralization has operated within larger ebbs and flows of "back to the land" rhetoric, which became commonplace and seemingly permanent after recurrent shortages of fuel and other goods in the 1970s (Brown, 2011). Some men today may similarly have difficulties identifying with a "soft" masculinity that is associated with an increasing number of jobs whose exertions have been made easier and whose dangers have been at least partially mitigated through technology, relative to the physical labor captured in the myth and perhaps still required of their fathers and grandfathers (Du Mez, 2020).

Rural spaces and their seduction of self-sufficiency can be a temptation to large segments of the population, however, and not only to the white men who have comprised the majority of those attracted to organizations promoting the restoration of rural virility. Historian Dona Brown's examination of the back to the land movement's history says that second-wave feminists encouraged women to move to rural environments to be self-sufficient away from oppressive men, inverting the appeals more typically directed toward men. Brown also recounts how others in her field have argued that people, especially Black folks, moving to the suburbs in the early 1900s were not only seeking more affordable housing and property ownership, but also food security that was at least potentially more accessible on one's own land than in rapidly growing cities (2011). Anthropologist Anna Maria Bounds' (2020) ethnography with New York preppers shows how, a century later, continuing distrust regarding the government's ability to care for its citizens during emergencies is still a major factor that incentivizes participating in urban prepping for preppers of color. Olson's quote from the last chapter also reflects this idea when he asserts that city dwellers will flee from violence and chaos surrounding their homes when the federal government eventually and inevitably fails to manage some large-scale emergency. But he says it will already be too late for them to be saved alluding to the Biblical apocalypse of Revelations. Instead of finding refuge, he says, those who flee will find only more hardship as they are confronted by people who had the foresight to prepare a safehold in the country well before disaster struck.

Brown suggests that very real experiences with the government's inability to manage crises undergird contemporary efforts to reduce food insecurity through the locavore movement and community gardens in cities like Detroit (2011).[1] When the COVID-19 pandemic began in early 2020 and the virus negatively impacted global shipping chains and affordable food, some Americans fancied themselves Victory Gardeners and kept busy during lockdowns by planting small vegetable gardens, acting in the lineage of forebearers who bolstered morale and food supplies during earlier national crises (Mayer,

2020). These recent examples of people embracing at least some aspects of a back to the land approach are a reminder that there are rational, practical reasons to engage in some behaviors for which militias advocate. Even the Department of Homeland Security (DHS) has, for more than a decade, recommended that everyone have an emergency kit that includes several days' worth of food and water and hard copies of local maps in case some disaster forces people to search for security outside their homes. Framing "getting back to the land" exclusively as an extremist impulse, or exclusively as a uniformly white and male endeavor, risks overlooking how Americans across the political spectrum share some interests and even actions with nostalgic groups. It also risks falsely excluding the possibility of women and men of color being "red-pilled" or radicalized into extremism, including exclusionary and potentially violent nationalism, which is a growing problem.

Even so, sociologist Allison Ford argues that preppers in her sample (not all of whom were white or rural) still "rely on qualities of hegemonic whiteness" (2021, p. 471), in part because appeals to the value of rurality and learning to subsist on the land are created in contrast to perceptions of urbanity. A city's visibly modernized and industrialized environment may alone foster nostalgia for open spaces and tradition (Boym, 2002), but as Katherine Cramer writes in her apposite *Politics of Resentment*, allusions to cities or to urban environments are very often stand-ins for people who are not white. While these perceptions are not necessarily about race alone because of how class, politics, values, and other identity characteristics are coded into racial stereotypes, Cramer writes, "these conversations are about race even when race is not mentioned" (2016, p. 86). Perceptions of the city and its inhabitants are suffused with ideas of threats caused by population density including potential scarcity, crime, and a habituated reliance on convenience or on a government that makes people less self-sufficient and dulls their instincts. Stereotypes about Black people intersect with these threats in inseparable ways, such that racism is a subcurrent of the contempt for urban environments even for people for whom race is not consciously strongly salient.

John, a white-collar worker in his forties, for example, recounted his time in the Navy as an eye-opening experience that allowed him to see truly destitute parts of the world and appreciate how he "had the same opportunity as anyone else" by virtue of being born in the US. He said he was quite pleased with his life, but seemed to sense that I was about to ask about the visible and well-known racial and economic disparities in his hometown of Detroit as he continued:

> I've grown up in Detroit, I've grown up in Michigan, I went in one direction and other people went in another direction, and I'm asking, 'Why?' Why should these guys who are here with the same opportunity as me, we work together, why would they go in another direction? They're no different than me. They're no better than me. They're no worse than me. Why? And the only thing I can figure is that it's something to do

with cities. What is it that cities breed? Cities around the world. Cities breed a certain . . . subculture? If you can call it that. It's not something that was around with our grandparents or great grandparents. It's something that just . . . evolved. It developed from, I guess you could say, unions making sure that everything was taken care of. . . . So, they want to rely on something like that—a service to take care of them.

John is very plainly referencing a perceived "softening" effect developed from living in cities that results in a sense of entitlement to being promised job security and other things, he thinks, rather than earning everything through individual hard work. He implies that all city dwellers are susceptible to this "subculture," as he called it, and that he only escaped it because his military service broadened his perspective. However, his characterizations are, whether he acknowledges them or not, inextricably tied to racist stereotypes of Black workers, specifically: their supposed entitlement, laziness, and reliance on unions, which are a conceptual stand-in for Democrats and other social welfare policies that many conservatives believe discourage honest labor. Although John attributes the same attitude to cities around the world, these stereotypes are even more evident as he references majority-Black Detroit.

Likewise, members' stated reasons for militia participation are not necessarily clearly rooted in overt, conscious racism, or even in an open desire to leave the city. Rurality is nonetheless almost fetishized for many of them. Only a relative handful of members whom I have encountered homestead or own property in remote locations that they use for personal retreat (or, sometimes, for their unit's training activities). And yet, most fantasize about living this way, reliant on few people but themselves, while expressing envy for those who do own rural property or talking about how such ownership, "is the dream. Assuming I'm ever able to retire," as Phil, a 48-year-old construction worker wistfully admitted to me while gazing at an open soybean field that served as his unit's regular training site. Many Michigan members specifically fantasize about escaping to the state's Upper Peninsula, a place whose landscape and presumed culture form a frequent conversational contrast to the reality of members' suburban surroundings. At the first training I attended with a unit located in the southeast part of the state, for example, some members were talking about their experiences in the peninsula. One mentioned he had once been stationed at a military base there and had been talked into shooting icicles (which can grow to more than 20 feet long and end in a deadly point)[2] off a large waterfall during his downtime. He recalled questioning the legality of this unique target practice but said his companion had merely responded with a shrug, asking, "who's going to catch us?" reflecting both the remote environment and a culture of independence away from usual authority structures.

Rather than being rural dwellers, it is more appropriate to think of the militia movement as having what might be called a rural *mentality*, an aspiration for a lifestyle and an identity that the rural represents to them. This means that the movement does indeed have a connection to the land and to ideas of land ownership, as Olson claimed, but this relationship is much more symbolic than it is reality. What we sometimes neglect in our analyses of a "symbolic consumption of the rural," as other scholars have termed similar practices (Campbell et al., 2006, p. 15), is that militia-style excursions into nature are not merely passive consumptive practices that occur in rural spaces. They are also *performative* practices where their peers, families, and, to some extent, the government are audience members. Wearing camouflage, camping in the elements, target shooting, and practicing survivalist tactics are physical embodiments of traditional masculine tropes of independence, self-sufficiency, and self-defense. Sometimes the audience may even include the actor, the militia member himself. Mark, a member without military experience in his early thirties told me, "I kinda just wanted to see if I could do it," during an annual training dubbed Snow Dawg that occurs in Michigan's frigid February temperatures. He and many other members who have echoed similar ideas to me are testing their own mettle to tolerate nature in one of its more hostile forms, in part to evaluate their own ability to do so during a true emergency that forces them from the safety of their homes.

Figure 5.1 Two members at a winter training called Snow Dawg. One takes aim at a distant paper target, and the other watches as he waits his turn.

Source: Photo by the author.

The curtain does not close on these performances once members leave those rural spaces, either. While training, members continue to learn presentations of self (Bounds, 2020; Goffman, 1959), including supplies and techniques that are both practical and rhetorical, that enhance their abilities to convey the image of a "real" militia member and a "real" man. New members, for example, may first attend with the limited gear they have on hand or that they can immediately afford to purchase but, if planning long-term membership, quickly adopt weapons, tactical vests, and other equipment that their unit considers to be ideal, sometimes for aesthetic reasons as much as practical ones. Adoption of various techniques encourages further investment in a member's militia identity and facilitates the costuming, both literal and metaphorical, of performances that some engage in during open carry rallies, protests, or other events where they aim to overlay their idealized rural mentality onto the suburban and urban spaces where they reside, work, and vote. Most want their collective actions to instill change that is not merely symbolic, as with any protest, and the symbolic aspects of their performances become a guiding light for their lives well beyond militia training grounds.

Nostalgic Nationalism

Nostalgia ideologically supports the symbolic appeals of rurality and untamed land for militia members while forming the shared metaphorical soil that fosters connections with people outside the movement. Cultural theorist Svetlana Boym wrote that nostalgia could be thought of as a "longing for a home that no longer exists or has never existed" (2002, p. xiii). That sense of longing includes a wistfulness and feelings of loss or irretrievability alongside positive recollections of the past. Psychologists who have studied nostalgia believe it is a sensation that is fundamental to the human experience, that we all may feel it around certain elements of our own biographies, and that it, overall, serves positive functions for identity exploration and self-esteem (Batch, 2020; Sedikides et al., 2004). Boym says this kind of nostalgia allows for reflection of past events that may be culturally instructive and may help affirm one's sense of belonging and place in society.

But people can also feel nostalgia outside their own biographies for a time or place they have never personally experienced, and even a time and place that perhaps no one has experienced. Nostalgia can be "a preference for things as they are believed to have been" (Dudden, 1961, p. 517), for "a story that feels as if it were true" (Hochschild, 2018, p. 16) even if it is incompatible with both past and present realities. Militias and other nostalgic groups, as historian Darren Mulloy says, long for the mythologized history of the nation's founding because "of the purposes to which it can be put. [They] use the past to bolster their sense of identity, to confer significance on their activities, and to legitimate their concerns" (2008, p. 62). Political scientist Andrew Murphy argues this kind of concrete nostalgic reference point

98 Settling for Nostalgia

creates a "politics of constraint" (2009, p. 131) that draws boundaries on the present based on the collectively imagined past. These limits may include ideas about the direction of the country, about the content of its culture, and about which groups are allowed to succeed, and which are allowed to fail. White men, whose political and economic paths should statistically be easier than other groups because they have not been limited by centuries of racism and sexism, may feel especially aggrieved when they are nonetheless unable to achieve the American Dream—their birthright, as Murphy calls it (*ibid.* 134), alluding to ideas of land ownership and other visible signs of economic achievement being missing from their portfolios.

Nostalgic groups almost feel a kind of diaspora for the mythological past that they believe represents the birth of the Dream and the peak of American freedom and independence (Gibson, 1994). The more jarring reality, however, is that many members think that most any point in our history is somehow superior to the present time. The mythologized heroism of World War II, the supposedly tranquil and economically stable 1950s, and the ostensible morality of Ronald Reagan's Presidential administration are all mentioned as specific examples that members believe are emblematic of Golden Ages within US history.[3] Members still value the Revolutionary War and its actors above all other symbolic reference points, but these alternatives are second-best options that still capture the nostalgia of a past that is supposedly better than the present. Militia members I have spoken with have often gone on diatribes filled with longing for simpler times, lamenting increasing specialization and the loss of broader skills in modern society. Josh, a 27-year-old customer service representative, flatly told me in the middle of such a speech,

Figure 5.2 Two men practicing field sutures on cattle tongues during a multi-unit even intended to bolster emergency medicine skills.

Source: Photo by the author.

"I grew up in the wrong decade. I should have been born in like the '40s or the '50s."

When members give specific examples of the skills people need to reclaim, they are almost always traditionally male-coded activities like automotive or plumbing repair, not cooking from scratch or mending clothing. There was one partial exception I witnessed that occurred during a combat medicine seminar in which members from multiple units participated. A 14-year-old boy attended with his father and balked at the portion of the training where people in attendance practiced doing sutures on beef tongues that the organizer had picked up from a local butcher and then sliced deeply with his pocketknife. Rather than openly acknowledging his son's obvious queasiness at the prospect of touching raw animal anatomy, the father showily told him that sewing, "Isn't just for women! It's a life skill. And it will be really helpful when you're older and your wife or your girlfriend is mad at you and doesn't want to sew up a hole in your pants!" Sewing may be a life skill, but one that men should be able to do only when women are not willing or available for the task.

Nostalgia can feel therapeutic and may reaffirm interest in traditions and rituals of the past when social or cultural change triggers a sense of threat or alienation (Sedikides et al., 2004). When such change feels like it is happening very quickly, nostalgia may also serve to mentally slow down time, to allow one to maintain a sense of identity and avoid *anomie* (a sense of being without social norms). It may also build imagined communities around the shared myths at its heart while strengthening connections to others within the same imagined community (Anderson, 2016; Boym, 2002; Marks, 1974; Murphy, 2009; Sedikides et al., 2004). This leads to a self-reinforcing cycle: as people experience threat, they turn to nostalgia for comfort; but their nostalgia-shaped vision then enhances the contrast between their idealized past and their supposedly degraded and inferior present; their feelings of threat grow, as does their desire to do something to manage those threats and attempt a return to the mythologized past.

Weaponizing Nostalgia

Politicians like Donald Trump who politically weaponize nostalgia take this cycle a step further. By imploring his base to make America great *again*, as it once was but is no longer, eager listeners are more likely to believe in a common interest that bridges other points of disagreement and to blame an outgroup for the purported decline of the nation (Berger, 2018). Outgroups are people we believe to be dissimilar to ourselves and our interests; in contrast, our in-groups are those people with whom we believe we have much in common and with whom we believe we would likely have positive interactions. We tend to make harsher judgments about outgroup members, especially when we assume someone's outgroup status based on easily noticeable visual features. Skin color, clothing, and general self-presentation are among the signals that can make us assume someone's race, gender, sexual orientation, religion, or socioeconomic status in a way that influences whether we start with a negative or positive assessment of them relative to our own experiences and values. People like Trump can amplify the outgroup salience of immigrants, people of color, or even Democrats among his supporters.

Disparate groups can most easily coalesce into active, organized, and possibly even violent conglomerations to achieve a shared end when they perceive a common enemy, especially one who has been openly labeled as a threat. Trump's appeal to a nostalgic vision of a once-great country capitalized on long-standing anxieties about cultural change that white men in particular can find threatening because of their historical monopoly on social, political, and economic power that is memorialized in the myth of our founding.[4] Nostalgia feels comforting when looking inward to one's in-group that is presumed to share one's interests and perspective, and, in cases like this, embracing nostalgia can make someone feel like they have found like-minded advocates for their desired society. As one of sociologist Johnathan Metzel's participants told him during his investigation of white identity's influence on health care, "Trump has given white men their voice back" (2019, p. 264).

Outgroups who are supposedly responsible for devolving the national culture are, within this particular nostalgic vision, blamed for in-group members' inability to achieve the American Dream. Their failure, in other words, is not due to some personal dereliction, nor any failure of our capitalist nation, which, in this framing, is also victimized by nefarious outgroup forces. Few militia members I encountered during my field work directly named immigrants for personal failures or missed job opportunities, though this rhetoric has become much more common and overt in their online communities in recent years after Trump's influence. Instead, they would more typically make false or at least questionable statements about the government extending undocumented migrants "more rights and more privileges than the citizens of this country" as 47-year-old civil designer Ralph insisted. Many claimed that completely free health care was a benefit that undocumented immigrants receive but citizens do not. Simon expressed this by telling me about a friend who had to spend $1500 out of pocket for each of six cancer treatments, but said:

> If it were some illegal [sic] though, they would get it for free, and they'd [the government] make sure their family was taken care of, too. I don't have anything against them, I feel sorry for them in some ways, but I just think you should take care of your own first.

Stories like this are meant to convey that we are nationally choosing to prioritize limited resources on out-groups at the expense of citizens who, by virtue of an imagined birthright, are more deserving. These members, some of whom have spouses or other close connections who were once themselves migrants, believe that the government shares at least equal blame with immigrant out-groups for supposedly threatening citizen's collective financial security. In their understanding, these attributions are not, however, about race, but are rather about culture, limited resources, and fairness. Militia members are not, in other words, simply employing a white supremacist's frame because they also oppose white and European migrants receiving such benefits.

Racial Threat

Much of the research on out-groups' perceived threats has nonetheless focused specifically on racial threat—the idea that white people use governmental mechanisms to try to maintain control when they feel their social, political, and economic power is weakened when non-white groups' power in those realms grows (Blalock, 1973; Blumer, 1958; Bobo, 1999; Metzl, 2019; Olzak et al., 1994). Racial threat has traditionally been studied for its influence on white people's political behavior, including voting patterns and gerrymandering that work to limit Black citizens' civic participation, and it is not a response that is limited to any political fringe (Bafumi & Herron, 2009; Behrens et al., 2003). Other work considers racial threat's deleterious influence on the criminal justice and educational systems (Drakulich & Crutchfield, 2013; Goyette et al., 2012; Jacobs et al., 2005; Novak & Chamlin, 2012; Olzak et al., 1994). Criminologists Kelly Welch and Allison Payne (2010), for example, find that school discipline becomes more punitive and more likely to include zero tolerance policies as the percentage of Black students rises.

Some scholars originally defined racial threat strictly in terms of white people observing a numerical increase in Black populations and tended to focus exclusively on white peoples' sensations of political and economic threat. However, others have observed the impact of perceived racial threat from immigrant groups of other races (Newman et al., 2012), and real population increases are not always necessary to produce threat. White people's anticipation or perceptions of change can be enough to provoke a threat response, and threat can include feelings of infringement on cultural or status markers, not only political and economic ones (Goyette et al., 2012; Pettigrew, 1998; Taylor, 1998). Lucas, a retiree in his sixties, for example, expressed a common theme among some of the older militia members I encountered when he said, "the Muslim religion and our Constitution and our way of life cannot co-exist. They can't do it," rather succinctly capturing these men's fear that Muslims would enforce a version of sharia law that trampled the individual rights fundamental to national identity.

White perceptions are highly susceptible to non-white groups' salience, not only their objective size, such that concerns like this about the Muslim population have unsurprisingly been very responsive to news stories covering histrionic claims about President Obama's supposed Islamic beliefs or other stories of foiled terror attacks that had been planned by people the media identified as Muslims. Racialized media representations of crime may especially enhance the importance of national stories in the formation of threat well beyond any local reality (Baybeck, 2006; Gallagher, 2003; Hopkins, 2010; Rocha & Espino, 2009; Taylor, 1998). A model of racial threat that is based on group position, rather than objective group size, is analytically advantageous because it explains why threat can grow even in the absence of population increases or other realistic group conflicts over economic or political resources (Cooter, 2012).

There are other threats that are largely driven by perceptions rather than reality yet contribute to white men's desire to prevent further cultural change. Chief among them are changes to women's roles in our society and especially in our economy. Some scholars understand emerging restrictions on abortion and other women's health care to be a kind of backlash toward women's growing autonomy, including their increasing presence in higher education, politics, and in various workplaces that previously over-represented men (Faludi, 2000; Flood et al., 2021; Green & Shorrocks, 2023). It is challenging to argue with that interpretation when states are considering legislation like that proposed in Idaho in March 2023 that is intended to criminalize inter-state travel for some women's abortion access (Durkee, 2023). Not all politicians or activists involved in such legislation are white or male, but white men comprise a disproportionate share of legislators who are proposing and voting for these regulations regardless of their constituents' wishes (Inglis, 2022).

General economic uncertainty also poses a threat to men's ability to adequately fulfill the role of family provider that is encapsulated in a nostalgia-informed ideal masculinity. The first generation of Americans who are not expected to economically surpass their parents are struggling to afford the fundamental markers of the American Dream (Dodge, 2022; Luhby, 2020; Rodriguez, 2022). Homes and college educations both require substantially more capital than used to be true, outpacing inflation, and this economic environment may increase threat among older generations who may have greater difficulty affording a comfortable retirement than they had anticipated and cannot subsidize their offspring's upward mobility.

The COVID-19 pandemic created another kind of threat not only because of its real impact on health and longevity (Greenhalgh & Simmons-Duffin, 2022), but also because of how it exacerbated preexisting economic and other insecurities. Many people, especially those in already-vulnerable economic conditions, lost their jobs early in the pandemic, and some struggled to provide basic sustenance for their families as prices for basic goods soared (Tracking the COVID-19 Economy's Effects on Food, Housing, and Employment Hardships, 2022). Many people, especially those connected to the militia milieu, resented and feared government efforts to control the pandemic's spread through policies like mask mandates and temporary lockdowns. These people denied the seriousness of the disease and collectively believed that the threat of government tyranny was worse than the threat of COVID's potentially debilitating effects. They were concerned, they said, that such mandates constituted a slippery slope because citizens could become complacent and blindly "follow orders" in a way that would threaten both gun rights and basic civil liberties. These fears fomented plots against several states' Democratic governors, most notably the elaborate plan to kidnap and try Michigan's Governor Gretchen Whitmer for treason (discussed in more detail in the next chapter), which resulted in the federal and state prosecutions of several individuals. For men who invest in traditional notions of masculinity and resent feeling controlled or being told what to do by powerful women, Governor Whitmer's efforts to intervene in COVID's spread likely felt substantially more threatening than similar efforts from other states' male governors' (Cooter, 2022).

Much of the research on perceived threats that trigger backlashes from powerful groups rightfully examines the aggregate impact that such attitudes have—how voting patterns are influenced by white fear or how women are statistically disadvantaged in certain workplaces because of men's resentment, for example. My focus on various perceived threats is more at the level of shared perceptions and how white people can contribute to systems of white supremacy even while thinking of themselves as non-racist, or how men can reinforce misogyny even while believing they are egalitarians.

Racism or Cultural Exclusion: A False Dichotomy

In earlier work (Cooter, 2012, 2013), I argued that at the experiential level, racial threat that militia members experience centers on *cultural* change rather than overt racism. They, for example, do not oppose immigration that follows legal policies, but believe that those who come here from any country without following procedures are signaling their premeditation to break other laws and pose risks to law-abiding citizens. Peter, in his late forties, expressed it this way:

> I have current family members who I am assisting to immigrate to this country. Do you realize the hoops my family and myself have had to jump through to come to this country? Many. . . . I do not fear Mexican immigration, I do not fear the 'browning of America' as some say, I have contributed to it. But open border immigration is a free ride. No hoops to jump through and no reason to adapt to a new culture or a desire to. [It's supposed to be] 'Out of many one,' not 'out of one many.' This adds to divisions and ultimately conflict. All immigrants have to earn citizenship! Or it has no value.

Many of the militia members I encountered are genuinely oblivious to the hurdles most people would face to legally immigrate and ignorant of how those procedures are even more complicated for people seeking asylum or refugee status (Amnesty International, n.d.). Many members are equally oblivious to much of our national history of racism and how both historical and ongoing racism continues to impair non-whites' ability to achieve the American Dream beyond what white people of similar economic and educational circumstances experience. Such a claim may seem inconceivable to some readers and certainly has been to some of my colleagues who grew up in diverse, liberal, academic circles. But this process is something I have personally witnessed. My rural hometown, according to Census data, is 90% white still today. When I was growing up there, confederate flags were almost as pervasive on flagpoles, clothing, and vehicles as kudzu was on the roadside. White people proudly displayed the flag as a symbol of individualism and rebellion against authority, and many of them genuinely did not know about the flag's racist meaning. They were never taught an accurate version of the Civil War, slavery, or the continuing legacy of racism in school, in the same way that my AP US history teacher vehemently denied the war was about slavery. There were very few Black people, who often have little choice except to remember and pass down more accurate histories of exclusion and racism (Nelson et al., 2013), in the town who could have informally corrected those lessons, and even fewer who would have felt safe or comfortable doing so.

An iteration of this same underlying problem of ignorance results in militia members who view their opposition to immigration and most social welfare policies as opposition rooted purely in cultural change without understanding the racial and racist implications of such attitudes, meaning their nostalgia can, even unintentionally, be weaponized against people who are not white men and thus help perpetuate white supremacy as a systematic force. Members' distinction between cultural and racial motivations is nonetheless important because possible routes for intervention are different for people who are overtly and knowingly racist relative to people who do not know basic facts about our social structures. At the same time, it is important to remember that such ignorance is socially constructed and, as sociologist Jennifer Mueller observes, "often claimed or projected in ways that exculpate one's responsibility to act" (2018, p. 9). That is, mass societal ignorance serves as a form of white indifference, as a convenient excuse to avoid dealing with systematic racism, and serves to perpetuate white supremacy as a taken-for-granted system.

White supremacy is most powerful when it is invisible to its beneficiaries because it gives the illusion of being normal and natural rather than an unequal barrier to fulfilling the Dream's promise. Mass ignorance is an ingredient in invisibility and is actively cultivated through boundary work and "conceptual obfuscation" (*ibid.*) that occurs, for example, through the intentional exclusion of certain topics from school curricula, or through making some religions' holidays into national holidays while completely ignoring others'. Boundary work of this nature is an act of forgetting as much as it is remembrance, so much that Boym referred to the volume of what must be forgotten to create nostalgic mythologies as an "abyss" (2002, p. 16). Collectively, we instrumentally forget those whose stories are left untold, whose voices are silenced, whose lives were snuffed out in the creation of our origin story. As sociologist James Aho writes, Americans are too often "blind to the despoliations, enslavements, rapes, and murders of the past that have provided them with the rights and privileges they enjoy today" (2015, pp. 44–45). Complicity in this process of forgetting occurs even when some individuals are unaware of what is being forgotten. That is, it is not necessarily some individual militia members' conscious choice to ignore certain elements of history that is at issue, but rather a systematic forgetting that is encoded in the myths we collectively teach white people. This kind of collective forgetting is a choice, an action, an activism that perpetuates white supremacist structures in its failure to interrogate ongoing oppressions.[5] White supremacy as a system and as a cultural force exists not only because of overt white supremacists but also because other white people (including, in some cases, those who consider themselves allies or even anti-racists) participate in social structures that were historically designed to racially discriminate; they often "forget" in this way the power they have to challenge those exclusionary structures and push us closer to a truly accessible version of the Dream.

Settler Colonialism

The lens of settler colonialism can help more clearly reveal what is forgotten and what is included in our shared stories. Settler colonialism is a kind of colonialism "in which the colonizers never left" (Carey & Silverstein, 2020, p. 5), where they instead maintain a permanent occupation and irrevocably influence the resulting culture (Gahman, 2020). A settler colonist's goal is not to pilfer resources for the benefit of a homeland, but rather to claim a new homeland, a process that entails conquest and theft of the physical land.

Settler colonialism is not a singular or concluded event, but rather an "ongoing structure" (Nakano Glenn, 2015, p. 4; Wolfe, 1999) that patterns power structures between the conquerors and the conquered in a way that is resistant to change and becomes self-reinforcing.[6] Power maintenance relies on white supremacy's lies that have been justified in part through ideas like Manifest Destiny, which asserted a Christian God's approval of the violence and erasure that settlement enforced in the name of claiming the frontier to establish God's kingdom on Earth. Puritan leaders framed conflicts against Indigenous populations as holy wars that would achieve this end and hasten Christ's return (Gorski & Perry, 2022; Halvorson & Reno, 2022). Presenting America as a nation righteously devoted to this apocalyptic outcome has ensured that threads of Christianity are embedded in the mythos today (such as ideas that America is a proverbial "city on a hill," meaning the obvious global moral and economic leader) (Braunstein, 2021). Scholars have argued that the religious connections are so evident within the myth that both "Christian" and "American" have become largely synonymous with "whiteness" in our collective imagination and, following Trump's influence, increasingly synonymous with "Republican" (Butler, 2021; Gorski & Perry, 2022). It is likewise no coincidence that Du Mez's captivating *Jesus and John Wayne* (2020) spends so many pages analyzing white evangelical Christians' investment in masculinity, traditional gender roles, and firearms as key pillars to their religious and personal identities. I witnessed this play out in my hometown evangelical community where, for example, some people would buy their eight- and nine-year-old male children BB guns, explicitly citing evangelical influencer James Dobson. Dobson insisted that boys are biologically driven to like guns and that denying those opportunities is a concerted attempt from "radical feminists" to "feminize boys" (*Kids*, 2010) and make them vulnerable to homosexuality, which he called "*the* greatest threat to your children" (Dobson, 2018, p. 127) (emphasis in original).

Selections from Norm Olson in the previous chapters show religion's influence on the militia's understanding of the nation's founding myth. Religious framings were explicitly embedded in the militia from its origins. They remain salient even for individuals who do not consider themselves part of that religious tradition due to their deep investment with the myth that is entangled with these religious ideas. Nelson, a militia member in his early twenties, for example, told me that he disagreed with claims that the US is a Christian nation or that the Founding Fathers were all Christians. When I asked him what he believed was the biggest issue facing the country, however, he responded:

> We've gone from being a Christian culture, or at least a culture that has accepted that there is a God, that there are certain moral principles we live by and things like the Ten Commandments or other things like that. We've stopped following those, so all of these other problems we are having whether it be greed, or taking on too much debt, or abortion or, anything else, it plays out of that. That's the base issue: it's the heart[7] of America is wrong.

Other members may not directly reference Christianity or "the heart" of America, but still long for the never-nation in their imagination while bemoaning how the national "character" or "mission" has drifted from its intended state in a way that alludes to some holy plan having been violated.

Trump has openly and successfully appealed to white evangelical congregations by utilizing the Christian themes of the myth (Gorski & Perry, 2022). At the launch of his "Evangelicals for Trump Coalition" on the campaign trail in January 2020, for example, he repeatedly referenced the idea that the country's founders had intentionally constructed a Christian nation and that religion is "under siege" in the US. He claimed that another electoral win would also be a win for God (Jenkins, 2020). Listeners who affirm the myth's

Christian origins can also easily hear appeals to those religious themes in Trump's other speeches even if they do not explicitly mention God or religion. One example was when Trump asserted "The only crime I've committed is to fearlessly defend our nation from those who seek to destroy it"[8] during his press conference following his arraignment for 34 counts of felony business fraud in April 2023. With this and related claims, Trump is trying to activate some of his evangelical base by implying that further legal action against him is an attempt to undermine God's will; it is not only a personal problem for him but also a celestial one that should motivate them into action.

Nostalgic Memories

The myth of America's founding relies on a nostalgia for an archetypal settler while simultaneously trying to forget the white supremacy of settler colonial reality. That imagined settler is a lone white man who, through the fruits of his own labor, carved out a unique democracy that is morally superior to any other nation in the world (Gibson, 1994; Grandin, 2019). Masculinity is important here. The archetypical settler is male even though the ultimately dominant pattern of British settler colonialism included women and children, in practice facilitating faster growth of the white population and settler values alike. Ideas of masculinity were already strongly connected during the settler era to notions of men (but not women) protecting the land and their families. Men, once more in contrast to women, were depicted as possessing necessary physical strength and acumen for farming even though many settler women were also involved in these tasks. Scholar Evelyn Nakano Glenn argues this male-specific connection to the settler concept was strengthened by how white settler women were legally "merged" (2015, p. 58) with their husbands and lost property and labor rights they may have possessed before crossing the Atlantic.

This strong connection between masculinity and settler imagery that is replicated in militia behavior today may help explain why only approximately 10% of militia members are women; since women are largely excluded from our collective imagining of settlers, they may also see themselves less as inheritors and reenactors of the mythologized founders. At the same time, women who become "one of the guys," as one of my female interviewees told me, by fully participating in militia trainings or similar behaviors and who opt into the settler persona receive enormous respect and admiration from men who invest in the founding myth.[9] Outside of militia ranks, other women may experience similar boosts to their status through this kind of persona adoption. Sarah Palin's popularity as a Vice Presidential candidate in 2008, for example, was facilitated by what we might call her settler femininity—a stereotypically feminine self-presentation alongside hunting and other skills connected to the myth.

Land during settlement was not, as the myth suggests, merely open and free for the taking when settlers arrived. They of course encountered Indigenous populations who were already occupying and using the land in a much more fluid manner than the European model of land use. Indigenous populations often moved with seasons and rotated crops to maximize resources instead of remaining stationary and attached to a single plot of land. Settlers were dismissive of the Indigenous approach, viewing it as an inferior use of resources and purported it reflected a laziness, an unwillingness to master the land (Nakano Glenn, 2015). Displacement and genocide of Indigenous peoples[10] in the interest of claiming land and establishing permanent settlements thus made land ownership a marker of Americanness, masculinity, and whiteness that was contrasted to Europeanness, femininity, and Indigeneity. Connections between Americanness, masculinity, whiteness, and land remain at the heart of our national myth (Inwood & Bonds, 2017). Open and tranquil rural spaces represent "natural purity, calm family life, idyllic safe communities, as well as a place where . . . good hard-working salt of the earth folks make honest livings" (Gahman, 2020, pp. 74–75). The frontier especially embodies this perspective. It is a space, almost an entity, that must still be conquered, and that represents and allows for personal freedom and exploration while maintaining an element of risk and a temptation to conquer that risk.

The Legacy of the Frontier

Frederick J. Turner's "Frontier Thesis" (1893) was among the first considerations of the frontier's dual practical and symbolic nature and spurred a host of other frontier studies. Building on this legacy, historian Greg Grandin (2019) says the imagery of the frontier and the idea of productive expansion was easily transposed onto other realms (i.e., culture, technology, and politics) once the frontier itself was effectively closed to further exploration. Pursuit of these expanding realms, he says, constituted "a constant fleeing forward [that] allowed the United States to avoid a true reckoning with its social problems" (*ibid*. p. 4). The frontier, he says, is thus "a state of mind" (*ibid*. p. 116) that, in other words, facilitates the Dream's illusion that progress is limited only by individual ambition.

Anthropologists Britt Halvorson and Joshua Reno note that "the pastoral imagery of the Midwest is . . . a key symbolic ingredient of American nationalism" (2022, p. 61). It is a symbol used by nostalgic fiction writers like Rose Wilder Lane and politicians like Trump alike. It is memorialized in paintings and film to normalize the ostensibly virtuous aspects of settler nostalgia (Grandin, 2019; Halvorson & Reno, 2022) and shape the public imagination of what the nation and its government supposedly should be. The strength of this symbolism linking the Midwest to the American ethos, to whiteness, and to masculinity has led sociologist Scott Melzer to use the term frontier masculinity to describe the ideal manhood that results from the myth (2012). For militia members and others with affinities for nostalgic groups, I suggest that *settler masculinity* may be a more accurate term. It captures nostalgia for the frontier and the skills the frontier's taming requires, but also encapsulates two more elements that are crucial for understanding how masculinity operates in these circles. First, it includes an orientation of rebellion toward the government that is central to members' identity. Second, it more clearly captures how oppression and exclusion happen (even, sometimes, unintentionally) through acts of nostalgic recreation; that is, how white supremacy is perpetuated through nostalgic group actions.

The strength of the interconnected symbolism of masculinity and Americanness may also help explain why we have traditionally seen militia groups be more active in Midwestern states compared to others. The allure of activity that harkens the settler era may be stronger when surrounded by the region's physical landscape and symbolism alike.[11] Even Norm Olson acknowledged the layered symbolic potential of this area in his statement immediately following Timothy McVeigh's terror attack, saying:

> The savage act of terrorism in Oklahoma City evidences the willingness and ability of America's enemies to strike the very heartland of our dear country. . . . It has been correctly noted that Oklahoma City is the 'Heartland' city of America. It also symbolizes the strength of America's Biblical and Spiritual roots. The beasts responsible for this tragedy are attempting to make a clear statement that neither our country, nor our common faith, nor our government are safe.

Nostalgia's cultivation also shapes what we collectively forget from the settler mythos. Identifying Oklahoma City as the heartland, as the epitome of the frontier and of Americanness, may have amplified the emotional impact of McVeigh's 1995 bombing there, as Olson suggests, when its devastation was ubiquitously labeled the largest terror attack to occur on US soil up to that point. However, we "forget" that more Black people were likely injured and killed in 1921, just over an hour and a half away in Tulsa, Oklahoma, when white people massacred a successful Black town because of racism and perceived economic threat.[12] Many people did not know about Tulsa until the 2019 television show "The Watchmen" dramatized the massacre in its opening episode (Vary, 2020), speaking to just how "forgotten" (i.e., intentionally omitted) stories like this are. We exclude them from the official history we teach many school children because we devalue the experiences of people who don't fit the classic white settler archetype. We, at best, gloss over stories that threaten the myth that everyone has an equal chance of achieving the American Dream by reminding us of racism and other intentional interference with some people's pursuit of life, liberty, and happiness. Attributing the label of largest terror attack to any single event similarly excludes the systematic terror and violence of both slavery and Indigenous genocide from the calculus.

Nostalgia for rural spaces and for the settler era is actively cultivated in the history lessons that pass on the myth of our founding, but we sometimes overlook how nostalgia can also be created and reinforced in militias and similar groups that act, as historian Le Goff says, as "nostalgia merchants" (1992, p. 95). During my fieldwork, it became clear that not all militia members joined the group with an equal investment in a mythologized past. Instead, members increasingly adopted the militia's political outlook, general concerns, and even verbiage the longer they were involved with a unit. Two members, for example, swore me to secrecy as they told me that they voted for Obama prior to joining the militia, but, within a short amount of time, both adopted a strong and unnuanced anti-Democrat stance that mirrored that of their units' other members. Around the same time, I also conducted a survey with Project Appleseed instructors that is indicative of the same pattern. This gun rights group does not consider itself to be a militia but nonetheless echoes many militia principles about the centrality of firearms for purposes of both self-defense and preserving the national character. They center their identity specifically on the tale of Paul Revere's midnight ride to warn of the British advance on Boston. Sixty-nine (83%) of 83 respondents reported that they knew nothing or next-to-nothing about this story before participating in Appleseed. To become an instructor for the organization, they are expected to know the story intimately and to help pass it to new members, and thus, according to their responses, adopted the story and its allegorical lessons only after joining the organization.

Nostalgia is something that is actively cultivated alongside group identity via repetition at events and through leaders becoming storytellers of anecdotes meant to solidify group identity and purpose. Militia units I have encountered have fewer formal history lessons during their events than Appleseed but still reference particular historical battles and figures, especially from the Revolutionary War. They also cultivate and refine stories about their own activities that highlight certain in-group-outgroup boundaries. They especially focus and find humor in stories that ridicule people who do not meet their standards, such as a white man who repeatedly failed to follow basic firearm safety procedures during a training until another member took away his weapon and told him he could only participate with a stick. This story is, nearly ritualistically, followed by questions like, "What caliber was the stick?" and heavy laughter. As sociologist Ruth Braunstein observes, stories like this are intended to simultaneously capture ideas of "who we are," "where we have been," and "where we are going" (2021, pp. 4–5). These stories altogether function as more than just an insider's script to militia culture and are treated almost like an oral holy text, one that serves as a yardstick for whether members and newcomers alike adequately understand and embrace militia values.

Nostalgia and Stated Motives for Membership

Shared commonalities are among the reasons that members cite when telling me why they joined a militia. In earlier writing based on my fieldwork, I found that their stated reasons could be divided into four categories: Comradery, Sense of Duty to Country or to Family, Personal Preparedness, or Political Expression (Cooter, 2013). I argued then that the most important common thread across these categories was masculinity. I still believe that to be true, but what I focused on less at the time was how the masculinity implicated in each category is essentially a settler masculinity that is imbued with nostalgia.

Ten interviewees[13] cited comradery as their reason for joining. They said they quickly met other members with whom they shared general interests and hobbies well beyond militia activities with examples including watching the Military Channel or specific TV shows, reading historical biographies, or visiting historical tourist sites. Others talked about how they thought militia participation would simply be fun. As Mark, a 42-year-old computer technician, laughingly told me, "I like to dress up!" thus recognizing some of the more performative elements of militia training but also reflecting an embrace of simpler times with fewer demands than exist in his daily life. Militia participation likewise allows members who share an explicit interest in historical events to discuss the past they value while engaging in activities that harken a return to a simpler rural environment.

Twenty-two total interviewees said a sense of duty was their primary impetus for joining a militia. Many of the 17 interviewees who cited a sense of duty to their country had previously served in the military and referenced having sworn an oath to uphold the Constitution and a desire to continue service to that oath after their military career ended. People stating this motive who did not serve expressed regret that they had been unable to do so because of health concerns or lamented that they had only become devoted to their country when they were too old to enlist. Regardless of military experience, members citing a sense of duty to country explicitly talked about believing their membership was a way to follow in the footsteps of the Founding Fathers and valorized the soldier-as-hero image that is at the center of the settler myth (Gibson, 1994).

Five other interviewees said a sense of duty propelled them into militia ranks, but their stated primary obligation was to family rather than country. These members all talked about embracing the hegemonic masculine role of protector and defender, which some members complained had fallen by the cultural wayside as people became more reliant on technology and less competent with individual physical skills and situational awareness. While somewhat separate from the soldier image above, people who were concerned about their families embraced a version of masculinity that is revered at the center of our founding myth.

Eight interviewees focused on their personal vulnerability as their reason for joining a militia unit. Some of these interviewees had traumatic threats to their own physical safety and security including a burglar in a childhood home, a murdered relative, and a spouse who unexpectedly died during routine surgery. These events all challenged these men's masculinity because they were unable to protect themselves or their family members from these experiences. Others who cited personal protection as their membership motivation did not report acute trauma but were each noticeably more invested in conspiracy theories about malignant global government actors than the average militia member and than the members citing other motivations for their militia participation. They wanted to find a group that would help them learn to defend themselves from whatever tyrannical attacks they imagined the government to be plotting, thus bolstering their masculine competencies. This segment of interviewees were the most likely to overlap with the off-gridder community, but not all did so; some focused exclusively on firearms training instead of the broad preparation marking off-gridders and focused rather exclusively on the government as the likely source of threat. All respondents in this category were, in other words, also referencing a masculinity that is virtually synonymous with the protectionism embedded in the settler myth.

Finally, eight interviewees referenced political motivations as driving their participation, which they generally believed sent a tangible message to officials in power that people like them are still willing to fight for the supposedly disappearing values present at the nation's founding. For them, voting was insufficient to capture their political will; they wanted to do something more to express their distrust of both parties and their concerns with the "direction" the country was going, once more relying on masculine expressions of strong, independent men, like our constructed image of the founders and other early settlers, who are willing to fight for what they want.

Nostalgia's Influence on Action

Narratives that are valued and repeated during a group's activities help sublimate individual identities to the group. They become a kind of pervasive and patterned thinking and a kind of moral philosophy—to use social movement terminology, an interpretive frame that shapes how members interpret various world events. The stories encourage listeners to value a pristine past over a degenerate present and future. They give touchpoints (places where different trees' branches overlap in my metaphor of nostalgic groups) that provide opportunities for collaboration or even merging with other groups. Revolutionary War figures and ideals connect militias to other gun-oriented groups that have interests in firearms or Founding Fathers. Concern for the national character and a longing for a purer, simpler past become the connection for many groups who have disparate ideas about race and gender inclusion. Nostalgia with specific touchpoints becomes a kind of lowest common denominator that provides opportunities for shared collective action across militias, neo-Nazis, Proud Boys, and others, as we've seen in recent years at social justice protests and January 6th alike.

Boym (2002, p. xvi) labels this a restorative nostalgia that she says desires to restore the past and

> tends to confuse the actual home and the imaginary one. In extreme cases it can create a phantom homeland, for the sake of which one is ready to die or kill. Unreflected nostalgia breeds monsters.

While "monsters" is suggestive of notable figures like Hitler who appealed to a kind of nostalgia centered on myths of ethnic purity, Boym goes on to

Figure 5.3 Militia members standing near a Gadsden flag as they wait on others from their unit to return from a qualifying walk.

say that restorative nostalgia is not "merely an individual sickness, but a symptom of our age, a historical emotion. . . . Nostalgia and progress are like Jekyll and Hyde: alter egos" (*ibid.*).[14] She suggests that progress cannot happen without a degree of longing for the past, one that becomes a hallmark of broader culture and that unfortunately comes at the cost of the wellbeing and safety of out-groups, who are the visible beneficiaries of that progress.

Boym's reference to average people being willing to die or kill for this vision is not an exaggeration in some cases. It is no coincidence that experts have raised warnings about encroaching global fascism, as we have witnessed an increase in hate crimes and stochastic terrorism in recent years (Li & Lartey, 2023). It is likewise no coincidence that "Molon Labe," Greek for "come and take them," and the "Don't Tread on Me" of the Gadsden flag are well-known visual identifiers of militia and militia-adjacent beliefs. For some people, these messages are not merely rhetorical but are instead indicative of a willingness to defend the status quo and potentially to violently lash out at attempts to change policy or culture that may seem central to an ideal national identity. Ongoing responses to gun control discussions and supposedly stolen elections are paramount examples here.

The restorative nostalgia that undergirds this belief system, as Boym says, "does not think of itself as nostalgia, but rather as truth and tradition" (2002, p. xviii). The worldview that emerges from our mythologized history, if reinforced and legitimized at the highest levels, risks becoming unyielding and unlikely to be influenced by other opinions or fact checking. It is fed by self-reinforcing and snowballing conspiracy theories that make the people who believe them even more insular and distrusting of other perspectives (Boym, 2002; Cooter et al., 2023; Rottweiler & Gill, 2020). It risks becoming a dogma that believers then attempt to enforce on others, sometimes with violent results.

The risk for dogmatic thinking is increased in already-insular online spaces that may become echo chambers for the ideas that caused users to seek them out in the first place. Militia members express their dedication to restorative nostalgia expressed in a variety of ways online, including in memes. For example, following school shootings like that in Nashville, Tennessee, in April 2023, slight variations on a particular meme have consistently been common in some militia and other gun rights social media circles. These memes show a person, usually a child, asking "How many children have to die before you would support gun control?" Another person, almost always an adult, white male, simply responds, "All of them." This meme, which I've most commonly seen shared by militia men who are fathers, comes across as beyond callous, especially immediately following a mass casualty event. Posters tend not to mean that they would willingly sacrifice their or other children for continued firearms access, as one might easily assume while viewing these images, but instead tell me they believe that there is no point in protecting children from what they see as rare and random gun violence if the trade-off is leaving a legacy of a tyrannical state where those children cannot be free. For these members, one's ability to defend themselves through firearm ownership is so central to individual freedom and American identity that giving them up would be equivalent to destroying the country for their children. Failing to fully understand the content and centrality of militia members' nationalism in their identity risks dismissing them as uniformly violent extremists who are beyond reasonable discussion. In reality, most members I have encountered are using aggressive cultural scripts to reflect issues that are shared widely among US citizens, and in-roads remain possible when conversations can be refocused on shared goals and values.

Firearms and Mythic Nationalism

Firearms are crucial to the identities of militia members and are also an integral actor in the mythologized story of our founding. They have a symbolic importance that supersedes their practical use and that can serve as another frequent point of shared interest across distinct groups; or as Melzer succinctly says of his NRA participants' goals, "Defend the guns. Win the culture war. Save America" (2012, p. 59). Some scholars argue that firearms or gun culture did not become an essential ingredient in settler masculinity until well after the frontier era, attributing gun manufacturers' and the NRA's influence in the 1960s and 1970s for wedding firearm worship to the settler myth long after the Revolutionary War ended (Lacombe, 2021; Steinhorn, 2013). Dunbar-Ortiz (2018) refutes this claim, in part citing data arguing that rates of firearm ownership were higher during the settler era than today and that guns were actually more common than Bibles among early male colonists' listed possessions. But Melzer (2012, p. 28) says, the bottom line is:

> Regardless of whether [gun culture] was real [during the settler era] or constructed afterward to sell stories and products, it continues to shape American culture and masculinity. Guns, masculinity, and freedom are intertwined and still resonate with Americans today.

However, we cannot ignore race and racism in the assessment of how these other variables are intertwined. Scholars Lindsay Livingston and Alex Trimble Young observe that the Second Amendment is, in practice, "conditioned, in deed if not in word, by the bearer's proximity to whiteness" (2020), based on a long history of denying Black Americans the right to bear arms. Armed Black people tend to be treated very differently by our legal system and our society as a whole because of stereotypes aligning blackness with criminality and danger.

For white people unencumbered by such stereotypes, firearms can more cleanly symbolize independence and a mythologized settler who is nobly striving for individual rights.[15] They also encapsulate a moral high ground that is presumed to come with that Revolutionary War victory, but one that is necessarily drawn in contrast to ostensibly inferior people who lost the battle (Gibson, 1994). This is part of why groups like militias and Appleseed value marksmanship. Shooting accuracy is not only a sign of firearms experience and a link to the legacy of the founders, but, to them, also a signal of a moral acumen that has been constructed through self-discipline and self-control that they believe to have been crucial for early settler survival. Firearms also symbolize power and resistance towards the government—a form of rebellion that is, to no small degree, parallel to the selective and contested symbolism that the confederate flag has in some white communities. Many non-militia people do not see revering firearms as a sign of strength but rather as a violation of a social contract or even as a symptom of a folly, rightfully observing how even the largest militia arsenal would have no chance of defeating a concerted government force. It is not, however, the case that most militia members truly believe they would be able to defend against a government intent on using tanks or other major weapons of war against them. Kyle, a 36-year-old commercial painter, told me that suggestion was "bull crap" as he talked about the necessity of limiting government tyranny through voting and protest before it ever reached the point of conflict. Members are instead trying to symbolically embrace the legacy that they believe the founders left to them to prevent a loss of liberties they see as fundamental to the national identity.

This is why the Second Amendment is so important to a variety of nostalgic groups and beyond: it is not only about potential defensive capabilities against a range of threats, both real and imagined, but also because of how firearms link their users to this mythologized past. Nostalgic groups and individuals who think like them consistently revile Democrats and efforts for gun control because they believe that such legislation indicates an outright rejection of an essential component of American identity. Groups that attach to any one or more of the symbolic meanings behind firearms can then use them as a shared reference or a rally point for collective action. Most militia members report disliking the NRA for various reasons, for example, yet support it when gun control legislation seems likely because they recognize the NRA's relatively unique and incredibly potent political power to fight for their common interest. Individual NRA members, likewise, often distance themselves from the reputation of groups like militias while nonetheless expressing the same justifications for firearm ownership and use. These justifications revolve around ideas of self-defense and rejection of government tyranny (Lacombe, 2021), and I observed as several men who said they were long-time NRA members eventually joined militia units because they wanted to do something "more than politics," as one man worded it, to personally support the Second Amendment.

Sheriffs Within the Nostalgic Settler Worldview

Ideas of politics, power, and corruption help explain why militia members tend to give local sheriffs the benefit of the doubt about their motives and trustworthiness, in contrast to usual militia views of government actors. Members see the federal government and its representatives as distant from constituents and as inherently corrupt but see sheriffs as an integral part of the communities they serve. Sheriffs are typically elected by the community, and members thus believe sheriffs are more likely to work in the interest of voters with whom they regularly interact and thereby be comparatively insulated from corruption (Cooter, 2022; Farris & Holman, 2017).

There is certainly truth to members' assumptions about sheriffs' local loyalties and general dispositions. Political scientists Emily Farris and Mirya Holman conducted a survey in 2021 for The Marshall Project and received responses from more than 500 of the nation's approximately 3100 sheriffs (Chammah, 2022a, 2022b). More than 300 respondents said they were willing to intervene between higher authorities and local constituents when they disagreed with the law those higher authorities were trying to enforce. This kind of "interposition" as it is sometimes known has been regularly expressed by sheriffs in numerous states regarding their unwillingness to enforce any proposed state or national gun control laws. Nearly half of this study's respondents also asserted that sheriffs' authority is higher than any other authority in the land, including the President's, while another quarter of respondents said they were "neutral," rather than disagreeing with that assertion.

Farris's and Holman's results show how sheriffs themselves rebel against control from higher authorities while resonating with a rural mentality and with recognizable fictional archetypes of independent, stalwart lawmen who exact their own justice in untamed landscapes. Sheriffs both represent and embody the settler colonist spirit, whereby settlers are valorized as operating "outside of the law and outside of the civilizing role of the state" (Inwood & Bonds, 2017, p. 12). Sheriffs are effectively an anachronistic outgrowth both of Founding Fathers who defied the British crown and of early frontiersmen who defied standards of civilized behavior in the interest of survival and conquest, personalities that are both encoded in our national mythos. Many who advocate for a rural mentality today find easy mental justifications for actions that violate civilized standards or even the law but fulfill individualism and self-advancement, as did the early settlers they reference.

Rebellion against authority for its own sake helps explain some breaches of decorum or even law breaking today, but the more consistent explanation members cite is self-determination. Militia members often espouse that individuals know what is best for them and their particular circumstances much better than the government or authorities ever could on topics ranging from self-defense to COVID-19 prevention to educational plans for their children. Some members, like many of the sheriffs in the above study, believe they have not only the right, but also the responsibility, to assess the legitimacy of any given law before deciding whether they will comply with it.

One member I spoke with, for example, told me that he refused to take out a required permit to build a fence on his rural property. He did not want to pay a fee to the government to modify something he believed he should have full control over because he owned it. Another was the sole employee of his own business. He used a certain chemical that individuals could use with no special dispensation, but he said the government required businesses to have a license to use it in the same quantity. He argued that such a distinction was illogical and also harmful to his ability to earn an income; so, in the unlikely event he was pulled over for a traffic infraction and an officer knew about this required license, he simply made sure to hide the chemical under other materials in his pickup truck when driving to jobs. It is an important part of most militia members' identity to insist they are law-abiding citizens, and these two examples of legal violations are rather minimal. However, the belief that individuals can decide whether something "really" breaks the law based on their perceptions of its legitimacy can obviously lead to much larger problems, such as believing one can reject the legitimacy of electoral processes and therefore insist an election has been stolen.

Many people did not realize the potential for sheriffs and other local law enforcement to ideologically align with nostalgic groups until Sheriff Dar Leaf publicly vouched for some militia members who had been arrested for planning to kidnap and try Michigan's Governor Gretchen Whitmer (Agar, 2020; Snell & Burke, 2020). But these connections are long-standing. Olson's documentation from the early days of the militia shows him interacting rather cooperatively with several different sheriffs, some of whom are quoted in local newspapers as openly supporting his militia-building efforts. During my fieldwork, I first observed how many sheriffs and other law enforcement in Michigan are aware of militia groups in their area and, like Leaf, not only tolerate but actively welcome their presence. In addition to public requests for militia help with search and rescue efforts (Higgins, 2010), members have reported to me that sheriffs ask them for assistance through less public channels for security for both private and public events. Members from a Michigan militia unit located in the western part of the state, for example, shared that they had attended a town hall held by a candidate for a state office and stood right next to the local sheriff while in camouflage and visibly wearing their sidearms. They had watched for his reaction to their open carry and happily reported at a multi-unit gathering that he "had no problem with it whatsoever." They chatted with him after the town hall, saying, "we did offer our services to him anytime he needed us, and he was very receptive to that." I have not personally witnessed those security requests, but similar ones were well documented (including in newspaper clippings) in archival materials from Olson's archive and continue to be reported as happening in some jurisdictions today.

Cooperative connections between militias and sheriffs may seem startling at first glance, but especially in smaller communities, LEOs are likely to be in the same social circles as militia members. Perhaps they attended high school together, or enlisted in the military at the same time, or, in some cases, are related to each other. Local LEOs with these connections view militia members as potential allies with shared interests and some shared skills and thus may underestimate the violent threat that some militia units could pose to their communities and beyond. This perceived allyship was perhaps best exemplified when 17-year-old Kyle Rittenhouse traveled across state lines with his AR-15 with the reported intention of protecting businesses from protestors who were demonstrating against Jacob Blake's death at the hands of police. Shortly before Rittenhouse shot three people, two fatally, a police officer offered him drinking water and told him that law enforcement appreciated the presence of armed citizens like him at the protest (Litke, 2020). Rittenhouse was criminally charged with several offenses related to the shootings and eventually acquitted of all of them. The acquittal not only cemented Rittenhouse's fame in a variety of conservative circles but also served as further "proof" of the legitimacy of the self-help justice embodied in the settler myth. I further explore how ideas of justice and those sworn to enforce it intersect with militia identity and action in the next chapter.

Notes

1. While food insecurity interventions like this may originate in social justice initiatives, their economic and social impact needs further study. For example, some people praise efforts to allow backyard chickens in suburban or urban spaces as a nod to nutritional self-sufficiency, yet may gloss over how these efforts seem to be frequently tied into gentrification and racist double standards, For example, Black families were accused of insufficiently modernizing their properties

and forced out of their homes in Knoxville, Tennessee, during so-called urban renewal if they possessed livestock (Kato, 2020; *Losing Home*, 2021).
2. See examples here www.mightymac.org/tahquamenonfallswinter.htm.
3. It is worth recalling once more that even within the overly rosy portrayals of these periods, they were certainly not particularly advantageous for people of color and for many white women.
4. White men are not the only demographic in which nostalgia can be weaponized. We have also seen this tactic in Black separatist groups, for example, and women of different races who have engaged with so-called "cottagecore" or "tradwife" efforts, especially online. My focus here is on what weaponized nostalgia looks like within the majority-white and male militia movement.
5. See geographer Joshua Inwood (2018) for an examination of how James Baldwin's concept of "white innocence" allows white people to focus on ideas of successful individualism in attaining the American Dream while ignoring the barriers that people of color have toward this end.
6. Critiques of using settler colonialism as an analytic frame rightfully note how much of the work centers the perspectives of the colonizers and their inheritors, rather than on the voices of the colonized. As a white researcher, I am attempting to write from my own trajectory and privilege to help better understand the lingering impacts that settler colonialism has on systemic white supremacy today.
7. Many Christian sects talk about issues like "changing hearts and minds for God" or "unhardening someone's heart" for salvation, a clear parallel within Nelson's message.
8. https://web.archive.org/web/20230000000000*/www.youtube.com/watch?v=r1WdFCtfwEw
9. This was my experience as well, and boosted my ability to conduct research in the field.
10. We also collectively "forget" how Indigenous populations were erased not only through violent genocidal attacks, but also through intermarriage, rape, religious conversion, forced schooling, and, later, through inducements to move away from reservations in effort to disrupt collective identity (Alfred & Corntassel, 2005; Nakano Glenn, 2015).
11. There is an ironic contradiction within this symbolism, however. Some militias use state parks for various training exercises, asserting individualism and independence from the same government that cultivates and maintains those spaces for shared public use—an action that perhaps gets as close as any US government intervention to the "Communism" that militias so despise.
12. There were 168 fatalities at Oklahoma City, with another 759 reportedly injured (Mallonee et al., 1996). The exact number of fatalities in Tulsa is not known but is believed to be as high as 300, with more than 800 others injured (*Tulsa*, 2018).
13. Three interviewees cited reasons in more than one category, and rather than asking them to rank their importance, I included them in both categories they mentioned such that the total reported in this section is 43.
14. It is notable that Boym speaks of nostalgia as though it is an entity with its own perceptions and consciousness. Perhaps this is an accident of translation, but it appropriately reflects her view here that nostalgia becomes a kind of cultural force, bigger than individual actors.
15. We have less research on gun owners of color even though their numbers increased dramatically during Trump's Presidency (Curcuruto, 2020), but while it seems that motivations for firearm ownership also focus on ideas of self-defense, their motives are more rooted in awareness of law enforcement failures to protect them (Bowen et al., 2023; Kramon, 2023) and less about embodying nostalgic archetypes. The Black Panthers similarly suggested that Black people arm

themselves as a form of protection in lieu of police (Chavez et al., 2020), echoing a history going back at least to notable journalist and activist Ida B. Wells who wrote, "a Winchester rifle should have a place of honor in every black home, and it should be used for that protection which the law refuses to give" (1892).

References

1921 Tulsa Race Massacre. (2018, November 1). www.tulsahistory.org/exhibit/1921-tulsa-race-massacre/

Agar, J. (2020, October 9). Sheriff who shared stage with militia defends their rights but not alleged governor kidnapping plot. *Mlive*. www.mlive.com/news/grand-rapids/2020/10/sheriff-who-shared-stage-with-militia-defends-their-rights-but-not-alleged-governor-kidnapping-plot.html

Aho, J. (2015). *Far-right fantasy: A sociology of American religion and politics* (1st ed.). Routledge.

Alfred, T., & Corntassel, J. (2005). Being Indigenous: Resurgences against contemporary colonialism. *Government and Opposition*, 40(4), 597–614. https://doi.org/10.1111/j.1477-7053.2005.00166.x

Amnesty International. (n.d.). Who is a refugee, a migrant or an asylum seeker? *Amnesty International*. Retrieved April 16, 2023, from www.amnesty.org/en/what-we-do/refugees-asylum-seekers-and-migrants/

Anderson, B. (2016). *Imagined communities: Reflections on the origin and spread of nationalism* (Rev. ed.). Verso.

Bafumi, J., & Herron, M. (2009). Prejudice, black threat, and the racist voter in the 2008 presidential election. *Journal of Political Marketing*, 8(4), 334–348. Batch, K. (2020). Nostalgia: The paradoxical bittersweet emotion. In M. H. Jacobsen (Ed.), *Nostalgia now: Cross-disciplinary perspectives on the past in the present* (1st ed., pp. 31–46). Routledge.

Baybeck, B. (2006). Sorting out the competing effects of racial context. *Journal of Politics*, 68(2), 386–396.

Behrens, A., Uggen, C., & Manza, J. (2003). Ballot manipulation and the "menace of Negro domination": Racial threat and felon disenfranchisement in the United States, 1850–2002. *The American Journal of Sociology*, 109(3), 559–605.

Belmont, C., & Stroud, A. (2020). Bugging out: Apocalyptic masculinity and disaster consumerism in offgrid magazine. *Feminist Studies*, 46(2), 431.

Berger, J. M. (2018). *Extremism*. The MIT Press.

Blalock, H. M. (1973). *Toward a theory of minority group relations*. Wiley.

Blumer, H. (1958). Race prejudice as a sense of group position. *The Pacific Sociological Review*, 1(1), 3–7.

Bobo, L. D. (1999). Prejudice as group position: Microfoundations of a sociological approach to racism and race relations. *Journal of Social Issues*, 55(3), 445–472.

Bounds, A. M. (2020). *Bracing for the apocalypse: An ethnographic study of New York's 'prepper' subculture*. Routledge.

Bowen, D. M., Barber, M., Gomez, M., Rooney, L., Ellyson, A., Rowhani-Rahbar, A., & Rivara, F. P. (2023). Black women & gun ownership in America: An exploratory study of motivations and strategy. *Violence and Gender*, 10(1), 38–44. https://doi.org/10.1089/vio.2022.0001

Boym, S. (2002). *The future of nostalgia* (Illustrated ed.). Basic Books.

Braunstein, R. (2021). The "right" history: Religion, race, and nostalgic stories of Christian America. *Religions, 12*(2), Article 2. https://doi.org/10.3390/rel12020095

Brown, D. (2011). *Back to the land: The enduring dream of self-sufficiency in modern America*. University of Wisconsin Press.

Butler, A. D. (2021). *White evangelical racism: The politics of morality in America*. The University of North Carolina Press.

Campbell, H., Bell, M. M., & Finney, M. (Eds.). (2006). *Country boys: Masculinity and rural life* (Illustrated ed.). Penn State University Press.

Carey, J., & Silverstein, B. (2020). Thinking with and beyond settler colonial studies: New histories after the postcolonial. *Postcolonial Studies, 23*(1), 1–20.

Chammah, M. (2022a, October 18). We surveyed U.S. sheriffs. See their views on power, race and immigration. *The Marshall Project*. www.themarshallproject.org/2022/10/18/we-surveyed-u-s-sheriffs-see-their-views-on-power-race-and-immigration

Chammah, M. (2022b, November 3). *Does your sheriff think he's more powerful than the president?* www.usatoday.com/in-depth/news/investigations/2022/11/03/county-sheriff-constitutional-power-richard-mack-oath-keepers/10627256002/

Chavez, N., Young, R., & Barajas, A. (2020, October 25). An all-Black group is arming itself and demanding change. They are the NFAC. *CNN*. www.cnn.com/2020/10/25/us/nfac-black-armed-group/index.html

Cooter, A. (2012). *Race and racism in the militia: Members' responses to Michigan's Black and Muslim populations*. www.amycooter.com/uploads/1/2/3/7/12374434/response_to_racialized_populations.pdf

Cooter, A. (2013). *Americanness, masculinity, and whiteness: How Michigan militia men navigate evolving social norms* [Thesis]. http://deepblue.lib.umich.edu/handle/2027.42/98077

Cooter, A. (2022). US Domestic Militias' intersections with government and authority: How a sociology of individualism informs their praxis. In D. Neubert, H. J. Lauth, & C. Mohamad-Klotzbach (Eds.), *Local self-governance and varieties of statehood: Tensions and cooperation* (pp. 31–49). Springer International Publishing.

Cooter, A., Taylor, M., & Hansen, T. J. (2023). Cultural change and conspiracism: How conspiracy theory trends reflect threat and anxiety. In M. A. Argentino & A. Amarasingam (Eds.), *Far-right culture: The art, music, and everyday practices of violent Extremists*. Routledge.

Cramer, K. J. (2016). *The politics of resentment: Rural consciousness in Wisconsin and the rise of Scott Walker* (Illustrated ed.). The University of Chicago Press.

Curcuruto, J. (2020, July 21). NSSF survey reveals broad demographic appeal for firearm purchases during sales surge of 2020. *NSSF*. www.nssf.org/articles/nssf-survey-reveals-broad-demographic-appeal-for-firearm-purchases-during-sales-surge-of-2020/

Dobson, J. C. (2018). *Bringing up boys* (Reissue ed.). Tyndale Momentum.

Dodge, K. (2022, May 31). College tuition inflation: A deep dive into the soaring cost of college over the past 60 years. *Academic Influence*. https://academicinfluence.com/inflection/college-life/college-tuition-inflation-deep-dive

Drakulich, K., & Crutchfield, R. D. (2013). The role of perceptions of the police in informal social control: Implications for the racial stratification of crime and control. *Social Problems, 60*(3), 383–407.

Dudden, A. P. (1961). Nostalgia and the American. *Journal of the History of Ideas, 22*(4), 515.

Du Mez, K. K. (2020). *Jesus and John Wayne: How white evangelicals corrupted a faith and fractured a nation.* Liveright.

Dunbar-Ortiz, R. (2018). *Loaded: A disarming history of the second amendment.* City Lights Publishers.

Durkee, A. (2023). Idaho abortion bill could be first ban on interstate travel for procedure. *Forbes.* www.forbes.com/sites/alisondurkee/2023/03/29/idaho-abortion-bill-could-be-first-ban-on-interstate-travel-for-procedure/

Faludi, S. (2000). *Stiffed: The betrayal of the American man.* Harper Perennial.

Farris, E., & Holman, M. (2017). All politics is local? County sheriffs and localized policies of immigration enforcement. *Political Research Quarterly, 70*(1), 142–154. https://doi.org/10.1177/1065912916680035

Flood, M., Dragiewicz, M., & Pease, B. (2021). Resistance and backlash to gender equality. *Australian Journal of Social Issues, 56*(3), 393–408.

Ford, A. (2021). "They will be like a swarm of locusts": Race, rurality, and settler colonialism in American prepping culture*—Ford—2021—rural sociology—Wiley Online Library. *Rural Sociology, 86*(3), 469–493.

Gahman, L. (2020). *Land, god, and guns: Settler colonialism and masculinity in the American heartland.* Zed Books.

Gallagher, C. A. (2003). Miscounting race: Explaining whites' misperceptions of racial group size. *Sociological Perspectives, 46*(3), 381–396.

Gibson, J. W. (1994). *Warrior dreams: Violence and manhood in post-Vietnam America.* Hill & Wang.

Goffman, E. (1959). *The presentation of self in everyday life.* Anchor.

Gorski, P. S., & Perry, S. L. (2022). *The flag and the cross: White Christian nationalism and the threat to American democracy.* Oxford University Press.

Goyette, K., Farrie, D., & Freely, J. (2012). This school's gone downhill: Racial change and perceived school quality among whites. *Social Problems, 59*(2), 155–176.

Grandin, G. (2019). *The end of the myth: From the Frontier to the border wall in the mind of America.* Metropolitan Books.

Green, J., & Shorrocks, R. (2023). The gender backlash in the vote for Brexit. *Political Behavior, 45*(1), 347–371.

Greenhalgh, J., & Simmons-Duffin, S. (2022, August 31). Life expectancy in the U.S. continues to drop, driven by COVID-19. *NPR.* www.npr.org/sections/health-shots/2022/08/31/1120192583/life-expectancy-in-the-u-s-continues-to-drop-driven-by-covid-19

Halvorson, B. E., & Reno, J. O. (2022). *Imagining the heartland: White supremacy and the American Midwest.* University of California Press.

Higgins, L. (2010). Bridgewater township official turns to militia for help; watchdog groups question decision. *AnnArbor.Com.* www.annarbor.com/news/bridgewater-township-turns-to-militia-for-help/

Hochschild, A. R. (2018). *Strangers in their own land: Anger and mourning on the American right* (First Trade Paper ed.). The New Press.

Hopkins, D. J. (2010). Politicized places: Explaining where and when immigrants provoke local opposition. *American Political Science Review, 104*(1), 40–60.

HoSang, D. M., & Lowndes, J. E. (2019). *Producers, parasites, patriots: Race and the new right-wing politics of precarity* (Illustrated ed.). University of Minnesota Press.

Inglis, J. (2022). Who is representing you? *The Boston Globe.* www.bostonglobe.com/2022/10/19/opinion/who-is-representing-you/

Inwood, J. F. J. (2018). "It is the innocence which constitutes the crime": Political geographies of white supremacy, the construction of white innocence, and the Flint water crisis. *Geography Compass, 12*(3), e12361.

Inwood, J. F. J., & Bonds, A. (2017). Property and whiteness: The Oregon standoff and the contradictions of the U.S. settler state. *Space and Polity, 21*(3), 253–268.

Jacobs, D., Carmichael, J. T., & Kent, S. L. (2005). Vigilantism, current racial threat, and death sentences. *American Sociological Review, 70*(4), 656–677.

Jenkins, J. (2020, January 4). In speech to evangelicals, Trump says God is 'on our side.' *Religion News Service*. https://religionnews.com/2020/01/04/in-speech-to-evangelicals-trump-says-god-is-on-our-side/

Kato, Y. (2020). Gardening in times of urban transitions: Emergence of entrepreneurial cultivation in post–Katrina New Orleans. *City & Community, 19*(4), 987–1010. https://doi.org/10.1111/cico.12476

Kids and Toy Guns. (2010). *Focus on the Family*. www.focusonthefamily.com/family-qa/kids-and-toy-guns/

Kramon, C. (2023, January 6). Fear of violence reshapes the face of gun ownership. *INDY Week*. http://indyweek.com/news/ninth-street-journal/fear-of-violence-changes-face-of-gun-ownership/

Lacombe, M. J. (2021). *Firepower: How the NRA turned gun owners into a political force*. Princeton University Press.

Le Goff, J. (1992). *History and memory* (S. Rendall & E. Claman, Trans.). Columbia University Press.

Li, W., & Lartey, J. (2023, March 25). New FBI data shows more hate crimes. These groups saw the sharpest rise. *The Marshall Project*. www.themarshallproject.org/2023/03/25/asian-hate-crime-fbi-black-lgbtq

Litke, E. (2020). Fact check: Police gave Kyle Rittenhouse water and thanked him before shooting. *USA Today*. www.usatoday.com/story/news/factcheck/2020/08/29/fact-check-video-police-thanked-kyle-rittenhouse-gave-him-water/5661804002/

Livingston, L., & Young, A. T. (2020). Introduction: US gun culture and the performance of racial sovereignty. *Lateral, 9*(1). https://csalateral.org/forum/gun-culture/introduction-performance-racial-sovereignty-livingston-young/

Losing Home: When Urban Renewal Came to Knoxville. (2021, May 13). [WUOT]. 91.9 FM WUOT, Your Public Radio Station. www.wuot.org/news/2021-05-13/losing-home-when-urban-renewal-came-to-knoxville

Luhby, T. (2020, January 11). Many millennials are worse off than their parents—a first in American history. *CNN*. www.cnn.com/2020/01/11/politics/millennials-income-stalled-upward-mobility-us/index.html

MacLeod, D. I. (1982). Act your age: Boyhood, adolescence, and the rise of the boy scouts of America. *Journal of Social History, 16*(2), 3–20.

Mallonee, S., Shariat, S., Stennies, G., Waxweiler, R., Hogan, D., & Jordan, F. (1996). Physical injuries and fatalities resulting from the Oklahoma City bombing. *JAMA, 276*(5), 382–387.

Marks, S. R. (1974). Durkheim's theory of anomie. *American Journal of Sociology, 80*(2), 329–363.

Mayer, P. (2020, May 9). Pandemic gardens satisfy a hunger for more than just good tomatoes. *NPR*. www.npr.org/2020/05/09/852441460/pandemic-gardens-satisfy-a-hunger-for-more-than-just-good-tomatoes

Melzer, S. (2012). *Gun crusaders: The NRA's culture war*. NYU Press.

Metzl, J. M. (2019). *Dying of whiteness: How the politics of racial resentment is killing America's heartland*. Basic Books.

Miller-Idriss, C. (2020). *Hate in the homeland: The new global far right*. Princeton University Press.

Mueller, J. C. (2018). Advancing a sociology of ignorance in the study of racism and racial non-knowing. *Sociology Compass, 12*(8), e12600.

Mulloy, D. (2008). Approaching extremism: Theoretical perspectives on the far right in American history. In *American extremism: History, politics and the militia movement* (pp. 17–33). Routledge.

Murphy, A. R. (2009). Longing, nostalgia, and golden age politics: The American jeremiad and the power of the past. *Perspectives on Politics, 7*(1), 125–141.

Nakano Glenn, E. (2015). Settler colonialism as structure: A framework for comparative studies of U.S. race and gender formation. *Sociology of Race and Ethnicity, 1*(1), 52–72. https://doi.org/10.1177/2332649214560440

Nelson, J. C., Adams, G., & Salter, P. S. (2013). The Marley hypothesis: Denial of racism reflects ignorance of history. *Psychological Science, 24*(2), 213–218. https://doi.org/10.1177/0956797612451466

Newman, B. J., Hartman, T. K., & Taber, C. S. (2012). Foreign language exposure, cultural threat, and opposition to immigration. *Political Psychology, 33*(5), 635–657.

Novak, K. J., & Chamlin, M. B. (2012). Racial threat, suspicion, and police behavior the impact of race and place in traffic enforcement. *Crime & Delinquency, 58*(2), 275–300.

Olzak, S., Shanahan, S., & West, E. (1994). School desegregation, interracial exposure, and antibusing activity in contemporary urban America. *American Journal of Sociology, 100*, 196–241.

Pettigrew, T. F. (1998). Intergroup contact theory. *Annual Review of Psychology, 49*(1), 65–85.

Rocha, R. R., & Espino, R. (2009). Racial threat, residential segregation, and the policy attitudes of Anglos. *Political Research Quarterly, 62*(2), 415–426. https://doi.org/10.1177/1065912908320931

Rodriguez, J. (2022). Sorry, millennials, you're never getting a good home. *Business Insider*. www.businessinsider.com/millennials-house-home-real-estate-mortgage-rates-rent-debt-boomers-2022-9

Rottweiler, B., & Gill, P. (2020). Conspiracy beliefs and violent extremist intentions: The contingent effects of self-efficacy, self-control and law-related morality. *Terrorism and Political Violence*, 1–20.

Sedikides, C., Wildschut, T., & Baden, D. (2004). Nostalgia: Conceptual issues and existential functions. In J. Greenberg, S. L. Koole, & T. Pyszczynski (Eds.), *Handbook of experimental existential psychology* (pp. 200–214). The Guilford Press.

Snell, R., & Burke, M. N. (2020, October 9). Plans to kidnap Whitmer, overthrow government spoiled, officials say. *The Detroit News*. www.detroitnews.com/story/news/local/michigan/2020/10/08/feds-thwart-militia-plot-kidnap-michigan-gov-gretchen-whitmer/5922301002/

Steinhorn, L. (2013, December 17). White men and their guns. *HuffPost*. www.huffpost.com/entry/white-men-and-their-guns_b_4419903

Taylor, M. C. (1998). How white attitudes vary with the racial composition of local populations: Numbers count. *American Sociological Review, 63*(4), 512.

Tracking the COVID-19 Economy's Effects on Food, Housing, and Employment Hardships. (2022). *Center on Budget and Policy Priorities.* www.cbpp.org/research/poverty-and-inequality/tracking-the-covid-19-economys-effects-on-food-housing-and

Turner, F. J. (1893). The significance of the Frontier in American history. *American Historical Association.* www.historians.org/about-aha-and-membership/aha-history-and-archives/historical-archives/the-significance-of-the-frontier-in-american-history-(1893)

Vary, A. B. (2020, June 23). 'Watchmen' cast and filmmakers on police, racism and the Tulsa Massacre. *Variety.* https://variety.com/2020/tv/news/watchmen-tulsa-massacre-racism-police-1234645870/

Welch, K., & Payne, A. A. (2010). Racial threat and punitive school discipline. *Social Problems, 57*(1), 25–48.

Wells, I. B. (1892). Southern horrors: Lynch law in all its phases by Ida B. Wells. *Encyclopedia Virginia.* https://encyclopediavirginia.org/entries/southern-horrors-lynch-law-in-all-its-phases-by-ida-b-wells-1892/

Wolfe, P. (1999). *Settler colonialism and the transformation of anthropology: The politics and poetics of an ethnograph event.* Continuum.

6 The Movement's Trajectory
The Early 2000s, the Trump Era, and Beyond

Nostalgia for an imagined past that is embodied in the mythical origin story of America's founding remains a crucial variable for explaining recent developments in the militia movement. Historian Dona Brown says that, as a nation, the US has always experienced ebbs and flows in the collective appeal to a rural mentality but that a resurgence of this outlook in the 1960s and 1970s never completely abated. She writes:

> At the turn of the millennium, a false crisis—the anticipated 'Y2K' collapse in the year 2000—was followed by a real one, in the wake of the 2001 attacks on New York and Washington. Two drawn-out and costly American wars ensued, and even these were often overshadowed by other calamities. Energy prices rose and fell with alarming volatility, and a series of hurricanes, floods, and droughts seemed to portend catastrophic climate change. When in 2007 a housing bubble burst, triggering a bank panic and a stock market crash, Americans were suddenly confronting nearly every kind of crisis that had threatened and inspired back-to-the-landers over the previous hundred years.
> (2011, pp. 228–229)

I would also suggest that a major source of the threat during this period went beyond the events that Brown mentions. Especially among nostalgic groups, perceptions of government mismanagement or outright tyranny in response to these troublesome events contributed to citizens' sense of danger and uncertainty. For some, crisis has never really ended.

Recent Militia Trajectory

President Obama took office in 2009 during a large economic recession, and for many conservatives, his power signaled a devolution away from an ideal nation. His tenure witnessed the first real spike in militia activity since the late 1990s, a spike that many commentators attributed to racism alone. Some voters who objected to Obama's presidency absolutely responded with unmitigated racism, loathing a Black man holding the highest office, or believing conspiracy theories that he was a Muslim or a foreigner who was ineligible to hold the position and who intended to destroy America's culture of individualism by promoting Communism.

My observations in the field revealed that dispersions of Obama went beyond racism for those who joined the militia movement at this time. Obama was the first Democrat to take office following the movement's dormancy after Olson's departure from it during the Clinton years. Militias usually have more responsiveness to Democratic administrations than Republican administrations (whether nationally or locally) because they see Democrats as more rapidly pushing the country away from their imagined nostalgic ideal. Even following the real and perceived threats from the terror attacks of 9/11, most militia units reported that they did not experience large or durable increases in attendance. Based on my numerous conversations with both short- and long-term members, it seems to have been the case that most people who might otherwise be attracted to militia activity during times of national duress had one of two responses. Some, who were young and healthy, joined the military so they could directly participate in the conflict. Others felt that Republican President George W. Bush, who, like his father, visually and audibly adopted a settler cowboy masculinity (Melzer, 2012), was adequately managing national security at this time and did not feel a strong personal need to join a militia to supplement national action.[1]

In contrast, militias and similar actors typically see Democratic administrations as operating in opposition to this cultivated national protector persona. They see Democrats' limited efforts to enact gun control, to loosen immigration restrictions, and to increase protections for LGBTQ+ people as possible threats to national identity and culture. Obama represented all of those things but amplified conservative stereotypes of culturally destructive Democrats who reject American exceptionalism even further by campaigning on promises to pursue universal health care. This represented a shift into more open "Socialism" and away from individual responsibility for many of his detractors. These Democratic Party variables were, alone, reportedly sufficient to drive some members I spoke with to join a militia as they insisted Obama's race did not matter and that they would be concerned about any candidate who made the same campaign promises that he did.

Disdain for what Democrats represent serves as another example of objections to change that are rooted in culture, rather than simple racism per se,[2] even as cultural objections are often still imbued with and strengthened by racist stereotypes. Militia members who, for example, believe the term "Muslim American" is an oxymoron say they think that Islam fundamentally rejects individual liberty and principles of religious freedom—a cultural attribution. They often simultaneously assume people whom they perceive to be Muslim based on their skin color, clothing, or other features both necessarily and uniformly adhere to this belief structure—a racialized attribution that blurs the line between culture and perceived race (Cooter, 2012, 2013; Naber, 2007, 2008). This racialized attribution is reinforced if, as other scholars have argued, there is a perceived equivalency between Christianity and both whiteness and Americanness (Butler, 2021; Gorski & Perry, 2022); otherized Muslims must, by extension of this parity, be something other than either white or American.

The biggest increase in attendance[3] for militia groups I was monitoring during that time did not occur in anticipation of an Obama presidency or immediately after he took office, further confirming that the membership response Obama triggered was likely due to factors beyond (or at least in addition to) his individual identity. In April 2009, a report from DHS leaked online and, following heavy media coverage, incited an enormous negative reaction from a variety of people. The report warned of dangers of "right-wing extremism," and, among other information, used rather vague phrasing to indicate that veterans returning from conflicts in the Middle East might be prone to recruitment by extremist organizations. Many people interpreted the report as saying that veterans were somehow especially prone to extremism and should be treated like suspected terrorists (Cooter, 2013). Veterans and active duty soldiers strongly embody the archetypal settler man in our collective imagination (Gibson, 1994), meaning that many people who were offended on veterans' behalf also saw this as an attack on the nation's ethos, so it was unsurprising when veterans and their supporters from across the political spectrum called for the report's retraction. The chairman of Vets for Freedom, for example, was widely quoted as saying:

> If anything, veterans have an allegiance to this country greater than the average citizen. Veterans have learned where their allegiances lie and are less prone to extremism. Something's wrong with the editing process, or [DHS officials] just don't understand veterans. The report demonstrates a true lack of understanding of who veterans are.
> (Fox News, 2009)

I spoke with numerous veterans who felt this same way and who were spurred to join a militia after the report's release. It was an ironic self-fulfilling prophecy and the opposite outcome of the report's intent. However, these new affiliates with whom I spoke, just like many of the veterans who joined the militia before them, did not have to be actively recruited and instead independently sought out militia units, in this case, to protest the report and its implications. They said they wanted to find something that allowed them to stand up to the government that they felt had betrayed them through this publication. Emmet, for example, a veteran in his twenties who had recently returned from Afghanistan, vented:

> I mean, here I am, I honorably served my country. I risked my life in the sand over there! I come back home and those fuckers call me a

terrorist? I was fighting terrorism. It was 'The War on Terror!' You bet I'm pissed!

Militia numbers stayed slightly elevated following this report through most of Obama's two terms.

Then, Trump announced his Presidential run in June 2015. In his opening campaign speech, he declared his intention to "fully support and back up the Second Amendment," cited economic threats from global competitors, and alluded to criminal and cultural threats from immigrant countries, which, he said, are "not sending their best" (*Trump Announces*, 2015). He thus hit directly on the core pillars of a nostalgia-informed national identity that were supposedly under threat. It nonetheless appeared for just a moment after he won and took office that we would see the usual pattern where nostalgic groups decrease in fervor during Republican administrations; we initially saw a decline in gun sales after his term began, as we would expect from typical gun purchasers who felt their Second Amendment rights and other core concerns were going to be protected by the Presidential administration (Dunbar-Ortiz, 2018). Once in office, however, Trump continued to appeal to the notion of the US as being the best country, but only precariously so and at risk of a dramatic fall without his ongoing intervention. These cautionary refrains legitimized and amplified the fears about out-groups that already existed among his base. Trump's warnings normalized exclusionary ideas (including racism, sexism, homophobia, xenophobia, and Christofascism) being openly discussed and heightened the sense of crisis and urgency for many of his supporters, including those within militia ranks. Gun sales reached a record high (Savidge & Cartaya, 2021), and militia numbers exploded as Trump continued to weaponize nostalgia to nurture the fantasy of an idealized national identity.

COVID-19's appearance in the US in early 2020, near the close of Trump's term, compounded the fears that his administration had cultivated in the previous three years regarding both economic precarity and threats to personal liberty. Alongside emerging protests about police brutality and racial justice nationwide, near-perfect conditions existed to push people who felt threatened by these developments into supporting Trump, as he brashly claimed without real content to have solutions for their myriad concerns. Some people were simultaneously drawn to militias and other nostalgic organizations as another way to self-manage their anxiety. Membership in such groups reached a peak in early to mid-summer 2020, when national media perpetuated perceptions of danger emerging from racial justice protests even as the images they shared of protestor anger were almost uniformly those of white men aggressively protesting COVID mitigation measures. While these images may have been frightening to some observers, they were inspiring to others who believed they should engage in similar actions to preserve their personal liberties and the safety of their own communities, no matter how far they were geographically from the protests. Trump's tweets encouraging protestors to "liberate" Michigan and other states that had implemented strict lockdown measures also legitimized these volatile pandemic protests (Collins & Zadronzny, 2020a).

One of my long-term militia contacts told me at the time that he was worried that smaller, community-based militias like his were losing momentum relative to larger units. These growing units constructed a recognizable public persona at events that eventually culminated in what was perhaps the most volatile COVID lockdown protest, occurring at the Michigan State Capitol in late April 2020, and producing viral media images of armed men yelling in the faces of state police officers. My contact said he was concerned because some of those groups were being led by people who "cared more about popularity contests than defending anything." When I pressed him further, he said the volatile nature of these larger units was making it hard to "keep tabs on them," something he typically took pride in doing to try to ensure both civilian safety and militia reputation. He said he was worried about possible violent undercurrents of these groups and felt helpless when one of these growing units started to pull a few antsy members away from his own.

Movement Evolution

Millenarianism and Accelerationism

In addition to individual incitement to action and overall membership increases, we witnessed two interrelated developments in the militia movement's composition during Trump's presidency. First was the movement's overall shift toward the millenarian end of the spectrum. Instead of making up only about 10% of militia units, as had previously been true, historian Robert Churchill and I have discussed how we both believe millenarian units became closer to 25% of the movement. While this is still a minority of the movement, the rapid increase was alarming. It was proof of how both units and individual members can slip along the spectrum into greater radicalization because of outside influences. There also seems to be a risk of a snowballing effect, such that further slippage into extremism may be exponential when these radicalized elements grow and are able to interact with increasing numbers of militia affiliates over time.

The second major change in the movement's composition during Trump's tenure was the rise of militant accelerationism. Accelerationism asserts that modern society is facing an inevitable and escalating decline. It may be a rather passive ideological strategy (Hughes & Miller-Idriss, 2021), whereby believers almost depressively attempt to prepare to weather an impending disaster, or it may be militant, whereby believers actively seek to bring about social collapse through "a set of tactics and strategies designed to put pressure on and exacerbate latent social divisions, often through violence" (Kriner, n.d.). Militant accelerationists believe they live in a dystopia that is "poisoned to its core" (Berger, 2013, p. 70) and that no solution to society's ills can be found through politics or other legitimate means and thus resort to such violence to hasten collapse and establish a new social order (Kriner & Cooter, 2023).

Accelerationism is different from millenarianism, but the two frameworks can have blurry boundaries, especially because accelerationist principles have been a major variable that has pushed militia members who were formerly constitutionalist in orientation to the millenarian end of the spectrum. I witnessed this playing out in real time among some of the groups I follow, and it was, to be frank, frightening to see this shift happen. Members who had belonged to constitutionalist groups for many years started adopting the conceptual aspects of accelerationism as they discussed "riots" and "antifa" and "anarchy" around the social justice protests of summer 2020. Most members involved in these discussions were focused on their fears and preparations for the chaos that might ensue rather than on direct action to make that chaos happen.

However, a small number of members, including some people I had previously observed in person as being cool-headed and openly dismissive of conspiratorial thinking, slipped even further from their constitutionalist affiliations after accelerationism's influence. The usual pattern that I observed was that these members would, first, start regularly sharing memes or fake news stories about conspiracy theories, such as the resurging interest in Pizzagate and, later, in Hunter Biden's laptop (Collins & Zadronzny, 2020b; Kang & Frenkel, 2020).[4] I asked one of my long-time contacts why he was suddenly interested in such stories after openly mocking similar tales in earlier years. He told me that he doubted their veracity but felt like it was good operational security to encourage others to be aware of the allegations "just in case." But he did not include that disclaimer as he shared the dubious information with his unit and family members alike.

It became clear that the more he shared these stories and the more others commented or speculated about them on his social media threads, the more he believed they and related conspiracy theories were likely to be at least partially true. I watched as members like him became more engrossed with finding the "truth" and more angry as they became increasingly convinced that elites were both hiding important information and acting nefariously against the common good, with children often the stand-in for both innocence and vulnerability to social change within these conspiracy theories' frameworks (Breland, 2019). Some members like this started expressing frustration that more of their constitutionalist unit companions were not as concerned as they were and began looking for millenarian units that more closely aligned with their evolving outlook. Efforts to "stop the steal" and keep Trump in office became both a logical and moral conclusion for some people caught up in this process because Trump had become a hero within these conspiracy fantasies, supposedly the only person bold and powerful enough to stop degenerate Democrats.

The precise distinction between accelerationism and millenarianism is difficult to pin down because of the overlapping membership and ideology they share, but there are at least three points of general divergence. First, millenarians tend to believe they are joining in an apocalypse that has already been initiated and that would continue with or without their engagement. Accelerationists, in contrast, are more likely to believe that their personal involvement is a necessary ingredient in their desired social cataclysm. This distinction has a subfacet, which is that accelerationists are eager for social upheaval, while millenarians see that disruption as inevitable but not necessarily positive.

The second difference between these frameworks is that millenarians tend to have much more restricted in-groups than accelerationists. A person probably already needs to be a member of a millenarian's group before major apocalyptic preparations occur for them to be someone that millenarian wants to help shelter from their prophesized doomsday, whether that group is a militia unit, religious community, or other organization. By virtue of that preexisting membership, that person probably also shares other features like socioeconomic status, educational level, or city of residence with other millenarian members. Accelerationists can also have an insularity that is driven by interrelated ideologies, but that insularity tends to include people who have a common goal, even when their methods or motives for reaching it are different from their own. As scholars Brian Hughes and Cynthia Miller-Idriss say, "accelerationism is uniquely capable of sidestepping the ideological and operational conflicts" (2021). This means that people across the political spectrum can believe in an inevitable social decline, even if they perceive that trajectory as happening differently. In extreme cases of ideological nullification, some white supremacist organizations that, by definition, loathe anyone who isn't white have endorsed working alongside Black separatists or others who share the same goal of ending a racially integrated society (Hopper, 2017).

The third rule-of-thumb difference between accelerationism and millenarianism is that millenarians tend to robustly frame their anticipated doomsday with more overt religious appeals than are present in accelerationism. The religious belief of a millenarian group can be one possible foundation for how they form their in-group and also tends to shape their responses to perceived disaster in important ways, namely through adding spiritual requirements to believers' mandatory preparations for the apocalypse. Various cults whose members have been convinced that the end of the world was imminent, for example, have consumed poison or participated in other self-harm in an effort to join some cataclysm or in desperation after their prophecy did not come to pass. Even some responses to Y2K included directives from religious leaders that encouraged their congregations to make sure they were "right with their maker" or to enhance proselytization efforts in their communities.

Accelerationism is different from a nostalgic orientation, but a heavy investment in nostalgia can help drive someone to accelerationist messages. Accelerationism is, in other words, a logical outgrowth of restorative nostalgia that shares a rearview nationalism with the settler colonialism framework. It relies on what some have called nostalgia's "double distortion," where the past is viewed overly positively relative to its reality while the present is viewed overly negatively (Murphy, 2009, p. 128). Accelerationism entails forgetting the objective social progress that has been made relative to past eras, especially because that progress has been less beneficial and less noticeable to the white men who are at the center of the settler myth's framework. Many accelerationists have no specific plan for the future, they only believe overthrowing the current social system will lead to something better. They use the mythologized past as a kind of goalpost and their nostalgic vision provides "narratives of original perfection, decline, and potential restoration" (Braunstein, 2021, p. 96). They know that an unspecified future, while perhaps frightening in its uncertainty, simply must be better than the degenerate present. They, in other words, know what they want the future to *not* be.

Features of both millenarianism and accelerationism existed in nostalgic groups before researchers started using these terms. Some neo-Nazi groups have, since at least the early 1980s, advocated for "racial holy wars" to attain a "pure," all-white nation. They have insisted that such a conflict could come at great cost and that members should be prepared to defend their families from backlash while so-called lone wolves make strategic early strikes of violence against Black people and other oppressed groups. These earlier groups, which we might call proto-accelerationists, rarely mentioned overthrowing entire political systems as they outlined their desired social revisions. They usually left those systems entirely unaddressed or contextually implied that power frameworks would be left relatively unscathed but with white men reinstated to their proper seats within them.

The first openly accelerationist organization to directly call for terroristic action that was intended to create full social collapse was Atomwaffen Division, which was formed in 2015 (CTEC, 2023). One example of their typical accelerationist framing can be found on an archived version of their website. It captures nostalgia for a lost, superior past alongside the belief that, to be reclaimed, society must be re-established from the ground up.

> There is nothing that can be fixed in a system so inherently flawed, National Socialism is the only solution to reclaim dominion over what belongs to us. The west cannot be saved, but it can be rebuilt and even stronger without the burdens of the past.[5]

Atomwaffen Division became a sustained organizational influence that caused calls for upheaval to become a more obvious and identifiable feature of numerous nostalgic groups leading up to and during Trump's presidency (Newhouse, 2021). Accelerationism became an especially noticeable ideological and tactical presence following the 2020 racial justice protests that followed several high-profile police shootings. Militant accelerationists have been involved in numerous crimes in the last several years, including murders and other violent attacks on police officers, support for terrorist organizations, plots to destroy infrastructure, and plots to cause chaos at protests (Blankstein & Collins, 2020; Choi, 2021; DOJ, 2020; Price & Sonner, 2020). They believe stochastic acts of violence, especially if directed at law enforcement, could be enough to foment a mass uprising that leads to the government overthrow that they desire.

Boogaloo's Emergence

Boogaloo affiliates perhaps best exemplify what accelerationism has looked like in action since Trump took office. Boogaloo emerged around 2012, first simmering for several years in online spaces via meme culture before coalescing as a meaningful offline phenomenon in 2020. Boogaloo received its name from a movie called *Breakin' 2: Electric Boogaloo*. A critically panned sequel with a large popular following, the movie's name became a humorous stand-in online for any sequel or second act before being adopted by those specifically hoping for a second Civil War[6] that would result in a revamped society and government (Daymon, 2020; Kriner & Lewis, 2021). Not all Boogaloo affiliates are the militant variety of accelerationist. Some I have spoken with believe that racial justice protests cause more people to reject public powers and push for law enforcement reform through traditional, though substantially modified, legal and political channels. I started a survey of affiliates on large Boogaloo Facebook groups very shortly before they were deplatformed to further understand affiliates' opinions on protests related to both George Floyd's murder and to COVID lockdown measures. One respondent who identified with the ideological aspects of accelerationism wrote in reference to the Floyd protests, "The protests are extremely valid. Nothing represents state violence more than a cop kneeling on someone's throat. I hope they create positive policy changes." On a later question when I asked what more needed to be done for durable changes in policing to happen, this same respondent simply replied, in all caps, "LEGISLATION." Another answered, "civilian oversight no more internal affairs," similarly referencing a revamping of current political-social structures, a modification that sounds rather straightforward but that tends to be stridently opposed by those in power,[7] opposition which may then be cited by militantly inclined actors as a justification for more a more aggressive response.

Boogaloo affiliates who are militant accelerationists reject any attempt to work within or settle for modifications to the existing system and have been heavily involved in a variety of crimes, including the plot to kidnap Michigan's Governor Gretchen Whitmer. One of my survey respondents on this end of the spectrum who indicated he was a "Native American/White Skilled Tradesman"[8] answered my question about durable changes to policing by saying, "Fuck the Police. Eat the Rich. Guillotine the Oppressors." This was one of three questions he answered with a reference to guillotining on the

25-question survey, and another of his answers included, "No mercy for the police." On an open-ended question asking his opinion about Black Lives Matter protesters, he also said, "I support them more every single day. US Gov't ought [to] be burned to cinders, it's far too big for its own britches." He did not use the phrase "Civil War" in any of his responses, but the vitriol across his answers is as evident as his belief that the current social structure is beyond salvaging.

Boogaloo's Influence

Boogaloo has likely permanently shifted the nostalgic group milieu (Kriner & Cooter, 2023) for two reasons. First, because of how it comfortably housed both branches of accelerationism and thus became one of the key forces (a kind of "wind" in my metaphor) that facilitated the intermingling of militias, neo-Nazis, Proud Boys, and others in pursuit of chaos who use nostalgia as a reference point for their varying ultimate ideals. While some people at protests identified simply as a Boogaloo supporter, others identified as both Boogaloo and a militia member, and others as a member of both Boogaloo and a neo-Nazi organization; when they all dressed similarly and stood on the same side of a protest line, they spent little time interrogating each other's motives or affiliations, instead prioritizing common interest and planting proverbial seeds for more future interactions.

The second reason that Boogaloo had such a strong influence on nostalgic groups is that, unlike many similar groups or even political action organizations that try to motivate a response to social change, Boogaloo incorporated easily identifiable elements of play and fun alongside their dire expectations about societal collapse. Hawaiian shirts were the most publicly visible signal of Boogaloo support that allowed people with different motivations for attending a given protest and who had different ideas about their role within accelerationism to easily identify and feel connected to each other. Less noticeable but equally meaningful symbols and phrases that spun out from the original Hawaiian theme also served as visual identifiers of in-group belonging and made adherents feel like they were part of a private club that used coded language to communicate with each other under the noses of those they sought to undermine. References to "luaus" or "pig roasts," for example, were common stand-ins for both fantasized and actualized attacks on police. Once major social media platforms started censoring these expressions, some groups believed themselves very clever as they shifted their Facebook group names to things like Big Igloo (a play on Boogaloo's pronunciation) or second-order derivatives from the original, like Ice House. A patch with an igloo replacing or supplementing the stars on a black and white American flag also became quite standard on Boogaloo affiliates' tactical vests or other gear. In my earlier work, I observed how elements of play were essential to the camaraderie that militia members established with each other at in-person events (Cooter, 2013). I observed the same effect in

Boogaloo Facebook groups and other online spaces when members joked about one-upping each other's Hawaiian shirt purchases, trying to find the most outrageous colors or loudest prints, or when they participated in long threads competing to see who could come up with the most clever (or most lewd) uses for the word "Boogaloo" and its alternatives.

Boogaloo adherents were a target of media fascination across several protests with different focal areas in 2020 and 2021 in part because of their easy visibility at these events. They were also alluring to people already inside or loosely connected to the nostalgic group world who found the seduction of belonging to an edgy in-group that was willing to act on their beliefs too strong to ignore. It is likely that Boogaloo became the second largest catalyst (with Trump being the first) for driving the size and visibility of nostalgic group action leading up to January 6th because of its ability to both attract and connect people across nostalgic group lines.

Today, however, nostalgic groups seem to have mostly moved on from overt Boogaloo associations even while its influence on their goals and overall culture clearly lingers. Some groups still affiliate with that Boogaloo label, but we have seen many fewer of the recognizable Hawaiian shirts and other visually identifying gear since Biden took office. Despite some temporary surges, Boogaloo has also been less active in social media spaces (Shapero, 2022). Groups I personally observe online have all-but stopped the use of Boogaloo talk, including previously pervasive jokes and memes. The relative inactivity may largely be because of Boogaloo involvement in the January 6th insurrection[9] and the general backlash nostalgic groups faced after their failure to prevent a Biden Presidency. We may yet see a resurgence of Boogaloo expressions in the future, including around the 2024 Presidential election cycle, but given the failed coup—a decidedly lost Civil War effort for some—it seems more likely that this particular instantiation has played itself out and nostalgic group evolution will adopt different markers and points of convergence in the future.

Militias in the Trump Era

The original Boogaloo surge and the overall dramatic momentum of the nostalgic group network that was growing in summer 2020 was fortunately disrupted when Facebook deplatformed militia groups and individuals whose profiles marked them as obviously associated with militias in early fall 2020 (Kriner & Cooter, 2023; Wong, 2020). Facebook had been the primary social media platform for most of these organizations, and when group pages disappeared without warning, most units were left floundering with their members attempting to connect across multiple other platforms with overall limited success. Numbers dwindled as it became a greater burden for many people to maintain militia connections without the ability to network and communicate online so easily both with one's own unit and with other units. I think it is safe to say that Facebook's deplatforming was the single biggest disruption in the history of the militia movement, even bigger than the fallout from the Oklahoma City bombing and Olson's response to it. Facebook had given the movement much more effective traction then the fax network from the 1990s or any other previous technology in building a cooperative, national militia network, and the unexpected deplatforming has thus far proven impossible to repair on any combination of other platforms. The movement's decline was further amplified when the movement received negative public attention a few months later as members of the Wolverine Watchmen were arrested and details of their elaborate plot to kidnap and try Michigan's governor became public. Some wanted to distance themselves from a movement that had fostered such violent action—similar to what happened after the Oklahoma City bombing in the 1990s—while others simply had even less of an incentive to invest the extra time and energy needed to maintain movement connections after deplatforming.

Members who remained involved despite these barriers, however, were true believers in the militia mission. Some were constitutionalist groups who believed they should operate as usual because they had done nothing wrong and insisted that those who were arrested were not representative of real militia members. Others, especially those who transitioned to Parler and Telegram because of those social media platforms' looser content regulations, may have been more extreme than the average member before the Facebook disruption because of the dedication required to switch platforms and maintain connections across fragmenting groups. Militia researchers believe that the most extreme elements were also using more private and encoded forms of communications such as the app Zello, which a militia group in Kansas had previously used in 2016 to plan an attack on a Somali refugee community in Kansas (Lehr, 2021).[10]

These alternate platforms became the primary sites where the January 6, 2021, insurrection began, with some groups discussing possible actions openly and others more secretively. Fallout from the violence at the Capitol included a further decline in militia numbers, particularly as the judicial system has successfully prosecuted cases against one of the largest militia organizations, the Oath Keepers. It would be a mistake, however, to assume that the militia movement is truly disbanded; just as was true following the Oklahoma City bombing, we should think about the militia movement as being in a state of abeyance with members who can and likely will be easily reactivated in future situations that reignite their fears and create opportunities for their potential success. Reactivation with new recruitment and new possible violence is very likely during the 2024 Presidential campaign as Trump and others who are trying to take up his mantle enter the field.

Case Studies

Three earlier militia groups that faced criminal charges are instructive for understanding possible future trajectories with law enforcement, politics, and other power structures: the Hutaree, the Crusaders, and the Wolverine Watchmen. I focus heavily on the first case because it has received much less public coverage, though I don't recount every possible element of any of the three alleged plots. I have had some degree of personal involvement with each of the below investigations, and hope that my viewpoint of some of the successes and failures in these cases can help inform knowledge-building and best practices as we move forward.

The Hutaree

In late March 2010, a total of nine people were arrested for allegedly plotting to murder a police officer and then use a large explosive device to murder other officers who attended the funeral of the first. Allegations against those arrested included attempted use of weapons of mass destruction, teaching the use of explosive materials, possessing a firearm during a crime of violence, and a then-obscure charge of seditious conspiracy (DOJ, 2010). An Indiana militia leader rejected the Hutaree as a legitimate part of the militia movement because, he said, "They had indicated they were looking to foment unrest" when they had previously been in contact with his unit (*Indiana Militia*, 2010).

The Hutaree nearly perfectly exemplified a millenarian unit. They anticipated social disruption and were a closed in-group that was concentrated around shared religious principles that referenced apocalyptic ideology. Their name was a word unit leader David Stone created, saying it meant "Christian Warriors." Stone called himself a pastor, insisted the other members of the unit attend his church, and may have believed they had a part to play in bringing about the End Times (Buchanan, 2010). Before it was taken down,[11] their website was replete with Bible verses and other religious references, especially to the book of Revelations. Their "About Us" section included "First we are Christian, we have Jesus Christ as our foundation. We see the end of the age coming quickly, and with it some very rough times ahead, as foretold by God's word." They indicated that militia, then survivalist identities respectively came second and third in importance after their religious identity. The website also had a section entitled "Beast Watch" that must have been intended to have frequent updates on modern signs of the apocalypse. But it contained only three listings: one on implanted microchips, another on European integration, and a list of jokes[12] about the number 666 that seemed to come from a source meant to ridicule apocalyptic believers, an angle clearly lost on the Hutaree member who shared them. The only other militia unit with whom the Hutaree regularly interacted had numerous older members who had first begun their nostalgic group affiliations with Sovereign Citizen or even Posse Comitatus groups, so vitriol for LEOs and the authority they represent were heavily imbued in the group.

The real difference from an ideal-type millenarian unit is that the Hutaree allegedly wanted to take an active role in starting social disruption rather than merely riding a wave of its inevitability. When members were awaiting trial, a Detroit FBI agent told a journalist covering the case, "Like any extremist group, I don't think in reality they believe that they're going to personally overthrow the US government. The plan is to basically be the match or the spark to ignite the revolution" (Temple-Raston, 2010). That sounds like an accelerationist aim, yet the Hutaree themselves did not articulate this goal quite so clearly. The "unrest" that Hutaree members desired obviously implicated harming police officers as surrogates of government power, just as some Boogaloo affiliates have more recently done, yet it's not certain what, if anything, they planned to happen after slaughtering police officers. This means that the Hutaree are likely best categorized as both millenarian and proto-accelerationist, rather than firmly accelerationist.

The Hutaree trained in Southeast Michigan where seven of the members lived, with the other two members crossing nearby state borders with Ohio and Indiana to participate. Other Michigan militias were very aware of their presence and activities. I first heard about them two years before their arrest at the second militia meeting that I attended in April 2008. That unit's members were weighing whether to purchase or rent a porta potty to use at a remote training ground, and the leader replied that he was afraid of semipermanently leaving one on-site because the Hutaree, who also used the property as a training ground at different times than this unit, might "machine gun it." I asked someone else to explain the context for this remark, and he replied that Hutaree members had previously destroyed community property and had generally practiced unsafe behavior during the two trainings hosted by this unit that Hutaree members had attended a few years earlier.[13] One of those Hutaree members was responsible for the infamous "what caliber was the stick?" story, and this meeting was the first time I heard it shared. The militia member recounting this tale warned me to be very careful if I approached any Hutaree members for my research because he thought they were dangerous, and another member who was listening to our conversation chipped in that he stayed away from them and that I should, too.

I decided to heed their advice and made no attempts to attend Hutaree training exercises. My goal during my fieldwork was to understand the typical militia member at this time, and I had to balance that with practical concerns about my safety. The prospect of heading to a remote location with, as one person called them, "crazy" and apparently angry men of whom even other militia members were wary was simply not compatible with my safety plan. I did eventually talk with several people who had close connections to that unit because they either occasionally trained or engaged socially with them. I attended a large meeting of the unit that had close ties to the Hutaree, and in whose training events the Hutaree often participated. I also interviewed two people who eventually became formally affiliated with the Hutaree after my encounters with them; both people were detained as a result of the initial raids on the unit, though only one of them was criminally charged.

When I interviewed this man, he was involved with a different militia unit. Even then, he characterized his relationship with the government as a state of "war," and said he strongly desired a violent confrontation with the government to assuage this anger. The source of his vitriol was a negative military experience that left him believing the government had no legitimate purpose in the Middle East and that the reason he had been deployed there was so the government could test experimental substances on service members for unclear reasons. That was the first time I heard a militia member intimate anything resembling proactive violence during my fieldwork, and no other member made me as uncomfortable as this person did during the interview. If other members I directly interacted with at this time held similar views, they were able to keep their anger under control enough to keep it substantially more hidden.

This man, however, had already made it a kind of patriotic or even moral mission to alert other people about precisely how the government could not be trusted even before joining the Hutaree. He gave me about two dozen DVDs out of a large suitcase in which I could see what must have been hundreds of copies of those disks, reminding me at the time of The Gideons International or other religious groups that hand out Bibles or tracts to persuade people to convert to their beliefs. The DVDs had titles like "Liberty in the Balance," "Psychiatry: Industry of Death," and "In Lies We Trust," and their content detailed different, specific allegations against the government. A couple of the films were fairly well-researched and balanced critiques of a particular issue, such as one film about the proliferation of genetically modified foods, but most of the films were rooted entirely in pseudo-science, mere speculation, or outright fabrications. Their topics covered things like Linda Thompson's claims regarding the "real" causes of Waco and other conspiratorial assertions, such as "proof" of the government's involvement in the 9/11 terror attacks. I watched all these DVDs, except for a couple that were improperly copied and unusable, while trying to suspend my disbelief and put myself in the mindset of someone who was convinced by the films' dire warnings. Viewing them, especially in rapid succession, helped me more viscerally understand the fear and anxiety from the threats that this man felt lurked within every shadow.

What I did not know at the time was that I was not the only person worried about the mindset and possible actions of the group this interviewee would ultimately join. The members who warned me about the Hutaree's dangerous firearms handling and urged me to steer clear did not tell me during our conversation that they had already reached out to law enforcement with their concerns, something that was later revealed at trial (Higgins, 2010). The FBI's response to these warnings was, first, to place a civilian as a confidential informant (CI) into the group that had reported their concerns then, later, to move him into the Hutaree after he found no evidence of wrongdoing in the first group (Baldas, 2012). After the CI reported that the

Hutaree were making and detonating experimental explosive devices, the FBI placed a trained infiltrator with the group to gather more evidence (Temple-Raston, 2010), eventually leading to the nine arrests in 2010.

Other militia members I was in contact with expressed a variety of emotions when these arrests occurred. Some members expressed relief, saying they had been worried about the possibility of violence from the Hutaree. Others were concerned that they or their unit might illegitimately be caught up in the investigation because of their casual connections to one or more of the defendants. One was fearful of backlash because he spoke out against the alleged plot. He had refused to help a Hutaree member avoid arrest after the FBI missed him in the initial round-up (Temple-Raston, 2010) and told me that he had received at least two threats from people in militia units outside of Michigan who thought he should have aided the man because they believed the arrests to be baseless harassment.[14]

By the time the trial started two years later in February 2012, rhetoric about the defendants had begun to shift more in their favor. More militia members began to doubt the legal case against the Hutaree after details of the evidence against them started emerging. Many, even people who had spoken negatively about Hutaree members before their arrests, started insisting that the alleged plot would have never happened. Some suggested the Hutaree members would have never been smart enough to carry out a successful attack at all, let alone at the scale they intended. The Hutaree leader's wife, who was among those facing charges, herself alluded to this idea saying, "We weren't dangerous. We couldn't overthrow F-Troop," referencing the bumbling soldiers of a 1960s black and white TV comedy (Kelleher & Damico, 2012). Others asserted that it was really the FBI informants who were responsible for radicalizing the group. They cited as evidence of this claim how one informant was arrested for firing a gun near his wife in a domestic violence incident while he was embedded with the group (Higgins, 2012), or how the professional infiltrator played up his genuine bomb-building knowledge as he was ingratiating himself with the unit (Temple-Raston, 2010), indicating, they believed, that he was truly responsible for designing the plot's details. Both these revelations fed into members' general distrust of the government and enhanced feelings that all militias might be targeted for arrest and persecution simply because the government resented their symbolic stance against them.

When the trial did begin, the allegations never made it to a jury. After hearing their case, District Judge Victoria Roberts declared that prosecutors had failed to prove the required facts for most of the charges and ordered that six of the defendants be immediately released from custody.[15] She ruled that there was not enough evidence to demonstrate Hutaree members had a specific plan for harm; the prosecutors failed to show that the defendants' comments about killing police officers or even officers' wives and children were sufficient evidence of a specific plan for action (The Associated Press,

2012). The other three defendants pleaded guilty a few months later to weapons charges, were sentenced to time served plus two years of probation and released.

I spoke with several people directly involved in the investigation. One told me that they believed Hutaree members were truly being trained to carry out the plot to murder police and that the prosecution had bungled what should have been a good case through questionable legal charges and other missteps. A off-gridder woman I met who cultivated social connections to the Hutaree and the militia they sometimes trained with gave an interview to the leader of a Florida militia about the defendants shortly after their trial began that seemed to confirm that specifics of the alleged plot did not originate with planted informants the way some had suggested. She shared, "I've never heard any talk of any explosives. I never heard talk of killing a police officer, or hurting a police officer," then, immediately contradicting that statement, she continued, "and even if I did hear that kinda talk, it usually included, like, doughnuts and laughter and um, you know, 'ha ha ha'—the typical stuff that people talk about" (New Colony Media, 2012). That she dismissed violent talk as "typical stuff" is quite telling regarding how far her personal Overton Window seems to have shifted after long-term exposure to this unit.

This woman organized a benefit for defendants the month after the final three were released, and the man who had been detained during the original round-up but never charged hosted the event on his farmland. Tickets were $25 each or $30 on-site, and the money was intended to help the defendants pay legal fees. The entry fee included barbeque that was still being cooked on a rusty outdoor smoker and pot-luck style sides brought in crockpots and sundry bowls by the organizer and unidentified others when I arrived about half an hour after the start time. Two local bands performed from the front deck of the property's large cabin, but even they had to use the single porta potty the landowner had rented for the occasion because he made it clear that he didn't want any of the 35 or so guests going into his home. This was a curious pronouncement given that he had personally invited almost everyone in attendance, and I couldn't help but note the irony of the attention given to the porta potty there after the way one had featured strongly in my initial introduction to the Hutaree. This one, at least, had escaped target practice.

The mood was more somber than should be expected for "celebrating the release and return home of our Brothers in Arms," as the promotional materials for the event read. For most of the time I was there, people stood or sat in relatively small groups, mostly talked in hushed tones, and sometimes suspiciously eyed other groups, as though experiencing permanently damaged trust from the last time an outsider had been brought into their inner circle. The veteran who had replaced one Hutaree member's firearm with a tactical stick at an earlier training was in attendance and tried to lighten the mood by sharing some home-brewed moonshine. The woods behind my childhood home held a decaying remnant of a still when I would regularly explore them,

The Movement's Trajectory   143

Figure 6.1 Some of the Hutaree supporters who attended an event to raise money for their legal expenses.

Source: Photo by the author.

and I couldn't help but recall my teetotaler father's pronouncement to avoid any moonshine with blue streaks as I held the offering to the light before taking a perfunctory sip, its brewer giving an approving nod as I did so.

The Hutaree's former unit commander David Stone was the first of several slated speakers, and the man who gave me copied DVDs also spoke. They both only briefly took the microphone to thank everyone for their support. Unlike what we have witnessed from more recent cases where nostalgic group members have run afoul of the law, no one took the opportunity to attempt inspiring future actions. The benefit's title on promotional materials and printed tickets, "Too Late to Apologize," had seemed to convey resentment and perhaps even nascent retribution toward the government for the two years the defendants and their families had lost for charges that were eventually largely dismissed, but that sentiment did not carry through to the event. I couldn't help but note the juxtapositions of the legal case, the subdued messaging at the celebration, and the large flag next to which speakers were addressing the audience. The flag, in common use by the Tea Party at the time, contained the numeral II in a circle of stars and was intended to convey a desire for a second American Revolution.

Other militias remained similarly stable following the Hutaree case conclusion. Most members I spoke with said they believed the case and its fallout had little to do with them because they rejected the Hutaree and the alleged plot as something legitimate militias who serve their communities would never do. One simultaneously accused the government of handling the case poorly and ridiculed the Hutaree's conspiracy theory orientation as a way to distinguish his unit from theirs:

> I guess the 'Evil New World Order'[16] had a change of heart? . . . The Feds blew this, in every aspect. They wasted a lot of money and time and energy. Maybe just the arrest and trial will keep folks like this from doing stupid shit in the future. I hope so.

Perhaps he had a point. No other coordinated militia unit plots made national headlines for several years.

The Crusaders

The next major militia arrests to receive attention happened a few weeks before the 2016 Presidential election. Three men who split from a larger militia called the Kansas Security Force were accused of plotting to bomb an apartment complex known to house predominantly Muslim Somali refugees. They were eventually convicted of conspiracy to use a weapon of mass destruction and conspiracy to violate the housing rights of their intended victims (a hate crime) and were sentenced to serve between 25 and 30 years (DOJ, 2019). I did not have preexisting direct research connections to the groups or individuals involved in this case when public defenders for one of the accused named Gavin Wright contacted me. They called themselves "clueless" about militias until being assigned to the case and said they needed someone to help them understand the basics of groups like this. They wanted me to help them understand how their client fit within militia culture,[17] in part because they had initially been inclined to argue that Wright, who called himself a survivalist, was not a member of any group, militia or otherwise. They thought this might work in his favor during his trial by presenting him as less dedicated to the plot and its supporting ideology than the other defendants.

The men resented how these refugees were supposedly getting benefits, like housing assistance, that natural-born American citizens like them did not receive. When I interviewed him in prison, Wright told me that unit leader Patrick Stein worked 16-hour days, lived in a mobile home, and still felt like he couldn't afford things that he wanted. He did not frame it this way, but he was suggesting that Stein's failure to achieve the American Dream in spite of his hard, physical labor made him even more resentful to see what he thought of has unearned advantages being given away to outsiders. That Stein was a farmer, an occupation that still captures so much of the idealized settler masculinity, may have further exacerbated this feeling.

Stein and other members of the broader Kansas Security Force were already on edge as 2016 began because of the shooting of LeVoy Finicum. Finicum was a compatriot of the Bundy family who had numerous confrontations, stretching back several years, with law enforcement[18] and that had garnered many militia and other nostalgic group affiliations while resonating with the broader nostalgia of settler colonial claims of entitlement to land use (Fuller, 2021; Inwood & Bonds, 2017). He participated in their occupation of the Malheur National Wildlife Refuge in Oregon and was lethally shot by an FBI agent at the end of this confrontation as he was reaching for a handgun. Many people on the nostalgic group spectrum appreciated the occupation as a symbolic step against federal government overreach and believed Finicum's death to be a targeted killing intended to disrupt a momentum they thought could be harnessed for further change; Stein uses the word "murdered" when talking about Finicum during at least one Facebook chat, and Wright told me that the incident created some "pretty mad people" in the Kansas Security Force who discussed the shooting across a variety of platforms. An FBI agent was eventually charged for lying about the circumstances of the shooting, spiking suspicion about Finicum's death even higher, and the fact that a jury acquitted the agent of all charges did nothing to allay those fears.

The Crusaders, like other militia members, also came to fear the spread of Islamic culture, which they believe is incompatible with American values. A civilian who became a CI for the FBI after reporting concerning chatter in the group said the bombing plot was spurred by the June 2016 Pulse nightclub shooting because they were "outraged that a Muslim was killing all these Americans" (*Informant*, 2018) and believed Muslims were a growing physical threat to true citizens. The refugees were highly salient in an otherwise predominately white town and became an easy target for the group's frustrations.

However, Patrick Stein, the unit leader, was clearly imagining racialized threat from Muslims before the Pulse massacre. He seemed particularly incensed by a comment that President Obama had made in February 2015, more than a year before the attack at the National Prayer Breakfast, about how religious violence was not limited to a single belief system and that Christians had committed "terrible deeds" during the Crusades (Gopnik, 2015). Stein's Facebook records, which were collected as evidence for the trial, include numerous comments referring to Muslims as "cockroaches," a turn of phrase that not only dehumanizes them but also efficiently captures ideas of infestation and contamination from their presence. He refers to Obama as the "cockroach in charge" or "king cockroach" and insisted Obama was a member of the Muslim Brotherhood and wanted to instill sharia law in the US.[19] Stein sometimes referred to himself as "Orkinman," a reference to the insect extermination company, and started calling his small group of plotters the Crusaders. I'm including here a lengthy comment from one of his April 9, 2016, posts to show the near-manic level of vitriol he already evinced on social media about Muslims before Pulse occurred. All typos and grammar errors are his.

> [The Crusades were] done in self-defense so they could survive and not go extinct at the hands of the cockroaches. . . . They slaughtered those fuckers just like they had been doing to them for how many hundreds of years. Yeah that was just payback fuckers!! The only thing they did wrong during the Crusades is they stopped before every single one of them cockroach no good Moslim motherfuckers were gone and eliminated completely from this planet!! We wouldn't brought it on themselves and their gonna do it again. They keep it up there will be another Crusades only on a much more massive scale that will not stop till everyone of those fuckers are eliminated. The bastards have to be killed just like cockroaches. You can't kill just one or two or three, you have to kill every single one of those fuckers without regard to age gender status or anything else for that matter. That's why we have the ORKINMAN!! We have to do the same thing to this mutated obscenity of cockroaches called Moslems!! The day that objective is completed is the day this planet will be a 10,000% better place to live. We gave them a second chance after the first Crusades and they obviously didn't learn their lesson so second chances are over with and it's time to exterminate the cockroaches forever!!! Just Sayin!!

The group planned their attack for November 9, 2016, the day after the Presidential election because they said they did not want to further undermine what they believed were Trump's already slim odds of success. Many political commentators still doubted a Trump presidency would come to fruition as that day approached. Even on election day, CNN, for example, kept highlighting a long line of women leaving "I Voted" stickers on Susan B. Anthony's grave in clear anticipation of announcing the first female President later that evening. Some nostalgic groups almost as openly feared a Hillary Clinton victory including Oath Keepers who talked about being willing and able to defend Trump even then from a stolen election (Jackson, 2020). Wright told me that his group had the same worry, that they were certain Hillary would win even if she had to cheat to do it. They believed that, once in office, she would only further Obama's "agenda" to undermine the Constitution by allowing more terrorists, whom Wright said they defined as both Muslims and undocumented migrants from the southern border, into the country. Another defendant, Curtis Allen, left Facebook records that expressed these sentiments about a stolen election and a Muslim "take over" as well.

The group wrote a manifesto that presumably was to be released to help explain their motives for the bombing. Journalist Dick Lehr listened to much of the audio secretly recorded by the CI on the case to write a thorough account of the Crusaders and their plot. He says that Allen, believed the manifesto would " 'trigger the other like-minded people across the nation to fucking stand up and start doing the same thing we're doing.' Which was going after 'Muslims and Government' " (2021, p. 208). The three-page, handwritten manifesto does not mention Muslims or immigrants; the closest it comes is an assertion in its opening lines that the mainstream media and government have been calling "veterans, Christians, and assorted groups" domestic terrorists, requiring the reader to impute other relevant parties in comparison. However, the document pleads with "America" to not call his group terrorists and instead to understand that they are "taking back control of our government," which, it says with a nostalgic nod, hasn't had transparency "since the 40s."

It is uncertain how bombing a refugee community would be exerting control over the government, but the carnage was intended to send a message well beyond the Muslim community the plot targeted in the hopes of stopping the perceived infiltration of Muslims into the country. The manifesto's author does clearly hope that others will engage in further unspecified mass action, concluding with:

> I call upon every American to hold our Elected officials accountable For this mess we now must sort out. The time is now my Fellow Americans. . . . We must Come together As a Nation Friends. The KSF sees the downfall of this nation near. We call on you to help SAVE IT.

These two appeals to Americans to "stand up" to save the nation are proto-accelerationist aims that, in context of the plot, exclude Muslims from the Crusaders' definition of American. Although the manifesto claims they are trying to *prevent* a cultural collapse, they also believe they are at an urgent tipping point and need to catalyze other patriots into action. They want to incite mass opposition to the government that they believe is exponentially moving away from their nostalgic, imagined, and idealized national culture. This action, though ostensibly working within the current system, would nonetheless accelerate its collapse.

The public defenders I worked with largely dismissed the manifesto as a rambling and angry rant that was devoid of any meaningful information about the defendants' alleged plot or even any real coherent message. They talked about how the anti-government rhetoric within it was not unusual relative to what someone would hear listening to Fox News or attending a Trump rally. Much of this conversation happened as I was riding in the car with them from their offices in Wichita to the facility where Wright was being detained. On the way, they pointed out a construction site for "survival condos." Someone was converting an old missile silo that, according to the project's webpage, which they showed me later, had been monitored and cleared by the EPA then remodeled into luxury, underground apartments supposedly capable of withstanding a nuclear bomb or lesser disasters. As I write, the website for the project (https://survivalcondo.com/) indicates that three of ten units remain available for the original asking price of either $1.5 or $3 million, depending on square footage. Although recent media coverage of the build indicates the silo is at a "secret location," part of the construction site was easily visible from the highway, and its intended purpose seemed to be common knowledge in Wichita. The attorneys pointed to this site as another example of how at least some of their client's survivalist beliefs and practices, which they first found odd or extreme as they were introduced to the militia movement, were substantially more mainstream than they had realized. They also mused that people who could participate in survivalist practices with a multi-million-dollar price tag would likely be viewed quite differently than their client who could not afford to pay an attorney for his own defense.

When I interviewed Wright, he told me that he never believed the plot was real. He called the conversations where the group would complain about immigrants, the southern border, and what happened at the Bundy standoff "bitch sessions," and insisted he believed even Stein was "blowin' and goin'"—blowing steam and going off about numerous things that angered him. I asked what other sorts of things Stein seemed to be angry at, and Wright exasperatedly responded, "Man, he was mad at the rain!" Despite dismissing the seriousness of the alleged plot, Wright repeatedly told me that he was embarrassed by his actions and that he didn't recognize the version of himself that he had heard on some of the CI's audio recordings. He told me that he was quite wary of sharia law spreading in the US but that, in reality, he had no problem with most Muslims. He claimed to have had a Muslim family that sublet from him for two years at some point in the past and indicated that he believed they were good people because they were "wanting to be American" and trying to assimilate to US culture. He said he had even been in the middle of selling a mobile home to a Somali family when Stein burst into his business one day, yelling at him about selling "to those people," and Wright said he had responded by throwing him out and chewing him out about interfering with his livelihood.

Wright also told me that he wasn't a particularly big fan of Trump, even though there was "no choice between" him and Hillary because of the deleterious impact he believed she would have. His attorneys had asked me to look for evidence that Trump, specifically, had influenced the group's actions and inspired the plot. The memes and posts I observed in the Facebook records for the case did overlap heavily with Trump's talking points, but those talking points amplified fears and hostilities that were already common among nostalgic groups before his candidacy. What I found instead was support for Wright's claims of backing anyone who was not Hillary.[20] For example, defendant Allen expressed in early May 2016 that he was uncertain about what kind of President Trump would be, but said:

> What I do know is this. Hillary Clinton cannot [be] allowed to be in office. Her actions as far back as an attorney in Ark[ansas] show her as

a lying manipulative beast that deserves to be In Prison. There is NO denying this!

One of Wright's attorneys still tried to explain how Trump's influence could have helped drive her client's words and actions at his sentencing hearing. Lehr (2021, p. 360) quotes her as arguing:

> [A]s long as the Executive Branch condemns Islam and commends and encourages violence against would-be enemies, then a sentence imposed by the judicial branch does little to deter people generally from engaging in such conduct if they believe they are protecting their country from enemies identified by their own commander in chief.

She goes on to say it would be "a pipe dream" to think that life sentences would have a deterrent effect on similar future actions (*ibid*. 360–361). Her client was nonetheless sentenced to 26 years, one more than Allen because of an added charge of lying to the FBI, but four fewer years than Stein, who was described as the plot's ringleader.

The Wolverine Watchmen

Some of the news coverage I saw at the time of the Crusaders verdict seemed to find the suggestion that Trump could be blamed for a violent, socially disruptive plot hard to believe. The Crusaders had been arrested several weeks before Trump won his 2016 election and three months before he took office. While people had already been criticizing Trump's otherizing and xenophobic language, just as Wright's lawyer later did, some people seemed to believe that his influence would have been limited before he took office. When a total of 14 men were arrested for elaborately plotting to kidnap Michigan's Governor Gretchen Whitmer and try her for treason in October 2020, shortly before Trump was attempting reelection, there was substantially less skepticism about possible causality between him and violent action.

By the time of the Watchmen's arrests, we had seen how hate crimes rose fairly steadily throughout Trump's tenure (Ruisch & Ferguson, 2023; Villarreal, 2020; *Hate Crime*, 2023) and collectively experienced a global pandemic that inflamed a variety of perceived threats—something we saw play out at both lockdown and social justice protests that received heavy news coverage. The 14 defendants, who variously faced both state and federal charges for the plot, were first spurred to meet because of how they perceived Whitmer's COVID mitigation efforts to be tyrannical infringements on individual liberties; several attended the infamous Michigan State Capitol lockdown protest at the end of March before the plot was fully drafted.[21] Trump had attacked several Democratic Governors who responded to the pandemic with lockdowns and restrictions on businesses, but Whitmer seemed to earn special attention from him, likely because she was a woman who was unafraid to hold him accountable for a poor response to the pandemic (Cooter, 2022a; Jabali, 2020). Trump had publicly and baselessly insulted Whitmer's intelligence and had, perhaps intentionally, slowed the federal response to COVID in her state in addition to tweeting "LIBERATE MICHIGAN" and other unmistakable support for the armed mobs protesting her orders in the spring of 2020, just as the Watchmen plot was in the early days of discussion (Bradner, 2020; Jabali, 2020; Liptak, 2020).

The details of the alleged plot seemed to contribute to public fascination with the case. Compared to some other terrorism cases, the plot was rather multifaceted and included discussions of Tasers, Molotov cocktails, potentially kidnapping Whitmer from her vacation home by boat and bombing bridges to impede law enforcement response. Some of the defendants conducted surveillance at this residence and at least some practiced tactical entry and exit from a mock-up home they constructed from PVC pipe. And yet, the plotters also considered the so-called Governor's Mansion on Mackinac Island as a possible kidnap location, apparently unaware that it has merely been a tourist location for the last many years rather than an actual residence.

When news of the Watchmen arrests broke about a month before the 2020 election, some observers briefly hoped this would effectively be a deathknell for the militia movement because it followed so quickly after Facebook had deplatformed militia pages and individuals with no notice starting in August of that year (Wong, 2020). Among the groups I follow, however, the constitutionalist elements distanced themselves from the Watchmen, again insisting they were not "real" militia members because of their apparently violent intentions, while millenarian groups only became more angry and convinced they were being unfairly targeted by a tyrannical government that was arresting people who had not yet conducted any crime. What's more, militia researchers watched as some members and other Trump supporters moved to Parler and Telegram (Collier et al., 2021; Jaffe & Gillum, 2021; Rondeaux & Dalton, 2022), which became even more intense echo chambers where discussions of action to "stop the steal" began even before Trump lost reelection.

I became connected to the Watchmen case when public defenders who doubted their clients' abilities to execute such a plot called me to once again ask about militia organization and culture, saying they wanted to understand where their clients fit on the militia spectrum. I heard most about Adam Fox, and attorneys described him as a bumbling, depressed, loner pothead who often rambled incoherently on the audio captured by a CI. They thought the conversations surrounding the plot were so detailed and so exaggerated that it could never have been mistaken as a real plan. They cited as an example how one defendant talked about having access to a weapons cache and the ability to remote control one of two different military helicopter models as he falsely claimed to be a former Navy Seal. The lawyers told me that as this defendant was bloviating to the group, he said that he would land the helicopter and exclaim, "Welcome to the Three Percenters, motherfucker!" to the pilot as they commandeered it. One of the attorneys remarked that listening to the audio of this exchange was "like being lobotomized" because it was so obviously ridiculous and far-fetched.

Others were not so quick to dismiss the plot's potential. Among them was, quite understandably, Governor Whitmer (2020) herself who openly identified Trump as a major cause of the planned attack against her. She penned an op-ed for *The Atlantic* shortly after news of the arrests broke and said:

> Every time the president ramps up this violent rhetoric, every time he fires up Twitter to launch another broadside against me, my family and I see a surge of vicious attacks sent our way. This is no coincidence, and the president knows it. He is sowing division and putting leaders, especially women leaders, at risk. And all because he thinks it will help his reelection.

Some members in other Michigan militias also thought there might have been merit to the arrests. In fact, some of them had already told me about Adam Fox months before he was arrested, sharing how he had attempted to pick fights with numerous people at different multi-militia events, including once being kicked out of another member's house for getting into a fight with that member's wife. A colleague who encountered Fox in person before his arrest described him as noticeably angry and more suspicious in a way that visibly differentiated him from other militia members at several gatherings. One of my longest-term militia contacts said he had believed Fox to be "a keyboard warrior who thought he was better than anyone else" and had difficulty getting along with any of the constitutionalist members in the area. The Wolverine Watchmen do appear to have been started by men who split off from one of the larger, public facing militias (one interested in "popularity contests," as my earlier source remarked), first forming a group called the Michigan Homeguard, and then splitting again into the core group of alleged plotters known as the Watchmen (Cooter, 2022b).

My militia contacts tell me that they believe, as is usually the case, these splits happened over disagreements about the tactics of the larger groups. Members of the Watchmen wanted to do more than hold public rallies on the Capitol steps and overall seem to have been more accelerationist than the average member of the other groups. Several of the defendants aligned with Boogaloo and included varieties of that word in their social media handles or wore Hawaiian shirts to various events. Among them were Fox and another defendant, Daniel Harris, who protested against police and in support of Black Lives Matter at a June 2020 event after George Floyd's murder (Proxmire, 2020), serving as another example of how militias and even accelerationists are not necessarily intentionally promoting white supremacist aims.

What does remain consistent, however, is distrust of or even hatred for government officials who do not adhere to nostalgic group ideals. Defendant Ty Garbin later testified that part of the Watchmen's goal had been to instill fear and disruption that they believed would ensure another electoral victory for Trump who, for them, had a stronger persona as an effective protector of the nation than Biden. Disrupting the elections seems to have been a secondary and opportunistic goal that came about after the Watchmen had already been discussing elements of the plot, rather than an original motivator for it (Cooter, 2022b; Goudie et al., 2022). This justification for the plot is an accelerationist-adjacent disruption to the democratic process that was intended to prevent Biden, whom they viewed as undermining American strength and culture, from obtaining the Presidency. This means that some of the Watchmen were comfortable working within the existing system, rather than completely destroying it, as long as they could control the political outcome. However, one FBI agent testified during the trial that the group was seeking the more quintessentially accelerationist, if not clearly defined goal, of a second Civil War (Krafcki, 2021; Reed, 2022). Fox, for example, was quoted in the criminal complaint as articulating this goal of destroying the current system in a recorded call with a CI, saying, "I just wanna make the world glow, dude. . . . That's what it's gonna take for us to take it back, . . . everything's gonna have to be annihilated, man. We're gonna topple it all, dude."

As of Fall 2023, five of the Watchmen—including Harris—were acquitted of the charges they faced, three pleaded guilty, and five were found guilty by a jury. Two of those, including Fox, did not receive their verdicts until a second trial following the first jury's inability to come to a unified decision. The mixed verdicts from the Watchmen seem to signal that juries are taking the charges and evidence in these militia plots seriously and evaluating them on their own merits, rather than filtering them through any simplified ideological lens.

The number of guilty verdicts in these cases and in the Crusaders' case may also indicate that juries, and therefore the American public as a whole, have started to understand the risks of violence from some militias and other nostalgic groups. Historically, charges and successful prosecutions for violent plots in the US have been stymied by broad First Amendment protections in the US (J. L. Walker, 2009). As was true with the Hutaree, it can be difficult to convince a judge or jury that defendants have taken meaningful steps toward enacting the plot or have done anything other than engage in "bitch sessions," as Wright called the Crusader's conversations. Some peer nations have greater restrictions on hate speech (Purtill, 2015; J. Walker, 2018) compared to how it has tended to be categorized as "lawful but awful" in the US (Keller, 2022). It may be that juries are starting to see a clearer connection between speech and the possibilities for violent harm (Cooter, 2022c), and it may also be the case that prosecutors had more convincingly argued that defendants in recent cases were taking concrete steps toward violent action, a task that became even easier for prosecutions of those involved in January 6th.

January 6, 2021

January 6th was a coup attempt.[22] It ultimately failed, but the goal of its angry mob was to "stop the steal" and prevent the certification of the 2020 Presidential election results so that Trump could stay in power. This event finally made it impossible to ignore the potential threat posed by organized nostalgic groups and their principles that resonate far beyond their official membership rosters. Distinct militia groups worked alongside Boogaloo, Proud Boys, neo-Nazis, and unaffiliated individuals from all across the country for the common goal of preventing a Biden Presidency (Tanfani et al., 2021).

In my metaphor of nostalgic groups where political winds can push different groups together for shared action, January 6th was a hurricane-force gale that blew them into a concerted, undifferentiated mob and may have permanently altered the nostalgic group landscape in the process. While the Oath Keepers in particular seem to have had some specific plans for the day (Shamsian, 2021; Walters, 2022), other actors were largely opportunistic and followed the lead of more intentional actors (Hosenball & Lynch, 2021). An estimated 89% of participants, based on early data, had no preexisting

Figure 6.2 Militia member Paul Bellar covering his face and codename while participating in a Michigan COVID-19 protest.

Source: Photo courtesy of Daniel Hud.

nostalgic group affiliations (Pape & Ruby, 2021). Researcher Michael Jensen (2022) has more recently found that 30% of those arrested had at least some knowledge of nostalgic organizations, including known engagement with various groups' social media profiles. Rather than affiliations, however, this type of engagement reflects how nostalgic group ideology has larger cultural and political appeal beyond those who join such groups, an appeal that can be activated for destructive collective action. Militias and other groups that have long-been considered political or social outliers in fact may simply be more open about views that are commonly but more quietly held in the broader population and can act as barometers for much deeper political currents.

One lesson that should be paramount from January 6th is that we need to pay more attention to how "normal" people can be radicalized. We sometimes prefer to believe that such actors are indeed outliers, somehow fundamentally, essentially bad and unreflective of our populace as a whole. This was part of why January 6th was so disturbing to many people who watched the insurrection's footage in horror, not only because of the day's violence, but also because it disrupted their imagined community, their shared notions of a coherent democracy. It created a realization that average people may become radicalized, sometimes rather quickly, after an appealing seed of exclusionary or conspiratorial thinking is nourished by groupthink and scapegoating before sprouting into fully fledged extremist actions. Powerful figures like Trump or, on a smaller scale, leaders of militias and other nostalgic groups, can still harness and channel these growing feelings, playing on the alienation and threat that some people experience during times of change, for nefarious purposes.

We must also remember that "extremist" or "extremism" does not necessarily mean statistically on the fringes of society; after all, a majority of Republicans may still believe the 2020 election was stolen (Murray, 2022). Rather, extremism reflects how, as J.M. Berger (2018) so artfully explains, an in-group can see no path forward except through the domination or elimination of an out-group. Radicalization, with its final destination in extremism, is, in other words, an extension of the commonplace process of in- and out-group dynamics. White men who, in the aggregate, already possessed greater social, economic, and political power were eager for Trump's empty promises to serve as an emotional balm to cool their rising frustration about social change, especially the increasing visibility and power of other demographic groups who are not represented in our settler-myth imaginings.

Other scholars have discussed how January 6th was the logical conclusion of the environment that Trump created during his tenure in the White House (Du Mez, 2020; Gorski & Perry, 2022). Nostalgic nationalism allows us to understand how those insurrectionary actors were strongly primed to respond to this cultivated environment where Trump stoked them into a frenzy about supposed threats that he promised only he could alleviate. Some insurrectionists believed their involvement was not only justified but also morally required of real patriots whose nation was on the verge of collapse. They saw themselves as following in the legacy of the Founding Fathers, with visions of the Boston Tea Party dancing in their heads as they assaulted police officers and breached the Capitol walls (Boryga, 2021). Others, in fundraising websites asking for help paying their attorney fees, echoed religious framing by appealing to a "higher calling" to justify their actions, or asserted that they were good husbands and fathers—to young daughters, they often specified (Wilson, 2022). These descriptions were clear efforts for defendants to present themselves as emblems of ideal, protective settler masculinity and as men who could not possibly be domestic terrorists and should not be treated as such in legal proceedings.

We've also seen some insurrectionists who have talked about having been caught up in the moment that day (Mallin, 2022), indubitably to attempt mitigating the legal consequences for their actions, but social scientists have also known for a long time that group dynamics can sometimes make individuals act in ways they normally would not (Postmes & Spears, 1998). Another example is Gavin Wright, the Crusaders defendant I interviewed who lamented how he had caved to a startling, yet simultaneously mundane, process of peer pressure. This, too, may merely be a case of regret after having been criminally charged, but nonetheless seems to have at least some kernel of truth behind it given his previous working relationships with Muslim individuals and what had been a close relationship to his adult child who is part of the LBGTQ+ community—a fact not very publicly known and left out of narratives portraying him and his militia unit as uniformly opposed to all social change. Mauricio Garcia, the Hispanic neo-Nazi who murdered eight people in a 2023 mass shooting in Texas, may be an example of someone who was radicalized into white supremacist action via similar group dynamics in online spaces after first falling deeply into rabidly misogynistic incel ideology (ADL, 2023).

The physical violence that happened during the insurrection, with damage to the Capitol building, five deaths, and more than 100 police officers injured (Farley, 2022), occurred alongside the symbolic violence that was also done to the integrity of US democracy. To be clear, democracy was far from pristine before this day. Pervasive issues like gerrymandering, felon disenfranchisement, and impediments to obtaining voter identification that disproportionately impact Black communities all act as a continuation of the settler colonial framework that nullifies any reality of democracy or the American Dream. It is no coincidence that polling places in Black communities were the ones that bore the brunt of threats to poll workers as part of "stop the steal" efforts. All these actions, including January 6th's attempted coup, function as a maintenance of systemic white supremacy by impairing the civic participation of people who are not white men. This is true even for some individuals who tried to "stop the steal" or who, armed, monitored ballot drop boxes believed only that they were performing a patriotic service in the interest of their nostalgic vision of the nation.

As of Fall 2023, more than 1,000 people have been arrested for their actions during the Capitol incursion (Mangan, 2023). Those arrested have disproportionately been veterans of the US military, with about 20% of the people facing charges having had military experience relative to less than 7% of the overall US population (Gilligan, 2022; Murphy, 2022). We need to do much more to understand why protecting Trump and "stopping the steal" appealed in this way to some veterans, but preliminary interviewees from one of my ongoing projects on extremist exploitation of veterans have confirmed that Trump encouraged some of their peers to embrace extremist talking points, especially around immigration. One interviewee, for example, noted, "All that rhetoric became more fervent under Trump. I try not to be political, but that's just a fact. I joined the military when Bush was about to leave, I was in through Obama, and it was never to the same level of rhetoric that we heard under Trump." The vast majority of military veterans are not extremists, but some veterans, especially those facing difficulties navigating a post-separation, civilian world may be especially vulnerable to nativist appeals, nostalgic messaging, and extremist exploitation.

At least half of the 14 Oath Keepers who have already been convicted for their actions that day were veterans (DOJ, 2023b; Lawrence & Toropin, 2022; Toropin, 2023). Six of the convicted Oath Keepers, including founder and leader Stewart Rhodes, and an additional four members of the Proud Boys have been found guilty of seditious conspiracy, the same charge that was previously unsuccessful against the Hutaree (DOJ, 2023a, 2023c). January 6th defendants clearly did more than merely discuss attacking the government, likely making charges easier to prove in this case. Despite conspiratorial claims to the contrary insisting the attempted coup was "just a protest" or fallaciously blaming the violence on antifa, the many videos and photographs of the violence that day made the insurrectionists' intent to disrupt the democratic process impossible to ignore. Their targets, politicians, including Republican Vice President Mike Pence who they perceived as thwarting Trump's reelection, were both physically and symbolically located within the nation's Capitol building during the Presidential vote certification.

January 6th and the events that led up to it have also done symbolic violence to our collective perception of acceptable political actions. As extremism researcher Sam Jackson (2020, p. 121) presciently observed after Rhodes' engagement with the Bundy family's occupation of federal land:

> The physical threat that Oath Keepers poses is not where the group's biggest influence lies. . . . Oath Keepers contributes to a broader discourse in American politics that pits the people against the government and that views violence as a legitimate form of resistance to government. . . . It shifts the Overton Window, or the limits of acceptable political discourse.

The same is true for other militias and additional nostalgic groups that acted in concert on January 6th and in other precursor events through Trump's presidency. Figures within the Republican party who repeat conspiracy theories insisting that the insurrection was nothing more than a protest or who openly support the insurrectionists and their actions further contribute to skewed perceptions of what is—or should be—acceptable in US politics. We have arrived at a time when juvenile name calling, harassment, or blatant disrespect from people who are supposed to be national leaders barely makes headlines in the cacophony of more egregious scandals about not just decorum but also national security. Some communities worry both about their physical safety in voting booths and the integrity of their choices in future elections, given the attacks on the democratic process. Anything short of open calls for violence almost feels like a welcome relief, and that is precisely the problem: that people have become accustomed to accepting threat and dangerous discourse as a normal part of our political process.

Future Militia Action

It is difficult to predict precisely how militias will evolve in this quagmire. The vast majority of active militia members nationally did not participate in "stop the steal" actions or earlier protests at statehouses. Some members I've spoken with or observed online were profoundly distraught over the January 6th insurrection, thinking it would damage the militia movement in a parallel manner to the fallout from Olson's response to the Oklahoma City bombing or worrying it would signal national weakness and instability to international competitors. Other members, especially those who are military veterans, expressed distress over what the insurrection signaled about the fragility of US democracy. Militia members have also never ubiquitously supported Trump. Disparate units that have different personalities, beliefs, and goals make perfectly anticipating militia action impossible. However, past behaviors are the best predictors of future action, and it is certainly the case that units that have already demonstrated radicalization toward millenarian, accelerationist, or other extremist tendencies have earned our attention.

In the aftermath of January 6th, the militia movement may seem to have dissipated, at least as an in-person rather than online phenomenon. It is true that there has been relatively little public activity from most militias either nationally or at the more local levels since then. The Oath Keepers, specifically, as a branded, national organization will likely never recover from the reputational damage of their prosecutions, even though some local units maintain the moniker and even though we may see some key players attempt eventual reinvention within the nostalgic group landscape.[23]

The militia movement should once more be understood as a movement in abeyance that is ready to coalesce around the right figure and the right messaging. They will almost certainly resuscitate the nascent cross-group coalitions that formed around Trump's encouragement and are likely to be highly responsive to the 2024 Presidential election and beyond. The militia-adjacent Proud Boys, for example, seem to have suffered less from their involvement in January 6th and are experiencing reinvigorated legitimation through connections to some chapters of Moms For Liberty (Gilbert, 2023). Moms For Liberty has been at the forefront of anti-LGBTQ+ and anti-CRT battles at school boards nationally. Their actions exemplify the bottom-up efforts to control both government and culture that will almost certainly replace further insurrectionary efforts to capture the highest office. That is, additional actions on the scale of the Capitol incursion that so blatantly attack both a practical and symbolic site of national power are unlikely, but efforts to revive a nostalgic frame can still be successful through aggregate gains from local wins.[24]

Anti-LGBTQ+ messaging, especially around transgender rights and visibility, currently has an enormous footprint in nostalgic groups' online spaces. I suspect this will continue as a core motivating issue through at least the next Presidential election. Nostalgic groups are both emotionally and cognitively responsive to issues that capture sustained negative attention from Fox News

Figure 6.3 Two militia members walking back toward their cars after a long day of training with forgotten pieces of shrubbery–part of their camouflage during an earlier activity—still tucked in their gear.

Source: Photo by the author.

or even more conservative outlets. They also opportunistically amplify these issues to gain resonance, members, and to continue pushing the Overton Window. It will be crucial to follow these emerging trends to understand likely points of conflict and even violence from these groups.

Trump has demonstrated that he is also adept at playing to the outrage of the day as presented in conservative news circles. He continues to stoke discord in his early efforts to regain the Presidency through, for example, his Memorial Day social media post that insisted in all caps that the country "has never been in greater peril than it is right now" (Bolton, 2023). His rhetoric is occurring while hate crimes continue to rise (Li & Lartey, 2023) and conditions are prime to once more legitimize white men's senses of threat and impending disaster caused by social change. Trump may not win the contest, but Trumpism already has. Its fascistic force has degraded acceptable political discourse and returned groups that had only recently won hard-fought protections to a very vulnerable status. Other contenders for the Republican nomination, namely Ron DeSantis, are mimicking and, in some cases, expanding on the Trumpian model by openly attacking transgender rights and visibility and criminalizing certain discussions of racism and gender identity (HRC, 2023; Papaycik, 2022). Regardless of who sits in the Oval Office in the future, militias and other nostalgic groups are likely to be an active presence in US political society for a long time. The question is merely how legitimized and mainstream they will be.

Notes

1. Some units also reported slight and temporary bumps following 2005's Hurricane Katrina and numerous news reports that followed about threats from nature, looters, and law enforcement alike (Berenson & Broder, 2005; Jackson, 2020).
2. See Mills (2021) for similar findings in the rise of the prepper community.
3. Accurately tracking the number of members of the overall movement is impossible because of a lack of membership rosters, secrecy, and internal dynamics that cause the numbers to shift dramatically over even short periods of time (Cooter, 2013). I tracked attendance at events that I attended in person and observed how both discussions and new membership activity in online spaces correlated across other groups over time.
4. The first of these conspiracy fantasies claims that Hillary Clinton was involved in a pedophile ring that, in part, met in a pizza parlor. This theory previously arose in 2016 and spurred other spiderwebbing conspiracy theories promoted by QAnon about pedophilia among global elites, especially other notable Democrats like Joe Biden. The conspiracy fantasy about Hunter Biden's laptop alleged that a computer that was mysteriously dropped off at a repair center contained information about Hunter Biden's purported dealings in Ukraine and/or China alongside "proof" that Joe Biden improperly used his authority to cover up his son's actions.
5. https://web.archive.org/web/20180211003022/https://atomwaffendivision.org/.
6. Some affiliates may prefer to reference the Revolutionary War as the event to be repeated but still foresee revolution against internal power structures and those who support them such that any conflict would also be a civil war.

7. For example, Nashville, Tennessee residents voted to instill a Community Oversight Board over police in that city after an officer shot a Black man in the back and killed him, but the board has faced many hurdles. The police union repeatedly tried and failed to overrule the voice of citizens in the board's formation, the state has since enacted several laws that effectively hamstring the power of this and similar boards in Tennessee's other major cities, and the police have refused to cooperate with the board during ongoing investigations (Hale, 2019; Pfleger, 2023; Torres Guzman, 2022). Most recently, state legislators have voted to abolish any citizen-led oversight boards, thus once more allowing officers to police their own, and it is unclear what further legal battles may follow (Max, 2019).
8. The questions for both race and occupation were both free-response questions, allowing them to write whatever they wanted without predetermined categories. "Native American" probably means someone who is racialized as white and who was born on US soil with attendant citizenship status. Numerous nostalgic group actors (especially men) I have encountered over my many years of research sometimes claim being "Native American" as a way to highlight their belief that race does not matter but citizenship does. It is worth noting how such a claim may be intended to disrupt racial categories but works to erase Indigenous people and their experiences. It also implicitly alludes to the racial appropriation done by various "back to the land organizations" that attempt to tap into perceived qualities of nature or even mysticism stereotypically connected to Indigenous populations. The other survey respondent I mention here who advocated only for legislative change wrote in "Human" as his race, as another kind of rejection of racial categories in favor of supposedly unified personhood.
9. There is no reliable count, to my knowledge, of how many people present at or arrested for their involvement in the Capitol incursion had Boogaloo affiliations, but their recognizable attire is quite visible across footage from the day.
10. Zello was mentioned numerous times in the charging documents for this case (see www.justice.gov/opa/file/903106/download), and I saw several records related to this app's use in the plot when I consulted on this case. The app nonetheless escaped media attention for several years, and a Zello employee later dubiously claimed the company only became aware of far-right groups using the platform in June 2020 (Gladstone, 2022).
11. The Hutaree website is archived and much of its content may still be viewed through http://web.archive.org/web/20100401191403/www.hutaree.com/. Some subpages of the archived site need to be highlighted (using <ctrl + a>) to view the white text on a white background.
12. Included on the list were, for example, "00666 - Zip code of the Beast" and "$566.66 - Price of the Beast at Costco."
13. At the time, I assumed, this person meant "use for target practice and repeatedly shoot," instead of thinking he was referring to literal machine guns, but some members eventually pled guilty to possessing illegal, fully automatic weapons, suggesting the speaker knew or had at least heard rumors about the Hutaree possessing these firearms at this early point.
14. The Hutaree investigation also led to my direct engagement with federal officers who asked what I knew about that unit and how they compared to more typical ones in the state.
15. Most had also been released on bond and electronic monitoring while awaiting trial.
16. The "New World Order" refers to a long-running conspiracy theory about global elites conspiring to hurt average citizens. See Cooter et al. (2023) for more on how this theory intersects with the militia movement.
17. I was not instantaneously comfortable with the prospect of working on behalf of defendants on a case with such abhorrent racist and Islamophobic allegations. Given the criminal justice system we have, I do think it is important that experts

do what we can to ensure all defendants have a fair trial and that prosecutors appropriately do their jobs to prove each case. This is something I was positioned to assist with in this case, especially given that the attorneys were seeking contextual information about the facts surrounding the case. I did not testify on the defendant's behalf and instead only provided information directly to the attorneys.
18. These confrontations continue today, with the newest iteration being an Idaho sheriff announcing he would no longer serve Ammon Bundy with papers related to an ongoing lawsuit with a hospital because Bundy was becoming increasingly aggressive. The sheriff walked that comment back following public backlash, but Bundy continues to bring supporters to his land and threatens to make a defensive stand (Blanchard, 2023; The Associated Press, 2023). It certainly seems Bundy is thinking about not only his history of confrontations with the government and its representatives, but also about the history of Ruby Ridge as he intimates a standoff over what he claims are illegitimate legal proceedings.
19. Stein also used racial and homophobic slurs when referring to Obama and other targets of his ire. It is interesting that homophobia is present in his commentary yet the LGBTQ+ victims of the Pulse massacre still stirred his sympathy as victimized "real" Americans, likely further highlighting the extent of Stein's anti-Muslim hate.
20. Wright told me that he had voted for Democrats in the past, including Bill Clinton, which, if true, would seem to indicate a strong misogynistic element undergirding his fear of Hillary taking the office.
21. One defendant who pleaded guilty and received a reduced sentence later testified that part of the unit's goal had been to instill fear and disruption that they believed would ensure another electoral victory for Trump, but this seems to have been a secondary goal that came about after the Watchmen had already been discussing elements of the plot, rather than an original motivator (Cooter, 2022b; Goudie et al., 2022).
22. Some political scientists use the language of self-coup or auto-coup to capture attempts that are conducted by the party that is, at that moment, already in power.
23. Rhodes himself seems to have been angling for this possibility in the memo he submitted while asking for a more lenient sentence for his role in January 6th. The memo presented the Oath Keepers as a "community service organization" that "functions within and for the benefit of society" (Dickinson, 2023). If Rhodes is pardoned by a second Trump Presidency or otherwise regains his freedom, this framing may be the foundation for once more constructing a false narrative about Rhodes' "true patriotism" and the sacrifices he ostensibly made in an effort to protect the nation.
24. It is worth noting that the second wave of the KKK took a similar approach to influencing politics and school curricula alike, with moderate success that was hampered by infighting and other internal problems (Du Bois, 1926; Laats, 2012; McVeigh, 2009).

References

ADL. (2023, May 10). Allen Gunman's writings reveal a disturbed, hateful man—but no clear motive. *ADL*. www.adl.org/resources/blog/allen-gunmans-writings-reveal-disturbed-hateful-man-no-clear-motive

The Associated Press. (2012, February 25). Michigan militia leader spoke of killing police, family. *Mlive*. https://www.mlive.com/news/2012/02/michigan_militia_leader_spoke.html

The Associated Press. (2023, May 8). Activist Ammon Bundy's latest standoff is in court. *Central Oregon Daily*. https://centraloregondaily.com/ammon-bundy-idaho-hospital-defamation-lawsuit/

Baldas, T. (2012, February 14). *In Hutaree trial, defense says key witness given special treatment*. Detroit Free Press. www.freep.com/article/20120214/NEWS01/120214051

Berenson, A., & Broder, J. M. (2005, September 2). Police begin seizing guns of civilians. *New York Times*. https://web.archive.org/web/20170801220821/www.nytimes.com/2005/09/09/us/nationalspecial/police-begin-seizing-guns-of-civilians.html

Berger, J. M. (2013, March 12). The hate list. *Foreign Policy*. https://foreignpolicy.com/2013/03/12/the-hate-list/

Berger, J. M. (2018). *Extremism*. The MIT Press.

Blanchard, N. (2023, April 21). Gem County sheriff will serve legal docs to Ammon Bundy. Hospital withdraws court request. *East Idaho News*. www.eastidahonews.com/2023/04/gem-county-sheriff-will-serve-legal-docs-to-ammon-bundy-hospital-withdraws-court-request/

Blankstein, A., & Collins, B. (2020, June 17). Alleged 'Boogaloo' extremist charged in killing of federal officer. *NBC News*. www.nbcnews.com/news/us-news/airman-charged-killing-federal-officer-during-george-floyd-protests-california-n1231187

Bolton, A. (2023, May 29). Trump wishes happy memorial day to those fighting 'misfits and lunatic thugs' within the nation. *The Hill*. https://thehill.com/homenews/campaign/4025169-trump-wishes-happy-memorial-day-to-those-fighting-misfits-and-lunatic-thugs-within-the-nation/

Boryga, A. (2021, April 2). Davie man accused of storming the Capitol and calling it 'our Boston Tea Party.' *Yahoo News*. https://news.yahoo.com/davie-man-accused-storming-capitol-154200349.html

Bradner, E. (2020, March 29). "That governor is me": Gretchen Whitmer takes on Trump as coronavirus cases rise in Michigan. *CNN*. www.cnn.com/2020/03/29/politics/gretchen-whitmer-donald-trump-coronavirus/index.html

Braunstein, R. (2021). The "right" history: Religion, race, and nostalgic stories of Christian America. *Religions*, *12*(2), 96.

Breland, A. (2019). Why are right-wing conspiracies so obsessed with pedophilia? *Mother Jones*. www.motherjones.com/politics/2019/07/why-are-right-wing-conspiracies-so-obsessed-with-pedophilia/

Brown, D. (2011). *Back to the land: The enduring dream of self-sufficiency in modern America*. University of Wisconsin Press.

Buchanan, W. (2010, March 29). Who is David Brian Stone, leader of the Hutaree militia? *Christian Science Monitor*. www.csmonitor.com/USA/Justice/2010/0329/Who-is-David-Brian-Stone-leader-of-the-Hutaree-militia

Butler, A. D. (2021). *White evangelical racism: The politics of morality in America*. The University of North Carolina Press.

Choi, J. (2021, February 12). FBI arrests two Kentucky men associated with the 'Boogaloo Bois' [Text]. *The Hill*. https://thehill.com/homenews/state-watch/538570-fbi-arrests-two-men-associated-with-boogaloo-bois-in-connection-with/

Collier, K., Schecter, A., & Kaplan, E. (2021, January 14). Telegram, a recent haven for the far right, purges extremist content. *NBC News*. www.nbcnews.com/tech/tech-news/telegram-recent-haven-far-right-purges-extremist-content-n1254215

Collins, B., & Zadronzny, B. (2020a, April 17). In Trump's "LIBERATE" tweets, extremists see a call to arms. *NBC News*. www.nbcnews.com/tech/security/trump-s-liberate-tweets-extremists-see-call-arms-n1186561

Collins, B., & Zadronzny, B. (2020b, October 30). How a fake persona laid the groundwork for a Hunter Biden conspiracy deluge. *NBC News*. www.nbcnews.com/tech/security/how-fake-persona-laid-groundwork-hunter-biden-conspiracy-deluge-n1245387

Cooter, A. (2012). *Race and racism in the militia: Members' responses to Michigan's Black and Muslim populations*. www.amycooter.com/uploads/1/2/3/7/12374434/response_to_racialized_populations.pdf

Cooter, A. (2013). *Americanness, masculinity, and whiteness: How Michigan militia men navigate evolving social norms* [Thesis]. http://deepblue.lib.umich.edu/handle/2027.42/98077

Cooter, A. (2022a). US Domestic Militias' intersections with government and authority: How a sociology of individualism informs their praxis. In D. Neubert, H. J. Lauth, & C. Mohamad-Klotzbach (Eds.), *Local self-governance and varieties of statehood: Tensions and cooperation* (pp. 31–49). Springer International Publishing.

Cooter, A. (2022b, August 25). Conviction of two Michigan kidnap plotters highlights danger of violent conspiracies to US democracy. *The Conversation*. http://theconversation.com/conviction-of-two-michigan-kidnap-plotters-highlights-danger-of-violent-conspiracies-to-us-democracy-189291

Cooter, A. (2022c, November 30). Oath Keepers convictions shed light on the limits of free speech – and the threat posed by militias. *The Conversation*. http://theconversation.com/oath-keepers-convictions-shed-light-on-the-limits-of-free-speech-and-the-threat-posed-by-militias-195616

Cooter, A., Taylor, M., & Hansen, T. J. (2023). Cultural change and conspiracism: How conspiracy theory trends reflect threat and anxiety. In M. A. Argentino & A. Amarasingam (Eds.), *Far-right culture: The art, music, and everyday practices of violent Extremists*. Routledge.

CTEC. (2023, April 12). *Dangerous organizations and bad actors: Atomwaffen division*. Center on Terrorism, Extremism, and Counterterrorism. www.middlebury.edu/institute/academics/centers-initiatives/ctec/ctec-publications/dangerous-organizations-and-bad-actors-4

Daymon, C. (2020, October 26). LOL extremism: Humour in online extremist content. *GNET*. https://gnet-research.org/2020/10/26/lol-extremism-humour-in-online-extremist-content/

Dickinson, T. (2023, May 8). Oath Keepers leader wants leniency for public service ... of creating the Oath Keepers. *Rolling Stone*. www.rollingstone.com/politics/politics-news/stewart-rhodes-leniency-creating-oath-keepers-1234731524/

DOJ. (2010, March 29). Nine members of a militia group charged with seditious conspiracy and related charges. *Department of Justice*. www.justice.gov/opa/pr/nine-members-militia-group-charged-seditious-conspiracy-and-related-charges

DOJ. (2019, January 25). Three Southwest Kansas men sentenced to prison for plotting to bomb Somali immigrants in garden city. *Department of Justice*. www.justice.gov/opa/pr/three-southwest-kansas-men-sentenced-prison-plotting-bomb-somali-immigrants-garden-city

DOJ. (2020, September 4). Two self-described "Boogaloo Bois" charged with attempting to provide material support to Hamas. *Department of Justice*. www.justice.gov/opa/pr/two-self-described-boogaloo-bois-charged-attempting-provide-material-support-hamas

DOJ. (2023a, January 23). Four Oath Keepers found guilty of seditious conspiracy related to U.S. Capitol Breach. *Department of Justice*. www.justice.gov/opa/pr/four-oath-keepers-found-guilty-seditious-conspiracy-related-us-capitol-breach

DOJ. (2023b, March 21). Six additional Oath Keepers members and affiliates found guilty of charges related to capitol breach. *Department of Justice*. www.justice.gov/opa/pr/six-additional-oath-keepers-members-and-affiliates-found-guilty-charges-related-capitol

DOJ. (2023c, May 4). Jury convicts four leaders of the proud boys of seditious conspiracy related to U.S. Capitol Breach. *Department of Justice*. www.justice.gov/opa/pr/jury-convicts-four-leaders-proud-boys-seditious-conspiracy-related-us-capitol-breach

Du Bois, W. E. B. (1926). The shape of Fear. *The North American Review*, 223(831), 291–304.

Du Mez, K. K. (2020). *Jesus and John Wayne: How white evangelicals corrupted a faith and fractured a nation*. Liveright.

Dunbar-Ortiz, R. (2018). *Loaded: A disarming history of the second amendment*. City Lights Publishers.

Farley, R. (2022, March 21). How many died as a result of capitol riot? *FactCheck.Org*. www.factcheck.org/2021/11/how-many-died-as-a-result-of-capitol-riot/

Fox News. (2009, April 16). *Napolitano apologizes for offending veterans after DHS eyes them for "rightwing extremism."* www.foxnews.com/politics/2009/04/16/napolitano-apologizes-offending-veterans-dhs-eyes-rightwing-extremism/

Full text: Donald Trump announces a presidential bid. (2015, June 16). *Washington Post*. www.washingtonpost.com/news/post-politics/wp/2015/06/16/full-text-donald-trump-announces-a-presidential-bid/

Fuller, J. (2021, November 25). The long fight between the Bundys and the federal government, from 1989 to today. *Washington Post*. www.washingtonpost.com/news/the-fix/wp/2014/04/15/everything-you-need-to-know-about-the-long-fight-between-cliven-bundy-and-the-federal-government/

Gibson, J. W. (1994). *Warrior dreams: Violence and manhood in post-Vietnam America* (Reprint ed.). Hill & Wang.

Gilbert, D. (2023, June 20). Inside moms for liberty's close relationship with the proud boys. *Vice*. www.vice.com/en/article/5d93qd/moms-for-liberty-proud-boys

Gilligan, C. (2022, November 11). United States veteran population, 2005–2021. *U.S. News*. https://datawrapper.dwcdn.net/CpPbw/3/

Gladstone, B. (2022). On Zello: A recruitment & organizing tool for the far Right | On the Media. *WNYC Studios*. www.wnycstudios.org/podcasts/otm/segments/on-zello-recruitment-organizing-tool-far-right-on-the-media

Gopnik, A. (2015, February 13). Obama and the Crusaders. *The New Yorker*. www.newyorker.com/news/daily-comment/obama-crusaders

Gorski, P. S., & Perry, S. L. (2022). *The flag and the cross: White Christian nationalism and the threat to American democracy*. Oxford University Press.

Goudie, C., Markoff, B., Tressel, C., & Weidner, R. (2022, March 24). New motive revealed in militia plot to kidnap, murder Michigan Governor Gretchen Whitmer. *ABC7 Chicago*. https://abc7chicago.com/murder-plot-michigan-governor-gretchen-whitmer-wolverine-watchmen-militiamen/11678667/

Hale, S. (2019, May 21). Nashville police union loses (again) in legal fight against community oversight. *Nashville Scene*. www.nashvillescene.com/news/pithinthewind/nashville-police-union-loses-again-in-legal-fight-against-community-oversight/article_b3e91dc1-2560-57c7-ad8e-7218d60c68dc.html

Higgins, L. (2010, April 15). Militia group gave FBI information on Hutaree two years ago, e-mails show. *AnnArbor.Com*. http://annarbor.com/news/militia-group-provided-fbi-information-on-hutaree-two-years-ago-emails-show/

Higgins, L. (2012, January 19). FBI informant in Hutaree case was arrested for firing gun during argument. *AnnArbor.Com*. www.annarbor.com/news/crime/fbi-informant-in-hutaree-case-was-arrested-for-firing-gun-at-wife/

Hopper, T. (2017, August 24). The weird time Nazis made common cause with black nationalists. *Nationalpost*. https://nationalpost.com/news/the-weird-time-nazis-made-common-cause-with-black-nationalists

Hosenball, M., & Lynch, S. N. (2021, August 21). Exclusive: FBI finds scant evidence U.S. Capitol attack was coordinated—sources. *Reuters*. www.reuters.com/world/us/exclusive-fbi-finds-scant-evidence-us-capitol-attack-was-coordinated-sources-2021-08-20/

HRC. (2023, May 17). Gov. DeSantis signs slate of extreme anti-LGBTQ+ bills, enacting a record-shattering number of discriminatory measures into law. *Human Rights Campaign*. www.hrc.org/press-releases/gov-desantis-signs-slate-of-extreme-anti-lgbtq-bills-enacting-a-record-shattering-number-of-discriminatory-measures-into-law

Hughes, B., & Miller-Idriss, C. (2021, April 27). Uniting for total collapse: The January 6 boost to accelerationism. *Combating Terrorism Center at West Point*. https://ctc.westpoint.edu/uniting-for-total-collapse-the-january-6-boost-to-accelerationism/

Indiana Militia: We're Not Like Hutaree. (2010, April 4). NBC Chicago. www.nbcchicago.com/news/local/indiana-militia-were-not-like-hutaree/2091934/

Informant: Kansas plot formed after Pulse attack. (2018, March 29). *KSNT 27 News*. www.ksnt.com/news/informant-kansas-plot-formed-after-pulse-attack/

Inwood, J. F. J., & Bonds, A. (2017). Property and whiteness: The Oregon standoff and the contradictions of the U.S. settler state. *Space and Polity, 21*(3), 253–268.

Jabali, M. (2020, April 8). Trump Waffles on coronavirus aid to Michigan because of sexism. *The Intercept*. https://theintercept.com/2020/04/08/coronavirus-trump-whitmer-michigan/

Jackson, S. (2020). *Oath Keepers: Patriotism and the edge of violence in a right-wing antigovernment group*. Columbia University Press.

Jaffe, L., & Gillum, J. (2021, January 28). "This is war": Inside the secret chat where far-right extremists devised their post-capitol plans. *ProPublica*. www.propublica.org/article/this-is-war-inside-the-secret-chat-where-far-right-extremists-devised-their-post-capitol-plans

Jensen, M. (2022). Extremist group/movement affiliations of the January 6 capitol rioters. *START.umd.edu*. National Consortium for the Study of Terrorism and Responses to Terrorism. www.start.umd.edu/publication/extremist-groupmovement-affiliations-january-6-capitol-rioters

Kang, C., & Frenkel, S. (2020, June 27). 'PizzaGate' conspiracy theory thrives anew in the TikTok era. *The New York Times*. www.nytimes.com/2020/06/27/technology/pizzagate-justin-bieber-qanon-tiktok.html

Kelleher, J. B., & Damico, R. (2012, March 29). Hutaree militia walk from jail after charges dismissed. *Reuters*. www.reuters.com/article/us-usa-crime-militia-idUSBRE82S1EX20120329

Keller, D. (2022, June 28). Lawful but awful? Control over legal speech by platforms, governments, and internet users. *The University of Chicago Law Review Online*. https://lawreviewblog.uchicago.edu/2022/06/28/keller-control-over-speech/

Krafcki, M. (2021, March 4). FBI testifies Wolverine watchmen were trying to instigate a second civil war. *WWMT*. https://wwmt.com/news/local/fbi-testifies-wolverine-watchmen-were-trying-to-instigate-a-second-civil-war

Kriner, M. (n.d.). An introduction to militant accelerationism. *ARC*. Retrieved April 16, 2023, from www.accresearch.org/shortanalysis/an-introduction-to-militant-accelerationism

Kriner, M., & Cooter, A. (2023). America's militant nostalgia: The role of accelerationism in the contemporary militia-patriot movement. In M. A. Argentino & A. Amarasingam (Eds.), *Far-right culture: The Art, Music, and Everyday Practices of Violent Extremists*. Routledge.

Kriner, M., & Lewis, J. (2021, February 18). The evolution of the Boogaloo movement. *Combating Terrorism Center at West Point*. https://ctc.westpoint.edu/the-evolution-of-the-boogaloo-movement/

Laats, A. (2012). Red schoolhouse, burning cross: The Ku Klux Klan of the 1920s and educational reform. *History of Education Quarterly*, 52(3), 323–350.

Lawrence, D. F., & Toropin, K. (2022, December 1). Convicted Oath Keeper leader preyed on veterans looking for meaning after service. *Military.Com*. www.military.com/daily-news/2022/12/01/convicted-oath-keeper-leader-preyed-veterans-looking-meaning-after-service.html

Lehr, D. (2021). *White hot hate: A true story of domestic terrorism in America's heartland*. Mariner Books.

Li, W., & Lartey, J. (2023, March 25). New FBI data shows more hate crimes. These groups saw the sharpest rise. *The Marshall Project*. www.themarshallproject.org/2023/03/25/asian-hate-crime-fbi-black-lgbtq

Liptak, K. (2020, May 1). Trump tweets support for Michigan protesters, some of whom were armed, as 2020 stress mounts. *CNN*. www.cnn.com/2020/05/01/politics/donald-trump-michigan-gretchen-whitmer-protests/index.html

Mallin, A. (2022, June 9). Just before Jan. 6 hearing, 3 Capitol rioters express regret, ask for mercy. *ABC News*. https://abcnews.go.com/Politics/jan-hearing-capitol-rioters-express-regret-mercy/story?id=85290390

Mangan, D. (2023, March 6). DOJ says at least 1,000 Trump supporters arrested for Jan. 6 Capitol riot. *CNBC*. www.cnbc.com/2023/03/06/doj-says-jan-6-capitol-riot-arrests-top-thousand-people.html

Max, S. (2019, October 23). Friction grows between Nashville community oversight board and police. *WPLN News*. https://wpln.org/post/friction-grows-between-nashville-community-oversight-board-and-police/

McVeigh, R. (2009). *The rise of the Ku Klux Klan: Right-wing movements and national politics* (Vol. 32). University of Minnesota Press.

Melzer, S. (2012). *Gun crusaders: The NRA's culture war*. NYU Press.

Mills, M. F. (2021). Obamageddon: Fear, the far right, and the rise of "doomsday" prepping in Obama's America. *Journal of American Studies*, 55(2), 336–365.

Murphy, J. (2022, January 5). *The veterans who stormed U.S. Capitol: Where are they now?* www.audacy.com/connectingvets/news/us-veterans-who-stormed-capitol-where-are-they-now

Murphy, A. R. (2009). Longing, Nostalgia, and Golden Age Politics: The American Jeremiad and the Power of the Past. *Perspectives on Politics*, 7(1), 125–141.

Murray, M. (2022, September 27). Poll: 61% of Republicans still believe Biden didn't win fair and square in 2020. *NBC News*. www.nbcnews.com/meet-the-press/meetthepressblog/poll-61-republicans-still-believe-biden-didnt-win-fair-square-2020-rcna49630

Naber, N. (2007). Introduction: Arab Americans and U.S. racial formations. In A. Jamal & N. Naber (Eds.), *Race and Arab Americans before and after 9/11: From invisible citizens to visible subjects* (pp. 1–45). Syracuse University Press.

Naber, N. (2008). "Look, Mohammed the terrorist is coming!" Cultural racism, nation-based racism, and the intersectionality of oppressions after 9/11. In A. Jamal & N. Naber (Eds.), *Race and Arab Americans before and after 9/11: From invisible citizens to visible subjects* (pp. 276–304). Syracuse University Press.

New Colony Media (Director). (2012, February 22). *Police in America #3 with Hutaree member and Antonio Buehler*. www.blogtalkradio.com/newcolony/2012/02/23/police-in-america-3-with-hutaree-member-and-antonio-buehler

Newhouse, A. (2021, May 20). The threat is the network: The multi-node structure of neo-fascist accelerationism. *Combating Terrorism Center at West Point*. https://ctc.westpoint.edu/the-threat-is-the-network-the-multi-node-structure-of-neo-fascist-accelerationism/

Papaycik, M. (2022, April 22). Florida's governor signs controversial bill banning critical race theory in schools. *WPTV News Channel 5 West Palm*. www.wptv.com/news/education/floridas-governor-to-sign-critical-race-theory-education-bill-into-law

Pape, R., & Ruby, K. (2021, February 2). The Capitol rioters aren't like other extremists. *The Atlantic*. www.theatlantic.com/ideas/archive/2021/02/the-capitol-rioters-arent-like-other-extremists/617895/

Pfleger, P. (2023, April 20). *Nashville and Memphis created police oversight boards seeking accountability. Now Tennessee's Republican supermajority is abolishing them*. https://wpln.org/post/nashville-and-memphis-created-police-oversight-boards-seeking-accountability-now-tennessees-republican-supermajority-is-abolishing-them/

Postmes, T., & Spears, R. (1998). Deindividuation and antinormative behavior: A meta-analysis. *Psychological Bulletin, 123*(3), 238–259. https://doi.org/10.1037/0033-2909.123.3.238

Price, M., & Sonner, S. (2020, June 4). 3 men tied to "boogaloo" movement plotted to terrorize Las Vegas protests, officials say. *ABC7 Los Angeles*. https://abc7.com/boogaloo-las-vegas-protest-news-george-floyd/6231077/

Proxmire, C. (2020, June 8). Lake Orion protest affirms Black Lives Matter movement. *Oakland County Times*. https://oaklandcounty115.com/2020/06/08/lake-orion-protest-affirms-black-lives-matter-movement/

Purtill, C. (2015, January 13). #FreedomOfSpeech: What that means in the US, Britain and France. *The World from PRX*. https://theworld.org/stories/2015-01-13/freedomofspeech-what-means-us-britain-and-france

Reed, K. (2022, August 11). Retrial opens of two men who plotted to kidnap the governor of Michigan in 2020. *World Socialist Web Site*. www.wsws.org/en/articles/2022/08/11/moar-a11.html

Rondeaux, C., & Dalton, B. (2022, January 6). What role did the far-right platform parler play in the Jan. 6 insurrection? *Slate*. https://slate.com/technology/2022/01/parler-jan-6-capitol-facebook-twitter.html

Ruisch, B. C., & Ferguson, M. J. (2023). Did Donald Trump's presidency reshape Americans' prejudices? *Trends in Cognitive Sciences, 27*(3), 207–209.

Savidge, M., & Cartaya, M. (2021, March 14). US record guns sales: Americans bought guns in record numbers in 2020 during a year of unrest. *CNN*. www.cnn.com/2021/03/14/us/us-gun-sales-record/index.html

Shamsian, J. (2021, March 3). A lawyer for an accused Oath Keeper Capitol rioter says the group's "quick reaction force" of weapon suppliers was actually just one guy. *Insider*.

www.insider.com/oath-keepers-quick-reaction-force-capitol-riot-overstated-lawyer-2021-3

Shapero, J. (2022, September 7). Violent extremist movement 'Boogaloo Bois' reemerges on Facebook: Report. *The Hill.* https://thehill.com/policy/technology/3632264-violent-extremist-movement-boogaloo-bois-reemerges-on-facebook-report/

Tanfani, J., Berens, M., & Parker, N. (2021, January 11). How Trump's pied pipers rallied a faithful mob to the Capitol. *Reuters.* www.reuters.com/article/us-usa-trump-protest-organizers-insight-idUSKBN29G2UP

Temple-Raston, D. (2010, April 12). How the FBI got inside the Hutaree Militia. *NPR.* www.npr.org/2010/04/12/125856761/how-the-fbi-got-inside-the-hutaree-militia

Toropin, K. (2023, January 23). 4 More Oath Keepers—including an army veteran—convicted of sedition over Jan. 6. *Military.Com.* www.military.com/daily-news/2023/01/23/4-more-oath-keepers-including-army-veteran-convicted-of-sedition-over-jan-6.html

Torres Guzman, D. (2022, May 2). Tennessee's community oversight boards restricted by state laws. *Tennessee Lookout.* https://tennesseelookout.com/2022/05/02/tennessees-community-oversight-boards-restricted-by-state-laws/

Villarreal, D. (2020, November 16). *Hate crimes under Trump surged nearly 20 percent says FBI report.* Newsweek. www.newsweek.com/hate-crimes-under-trump-surged-nearly-20-percent-says-fbi-report-1547870

Walker, J. (2018, June 29). *Hate speech and freedom of expression: Legal boundaries in Canada.* Parliament of Canada. https://lop.parl.ca/sites/PublicWebsite/default/en_CA/ResearchPublications/201825E

Walker, J. L. (2009). *Brandenburg v. Ohio.* www.mtsu.edu/first-amendment/article/189/brandenburg-v-ohio

Walters, G. (2022, October 5). The Oath Keepers' Jan. 6 texts sure do look damning. *Vice.* www.vice.com/en/article/n7zqjq/oath-keepers-trial-texts-recordings-opening-arguments

What is a hate crime, and what's the data behind it? (2023, May 1). *USAFacts.* https://usafacts.org/articles/hate-crime-data-value-expanding-our-sources/

Whitmer, G. (2020, October 27). The plot to kidnap me. *The Atlantic.* www.theatlantic.com/ideas/archive/2020/10/plot-kidnap-me/616866/

Wilson, T. (2022, April 11). Jan. 6 defendants raise more than $3.5 million through GiveSendGo. *Rolling Stone.* www.rollingstone.com/politics/politics-features/give-send-riot-jan-6-defendants-have-raised-more-than-3-5-million-through-christian-crowdfunding-website-1332787/

Wong, J. C. (2020, August 19). Facebook restricts more than 10,000 QAnon and US militia groups. *The Guardian.* www.theguardian.com/us-news/2020/aug/19/facebook-qanon-us-militia-groups-restrictions

7 Conclusion
Signals of Violence and Informed Best Practices

"Oh, you're the good guys," a female police officer reportedly told three militia members who were putting on Bluetooth headsets in a parking lot in Dearborn, Michigan, in Spring 2012. The headsets were intended to facilitate these members' communication with each other while they attended what they expected to be a contentious rally. Terry Jones, a virulently Islamophobic pastor from Florida was there to rail against Muslims just across the street from one of the largest Islamic Centers in the country. Most Michigan militia members I spoke with, including the three who attended this rally, said they did not care for Jones or his message but were concerned that his free speech rights had been unconstitutionally curtailed during a previous visit. They believed it was their duty to try to intervene should this encroachment happen again because, they said, they believed it would set a precedent for free speech being easily denied to other people under different circumstances if such incursions were not appropriately fought.

The officer approached these members who were dressed in regular clothes, not camouflage, and had no other visible signs of militia affiliation because, she told them, their identical headsets drew her attention. They were armed, and while all three reported having their sidearms appropriately concealed in compliance with Michigan law at the time, law enforcement and military members can often spot clothing bulges or other signals of a hidden weapon, so she may have at least suspected the presence of their weapons, too. She asked what they were doing there, and one member said he told her, "We're here to protect the free speech of both sides." She reportedly flipped up her sunglasses, gave her positive endorsement, and offered suggestions of behaviors in the crowd they could watch for that might signal impending violence: individuals praying alone or wearing heavy clothing that was incongruent with the warm weather as both could signal someone intending to use an explosive device.

This encounter has clear parallels to the interaction that would capture national media coverage eight years later between teenager Kyle Rittenhouse and police in Kenosha, Wisconsin. Police there gave verbal encouragement and water to Rittenhouse and other armed civilians with whom

DOI: 10.4324/9781003361657-8

they perceived allyship against people protesting the police shooting of Jacob Blake. The advice the officer reportedly gave the three militia members in Dearborn exemplifies an in-group versus outgroup mentality where police are not protecting both sides, but rather aligning only with people who are enforcing patterned white supremacy, even if unintentionally. Both the specific recommendations she gave clearly corresponded much more to possible behavior of Muslim protestors (many of whom were in traditional religious clothing in pictures I saw from the event) than to Jones' Christian supporters.

Both pieces of advice she offered were stereotypical of Muslims and their beliefs, but both were also rather superficial. They were indicators that had become very commonly represented in TV and other popular culture of terrorist violence, meaning that the officer did not really share any meaningful intelligence information or reveal anything these members should not have already known given their militia members' claims of having a refined situational awareness relative to the average person. She also declined, when they asked, to give them her personal cell phone number or a radio connection that would have allowed them to contact her directly if they observed a danger. Instead, she told them to call 911, just as any other person attempting to contact the police would need to do.

I couldn't help but wonder if, perhaps, the officer was not as sympathetic as these members believed. She was able to learn their names, their militia affiliation, and their stated intention while, in return, only giving a general sense of legitimacy to their already-planned surveillance actions. I say "only" because this example should be contrasted to instances of open alignment with militia groups or cases where investigational information has been inappropriately shared with them (Polantz et al., 2021), but a verbal endorsement of their character and presence is nontrivial and perhaps emboldening, as Rittenhouse's case demonstrates. I was unable to track down this officer to ask for her perspective on the encounter, but the interaction as the members recounted to me nonetheless shows how there is a potential for law enforcement to collaborate with militia members and how, at least in theory, this collaboration could be either helpful or detrimental to broader safety concerns. LEOs might use militia members as reliable sources of information about problematic activities of which militia members are aware. However, LEOs may take for granted the risk from some members, including cases where they see militias as potential enforcement extensions of their own prejudices. These options are not necessarily mutually exclusive given the role of policing in upholding systemic white supremacy more generally.

I've had innumerable interactions with local, state, federal, and international LEOs regarding my militia expertise, and those interactions increased in frequency after January 6th. They often want to ask what I think we can do to assess militia danger and help prevent violence in the future. I do not pretend to have perfect or complete solutions; these groups can vary enormously in terms of their motivations and tactics and the landscape as a whole will continue to evolve. There will never be a one-size-fits-all solution.

I nonetheless think there are some reasonable suggestions that my experiences can offer for initial assessments.

Millenarian or accelerationist units are both easy to identify, but only if we have access to their writings, conversations, or other materials. When a group has no real public presence, it can be very difficult to assess their ideological leanings, especially from a completely outside perspective. The factors I identify below are intended to help determine the potential risk a given unit poses, regardless of how they are labeled by either unit members or researchers. Drawing across my militia experiences, including the case studies I detailed in the last chapter and interactions with law enforcement, I've developed a list of red flags to help identify which militia groups are likely to pose the biggest risk of violence. These red flags fall under two broad categories: Behavior and Beliefs, and Network Characteristics.

Each item below has frequently been a factor in units arrested for alleged plots as well as in units closely connected to or supportive of those units. They are absent or very rare in other units with no criminal connections. The below assessment is intended to be more of a measurement index, where groups with more flags are more likely to be violent, rather than either a strict typology or a perfectly predictive framework. All these factors can, and often do, amplify each other, but because of the strong degree of interconnectedness of the flags subsumed under Network Characteristics, I provide the illustrative examples for that category after separately discussing each variable.

Behavior and Beliefs

Target Specification

Almost all militia units think of the government as an undifferentiated mass, and it is fairly common to hear comments like, "all politicians should be hung" at militia gatherings. While distasteful, such sentiments are largely symbolic and indicative of a belief that the country has already slid too far away from members' imagined ideal. Few, if any, members who express only this broad sentiment mean that they believe all politicians should literally die, let alone that they intend to participate in bringing about that end. The performative nature of the claim is underscored by the stated choice of execution by hanging—a method much more common in the US in a nostalgic past—instead of by the firearms of which they are so fond.

In sharp contrast, units or members who talk about specific plans for violent action or unambiguously identify concrete targets should immediately rise to the top of the concern list. Even minimal steps toward targeting specific individuals or physical spaces should be taken quite seriously. We saw examples of this when the Wolverine Watchmen definitively identified Governor Whitmer as their desired target early in their complaining about COVID restrictions and when the Crusaders pinpointed a specific apartment complex for their plot.[1] Members who introduce ideas of concrete violence can be radicalizing forces within otherwise peaceful units if they are encouraged or allowed to stay with those units because of how negative perseverations can be amplified by groupthink into fully fledged plots for action.

Cavalier Training Practices

The vast majority of militia units I followed in the field were incredibly conscientious of safety concerns, especially basic firearm handling procedures such as keeping the barrel of your weapon safely pointed away from people, ensuring a weapon is empty or at least on safety before handing it to someone else, or even checking that everyone at the range is using appropriate hearing protection.

I have less direct observational experience with units who did not use good safety during trainings, but different units' reports of unsafe practices at Hutaree trainings were later confirmed at their trial, and attorneys on both the Crusaders and Watchmen cases expressed disapproval of how some of those units' firearms usage appeared to have irresponsibly happened while under the influence of either alcohol or weed. Units that do not adhere to basic safety may be indicative of having leaders and members who have a problem with general rule following, and it is not a large stretch to think they may be more likely to break the law in addition to common sense safety regulations. It is also possible that they could be higher than average risk takers or have a general lower respect for preserving life that potentially makes them comfortable both defying safety procedures with their unit and with plotting to harm other people, even though legal and other consequences may follow from their actions.

Open Discrimination

Individual militia members have a range of personal prejudices. But when exclusion, whether on the basis of sex, gender, race, religion, or some other identity characteristic, is central to a militia unit's organizing principles or even used to define a unit's identity, that unit probably has greater than average antipathy toward anyone they believe to be an outgroup member. A few groups I have encountered, for example, exclude women from participation altogether or specifically exclude them from training and are openly invested in traditional gender roles in a way that enhances the hostility they feel toward women who challenge their prowess. One of my interviewees who sometimes trained with women, but only during multi-unit events, shouted, "permission to bring a woman aboard!" at his campsite as if it were a ship that I might doom with my presence when I arrived to speak with him. He later told me during the interview:

> You're probably goin' to get mad—my wife gets mad—but I think if women were more responsible with themselves and their bodies, we

wouldn't have the problems we have in this world. And that makes a lot of women mad. I don't know how you feel, but it's just, you know, it's like the game is like the fox and the hound, the way I look at it. You know, the guy saw the fox, the girl, and some girls are just so *stupid*. And I mean some girls are very respectable about themselves, you know, and you're not . . . uh, I'm sorry, but I do blame a lot of the problems in society on female behavior.

In this stammering response, this man, who was by far the most overtly misogynistic militia member I encountered in my field work not only victim blamed rape victims and, in the context of my preceding question, alluded to abortion being avoidable if women just controlled themselves, he also rapidly insulted women's collective intelligence and infantilized them by quickly shifting to calling them "girls" while also attributing broader but unspecified social problems to them alone. His voice rose loud enough during this part of the conversation that other unit members could easily hear him, and none seemed to object to his allegations.

When units, rather than just individual members, participate in exclusionary behavior, it means most of its members are likely strongly invested in stereotypes about various out-groups. Units like this are breeding grounds for those stereotypes and potentially for hate speech or violent action against those groups. If units in part form around notions of whiteness being somehow vulnerable to threat, they may be particularly susceptible to blending with or at least being influenced by overtly white supremacist organizations.

Religion[2] as an excluding factor potentially takes a key role with considerations of militia violence (Aho, 1995; Churchill, 2009), in part because appealing to a higher power makes religion-centered units much less likely to question their belief structures (Juergensmeyer, 2003). Members of the Hutaree and Crusaders all reportedly reviled Muslims and used their own contrasting Christian identity when selecting their unit monikers. A Muslim member from a different unit told me about his experience trying to cross-train with the Hutaree. He and two other members were told they would have to start attending the Hutaree church if they wanted to have regular interactions with Hutaree members. When my source revealed his religious affiliation during that conversation, he said they told him that he had to leave and was unwelcome on their property.[3] Refusing to interact with this man even casually after he revealed his Muslim identity shows how strongly the Hutaree defined themselves through exclusionary religious practices.

Conspiracism

Conspiratorial thinking is, generally, associated with an us versus them or an in-group versus outgroup mentality (Jolley et al., 2020; Swami, 2012). Conspiracy theories were so common in the early days of the militia movement that they were synonymous with it. They declined through the early 2000s, and have experienced a clear resurgence following the Trump administration's entanglement with QAnon theories and support (Miller et al., 2021; Wong, 2020). Some units that allegedly engaged in violent plotting have never let the older theories go. One man I interviewed who later became a Hutaree member, for example talked at length about the New World Order; several of his DVDs discussed how the US government was truly responsible for 9/11 and how it, alongside other attacks or disasters, were part of a "centuries-long" plan to somehow reduce the world population and enslave the remainder of humanity to vaguely benefit a handful of political and economic elites. Newer QAnon theories asserting that pedophilia is endemic to the Democratic Party are, in actuality, more a repackaging of these older conspiracy fantasies than they are entirely new creations. Both old and new versions present evil global elites as working against the common good and call for brave patriots, who, unlike most of the population, can cleverly see through their ruses, to salvage a declining nation.

The Wolverine Watchmen organized around a different but related set of conspiracy theories revolving around COVID-19 and its mitigation. Some of these fantasies insisted that following government mandates about curfews or business closures would be a rapid, slippery slope to more infringements on individual liberties and mass, unquestioning compliance with government overreach. Some went so far as to suggest there was no such thing as COVID, and that the whole pandemic was orchestrated by the government to achieve population control (Al-Ramahi et al., 2021). Other theories more specifically insisted that normalizing masks would usher in mass acceptance of other garments that covered the face, namely burqas, and thus open the door for the spread of Islam (Khalel, 2020). At least some Watchmen members shared memes or otherwise endorsed all these COVID conspiracy theories before their arrests.

Conspiracy theories are most dangerous when they are integrated into unit-level ideology and action plans like this. Repetitive focus on these theories' promised threats not only reifies them but also heightens the sense of distrust members have for the nefarious government that is perceived to be behind the threats. Unit-level support for conspiracy theories brews groupthink and likely feeds into paranoid thinking about a range of government activities that could reasonably foster violence in some individuals as their sense of desperation grows.

Secrecy

At the moment, the vast majority of militia groups are keeping a low profile. Many had no choice but to disappear from Facebook and move to more private corners of the internet when the company deplatformed them. Some of those groups instituted more rigorous vetting processes in these new spaces, trying to ensure that only true compatriots were added to their social media ranks, rather than detractors or infiltrators. Before this change, groups that were open and transparent were much less prone to violent expressions than units that hid behind closed groups. Closed groups allowed for keeping activities somewhat more hidden, perhaps bringing out truer sentiments or giving the false impression of safety from law enforcement investigations. More importantly, those closed spaces had the ability to make loners or people who felt alienated from other social groups believe they had found a place that was unique and special in its exclusivity. This desire to belong to something special because of its secrecy and exclusivity is perhaps suggestive of unsavory underlying motives for joining a militia group. Though the social media landscape has changed, we know that some groups have made their way back on to Facebook (Carless, 2022), and the general distinction between open and closed groups (and those who seek them out) is likely still relevant there and on other platforms.

Other units that chose to pull down their public facing websites and other social media presences after January 6th did not necessarily do so because they believed they were doing anything wrong, but rather because they believed they needed to avoid guilt by association. Those units have not uniformly slipped into extremism or violent plotting, yet it nonetheless remains true that units that are comparatively open and transparent about their trainings and other actions offer less cause for concern than those that are not so forthcoming. Units whose members take great pains to hide their identities and their faces, especially if their history of doing so predates recent changes, may be attempting to avoid identification while conducting criminal or at least questionable activities.

Network Characteristics

Strict Hierarchy

Most militias, like other organizations, have at least some degree of hierarchy that usually corresponds to a nexus of military experience and willingness to lead a group of people who reject authority figures as a main feature of their personality. Leaders tend to guide unit action, schedule trainings and other events, and present on political items of concern; however, they frequently encourage other members to share their skills and voice their opinions. They talk—or more typically, joke—their way through areas of disagreement, and generally develop a framework where other members can step in with no disruption to the unit if the leader is sick or otherwise unavailable for a planned activity. Units that defy this typical framework in one (or more) of several ways tend to be on the more problematic end of the militia spectrum.

Leader Worship

Units whose leaders take an authoritarian response by rebuking any and all critique or refusing to allow other members to contribute to the group's activities and priorities easily foster an environment where the leader's perspective is rarely questioned. Leaders like this may be charismatic and create a strong loyalty in the unit members such that they overlook warnings of radicalization and are reluctant to talk to anyone outside the unit about what they are witnessing.

Inverted Expertise

Militia members typically have great respect for military veterans and want to learn from them. In nonviolent units, this means that veterans are helping others refine their aim at the range or teaching survivalist-type skills while recounting their glory days. Because of their military experiences, including organizing and speaking with people from a variety of walks of life, veterans in these groups very commonly end up in leadership positions within their units. When veterans are, instead, subservient to a unit leader with zero military experience, it may be a signal that the leader is hoping to channel veterans' listlessness or anger from their military experiences into something dangerous.

Stolen Valor

Sometimes militia leaders with no military experience try to reinforce their authority by appropriating military titles like Commander or General for their units. From what I have observed, this is not only an instance of playing dress-up but also a further effort to legitimize themselves, especially in the eyes of real veterans in their unit. In other words, the hope seems to be that using a familiar terminological hierarchy may make it less likely these veterans would question their authority, despite the leader's inferior skills and knowledge. Military titles in militia units also frequently serve to further alienate these units from others who do not engage in this practice. Many told me that they viewed this kind of military rank structure as not only disingenuous, but profoundly disrespectful to those who had actually served. Some also viewed it as an inappropriate framing of militia units that they believe are supposed to supplement military and National Guard personnel, rather than replicate them.

Isolation

Most militias I have observed prioritize preparedness within their own communities but still believe it is crucial to be aware of other nearby militias so that they can coordinate in case of disaster. There are other units that are, in contrast, highly insular and paranoid even of other militia units. They tend to insist that their own trainings, goals, or tactics are both superior to other units' and, objectively, the only correct way to do things. Over time, this means members are increasingly isolated from different approaches not only to militia activity but also to politics or conspiracism. Militias that do not take this isolationist approach tend to believe isolating units have something to hide and, in my experience, have been unsurprised when members of such units are accused of violent plotting.

Familial Relationships

Insularity can also be amplified if multiple male members have familial connections within a given unit. Political ideology, perceived grievances, and other points of discussion more easily extend beyond militia gatherings when family connections exist in the unit. This can then further amplify the perceived urgency and importance of these issues as well as members' sense of despair or obligation to violently act to correct their perceived problems.

Network Characteristics in Practice

The case studies above all include examples of these structural and network red flags, which when present individually but especially in concert worsen processes of groupthink within a given unit. The Hutaree's leader, David Stone, did not have military experience but used a military rank structure in his unit. The man I interviewed who later became a Hutaree member was very angry about his military experience and told me that he was looking for a way to seek vengeance against the government. It became clear through their trial that Stone gave him a place where he felt both his experiences and his anger were valued even though he, himself, was not in a leadership position in the unit.

Stone cultivated an almost cult-like environment where the eight other core members of his unit included a woman he married (in a ceremony where an undercover FBI agent served as best man), his son, and his stepson. Additionally, all core members were also reportedly required to attend the church where Stone was pastor, and, according to a person connected to the case, were also generally required to participate in family events and other informal gatherings. This person told me that even some non-family members were expected to stay on the property, sleeping in a filthy trailer. The Hutaree members' primary social contacts happened only with each other. They were largely isolated from other people who were not members of the unit and were effectively withdrawn from many aspects of civil society. Stone's son and stepson had reportedly been homeschooled for most, if not all, of their education, further contributing to their limited view of the outside world. Stone allowed cross-training only very rarely with two other units whose leaders, like him, actively cultivated insularity and isolation for their members.

Patrick Stein, leader of the Crusaders, is unlikely to have been called charismatic by anyone. His authoritarian approach was much less subtle. Defense attorneys told me how he nonetheless seemed to be a persuasive influence on the other two defendants after they started pulling away from a larger militia unit and being more isolated. Stein's role radicalizing Islamophobic perspectives in the other men was also later noted in trial evidence (Levine, 2021a).

Stein, who at least sometimes used military rank terminology to reflect the unit hierarchy, had no military background and took the leadership position within the small unit over Curtis Allen, who would have been the more logical choice given his military experience and whose anger over his deployment experiences likely contributed to his involvement in the plot (Levine, 2021b).

Neither of the men identified as ringleaders for the Wolverine Watchmen's plotting served in the military, but all members held another member, Dan Chappel, in high regard because he was an Iraq War veteran. They turned to Chappel for inspiration about specifics of some of the plot and operational tactics (Krafcik, 2022). He, for instance, gave his opinion as to which model helicopter would be preferable for their mission when one of the plotters insisted that he could electronically commandeer one. What the Watchmen did not know was that Chappel was a CI and had been the one to report the unit to the feds after joining their message board and saying he had been concerned that members were planning to kill police officers (*ibid.*). The Watchmen also had a family unit, twin brothers Michael and William Null, who are still awaiting trial for their alleged role in the plot. The Watchmen were less insular overall, however, than some other units of concern including those comprising the other two case studies here. They regularly participated in other units' trainings, including across various state lines, sometimes using those joint events to try to recruit others to their plot. Unlike some of the other units, the Watchmen also relied on more of a communal planning strategy instead of a hierarchically rooted leader, perhaps because the unit was heavily infiltrated by law enforcement and CIs whose presence may have shifted conversational and other dynamics.

What Can We Do? Suggested Best Practices

Given the difficulty of observing red flags from outside a unit and given the likelihood of militias continuing to be an important social and political presence in coming years, what can we do about their potential for radicalization? I certainly do not have one-size-fits-all answers but share some of what I have learned from my observations and interactions with law enforcement without compromising investigational capacities.

Legal Strictures

Some researchers suggest that the best approach to handling US domestic militias is to legally ban them. This is tricky for a variety of reasons. Georgetown Law created a website that lists statutes from all 50 states that they say already make private militias illegal (*Fact Sheets*, 2020). However, many of these statutes are less clear-cut in their application than may seem to be true at first glance. For instance, many states' statutes include language about prohibiting activity meant to culminate in "civil disorder." Constitutionalist militias insist they have no such motives, and even some millenarian units with less of a militant accelerationist bent insist they are *restoring* order through their actions, thus potentially rationalizing even violent plots as being in the greater good. Militias' interpretations of these statutes as not applying to them have been reinforced through the lack of significant law enforcement or other legal interventions into their activities until recently, and most of the movement tends to view even those as necessary disruptions of problematic outlier units.

Many of the Georgetown fact sheets cite short snippets from state constitutions that say that paramilitary organizations must exist under the control of the state or, specifically, the governor. Most militias insist that they would follow legitimate orders in times of crisis and that they exist to supplement law enforcement or the National Guard when needed, thus, in their view, satisfying this legal requirement (Cooter, 2013). When all other responses to state legal strictures fail, members ultimately (and ironically) appeal to what they believe to be the unwavering federal supremacy of the Second Amendment over state or local legalities. They regularly capture this sentiment on clothing or online memes with the phrase "what part of 'Shall Not Be Infringed' don't you understand?"

The inefficacy of existing legislation is underscored by how several states are currently discussing new statutes to attempt to limit militia activities. New Mexico, for example, has proposed a bill that would prohibit "paramilitary organizations from performing drills with weapons in a group of three or more people" (Reynolds, 2023). Legislation like this will inflame passions well beyond militia membership rosters. Shooting clubs, competitive shooting organizations, and even concealed carry instructors may be worried about being impacted by this and similar laws and fight their implementation alongside the NRA and unaffiliated Second Amendment supporters alike.

Legislation like this, if passed, may have some small deterrent effect. If people are aware militia-type gatherings are being criminalized, they may avoid joining a militia unit. It is more likely, however, that in practice such legislation would be used after some other criminal action had occurred to increase a defendant's potential consequences. Militia members often gather on private property, even for trainings, and undoubtedly would cite their Constitutional right to assemble as nullifying state statutes like the one proposed in New Mexico if law enforcement did accost them.[4] Militias are likely to continue their activities regardless of any laws targeting them, especially if they are again openly encouraged by another President or teased with Presidential pardons. When directed at people who build a large part of their identity around defying illegitimate or tyrannical authority, legislation that targets militias without understanding the potential backlash effect may create more problems than it solves. As J.M. Berger (2018, p. 123) observes:

> Legitimacy is the most central component of an extremist in-group's identity construction—the most highly developed and best-protected asset that any extremist group possesses. So direct attacks on extremist

legitimacy may reinforce the notion that extreme measures are required to protect it.

LEO Rapport

I personally witnessed during my fieldwork and, later, in online spaces how problematic behavior including radicalization can result in militia ranks when members believe law enforcement are illegitimately targeting them (Cooter, 2013). I covered in my earlier work how law enforcement receive the most cooperation and respect when treating militia members like confidants who not only potentially inform them of problematic militia actors but also receive information about law enforcement concerns in return. Members who might otherwise inform on other units have a strong negative reaction to officers who, in contrast, treat them as presumptive criminals in the absence of evidence that would justify this label. In this circumstance, it is not only that members refuse to cooperate, some also engage in behavior that is actively disruptive to law enforcement goals. Some members remove themselves and their unit from public view or punitively cut off communication with other law enforcement contacts with whom they had previously cooperated, which makes signs of radicalization much more difficult to identify and prevent.

Other members do things like create cryptic memes or website messages that are intended to deplete the resources of the officers whom they believe to be monitoring these spaces. For example, several leaders of a unit I followed closely during my fieldwork were accosted by law enforcement, many of them while at their workplace, in the days leading up to the 2008 Pesidential election.[5] They had previously had what they thought was a good working relationship with LEOs in the area and were profoundly offended at their treatment and the assumptions about their potential violence that they believed were behind these interactions. Members who recounted how their local sheriffs had participated in the stop alongside federal agents were especially aggrieved because they viewed this as a betrayal from an officer who is sworn to protect the local community and its citizens. One man, still visibly irritated days after the interaction, told me that he called his long-term FBI contact and demanded to know why she was "stirring up a hornet's nest." In his view, these authoritarian interactions from LEOs were likely to create backlash of some kind within militia units who already distrust the government and its motives.

Another member made a graphic to be posted on the unit's website and distributed locally as a flier that advertised the "311 Militiapocalypse" for the day before the Presidential election. The background image looked, to me, to be a setting sun, but he said he chose it because it was ambiguous and could have been interpreted either as a sunset or as an explosion from an atomic bomb. Other members at that meeting were concerned the graphic would send the wrong message about their intentions but were quickly persuaded when the graphic's designer angrily talked about how FBI agents had cornered him at work in spite of years of attempted cooperation and how he intended this graphic to be retribution. He said he was sure that at least one FBI agent would be assigned the task of deciphering the message to discern the meeting's "real" purpose, and said he wished he could know how long it would take them to realize what the "311" meant even with "the 311th day of the year" being included on the image, underscoring his perception of FBI incompetence.

Some members have an even stronger reaction, not only attempting to distract law enforcement and waste their resources in a way that could damage urgent investigations, but by themselves becoming more radicalized. After the release of the 2009 DHS report on right-wing extremism that many interpreted as suggesting that returning veterans were prone to terrorism, anger toward the government was palpable in militia spaces, both from long-term members and prospective ones. Several people at those gatherings told me a version of classic labeling theory, saying, "if the government is going to treat me like a terrorist, I might as well *be* a terrorist." One member noted that as the government increasingly tried to control militia-minded people, the more they would be radicalized against the government as he said, "The tighter [government officials] squeeze, the more patriots will slip through their fingers."

We witnessed a similar radicalization in some members after Facebook deplatformed militia actors in 2020. Although Facebook is not an extension of the government, members saw the company as acting in bad-faith and perhaps based on incorrect or overgeneralizing information from law enforcement reports. Many also found this to amount to an infringement on free speech and free association given the platform's previous reach and accessibility, even if they recognized that free speech protections do not legally apply to private companies. Some members who were forced off the space talked to me and with each other on their new platforms about how they believed that this exclusion was a signal of more "persecution" to come and they needed to prepare both mentally and practically to fight against it. Some specifically discussed plans to buy more weapons because they believed there was a rapidly growing risk of direct confrontation with aggressive government actors.

Both the DHS report and deplatforming impacted all militia groups, but radicalization from perceived targeting can happen on a smaller scale as well, for example, if members of a unit are treated badly when another local unit is being investigated. This suggests that, when possible, LEOs should treat militia members with respect and assume that members generally understand how investigations work, especially given how some of them have military or law enforcement backgrounds and share their knowledge with others. One of the few publicly available militia articles that was written by LEOs also suggests this approach to establish proactive relationships to aid future investigations. The FBI agent authors write:

> How can law enforcement agencies determine which groups represent more of a threat than others? How can agency commanders assess the

specific beliefs and philosophies of the groups they may encounter in their own jurisdictions? In many cases, all they need to do is ask.

(Duffy & Brantley, 1997, p. 2)

It is, of course, crucial that LEOs maintain objectivity as they continue this dialogue. It is likely a best practice to have multiple officers who engage with a given unit and to have other oversights on these relationships to prevent overidentification because we know that some officers sympathize with militias' anti-federal government perspectives and may underestimate the risk that some units pose as a result (Agar, 2020; Cooter, 2013; Farris & Holman, 2023). Federal agents did not inform local law enforcement of their investigation into the Crusaders because of this very concern (Lehr, 2021).

Confidential Informant Movement

There will also be times that open dialogue between LEOs and militia members is obviously not possible, including when LEOs are infiltrating a unit to investigate them. One way that agencies seem to try to strike this balance is, at least in some circumstances, by placing a CI into groups that make a report on another unit. Legal proceedings in both the Hutaree and Crusaders investigations confirmed that a CI was first placed with the unit that made a report before the same CI was eventually moved to the unit they reported (Lehr, 2021; Reiter, 2012), Placing an informant in the reporting unit may be helpful for guarding against false reports that could be driven by the infighting that hallmarks nostalgic groups.

However, this approach also has risks. When the same CI is used across units, there is a concern that activities may escalate in the reported group before they are being meaningfully observed. If a group is truly engaging in dangerous action or plotting, they are also likely to become increasingly wary of newcomers as time progresses, making it difficult for the CI or other infiltrators to gain access later.

When the same CI is moved across units, it also increases the odds of a potential suspect discerning the CI's true purpose. People do change militia unit affiliations for a variety of reasons, but if a CI has raised suspicions about their intentions in the first unit, that information may be passed on to subsequent units. This is true even when there is acrimony between units because of how social networks can cut across them; friendships or other casual connections occasionally still exist across unit lines even if leaders or the units as a whole dislike each other. After court filings that the FBI had used a CI in its Hutaree investigation gained media attention, I saw how members of the unit that reported them quickly deduced the CI's identity on their private message board more than a year before his name was publicly confirmed at trial. They recounted how he had "disappeared" into the other group without the usual, slow disengagement that typically happens if someone is testing out different units for their personal fit. One long-time leader with military experience reminded others during that online discussion that he had told them he believed the man was likely connected to law enforcement when he very first joined their unit because he seemed to ask different questions than most newcomers. This particular suspicion did not seem to have filtered through to the Hutaree, but it exemplifies the kind of concerns that could be shared across unit lines in other cases. If a CI is outed during an investigation, that person may face serious danger and the investigation itself could be fatally hindered.

Further-damaged trust in the criminal justice process can also be a risk when court filings or testimony confirms that CIs have been embedded with a reporting unit. Members of the unit that reported the Hutaree insisted they had nothing to hide, and, because the CI attended events that were open to the public, were more retrospectively bemused than upset by his presence. However, they ridiculed the FBI and other investigators for "wasting time" investigating their unit in this way, saying they would have been happy to have face-to-face conversations that supplemented their already-extensive public materials online. Some recognized that investigations cannot assume that potential suspects are honest or forthcoming with relevant information, but the key take away from these discussions was government incompetence. Perceptions of incompetence grew when people began to believe the Hutaree's alleged plot had been exaggerated by investigators, and some members also retrospectively cited the CI's initial placement in the reporting group as further evidence that the government was attempting to unjustly criminalize "true patriots" in the militia movement as a whole.

Tidy Prosecutions

Prosecutors and other officials involved in later stages of legal proceedings against militias also influence militia perceptions of the integrity of a given case and beyond. The Hutaree's defense team criticized the prosecutor for giving preferential treatment to the paid informant on the case during his own serious legal troubles (Reiter, 2012) and lambasted FBI agents for their behavior during the case, which included mockingly calling one of the Hutaree members "toothless Tina" in internal email communications (Baldas, 2012). Such disparagement is not only unprofessional, but also contributed to the perception of agents as being classist, anti-rural, and condescending toward the concerns of average citizens. Agents' behavior fed into stereotypes that have grown even stronger in recent years among nostalgic groups about supposedly liberal, elitist government actors who do not represent their best interests.

A militia member who attended the trial also told me that testimony for the case revealed that the FBI agent who infiltrated the Hutaree by, in part, truthfully recounting his experience with explosives (Temple-Raston, 2010) was responsible for introducing plans and materials for the bomb that the group was alleged to have been intending to use at a police officer's funeral.

I'm not certain this was confirmed in news coverage of the case, but for him and other members, the activities of the investigators had started to feel like entrapment based on what they believed to be agents' inappropriate interference.

Allegations of entrapment were also part of the defense strategy for the Crusaders. The primary CI there seems to have been an upstanding citizen with no criminal record, but the FBI raised some eyebrows by compensating him more than $30,000, according to attorneys on the case, and giving him a car (Lehr, 2021). The car—though not exactly a top-tier model—was particularly ironic because, according to defendant Wright during my interview with him, the CI specifically recounted seeing a refugee driving a very nice new car and implied it must have come at taxpayers' expense. Crusaders' leader Stein was especially aggrieved by the notion that Muslim refugees were getting "free stuff" and "taking advantage of the government," and Wright said the CI habitually instigated Stein's emotions on this point. Wright went so far as to say that Stein "didn't have any issues with Somalis until [the CI] came around." This was a clear allusion to the claim that this CI, at the behest of federal agents, was the one ultimately responsible for the alleged plot. The perception of entrapment was also enhanced by how other investigators on the case posing as members of sympathetic groups were responsible for suggesting and providing Stein with certain weapons and bomb-making chemicals (ibid.) that he almost certainly would have been unable to otherwise obtain.

Allegations of entrapment and other investigational misconduct were even more salient for the Watchmen, some of whom are, as of this writing, are still seeking routes for appeal. Defense attorneys on this case discovered that one of the investigating FBI agents had been accused of perjury in a different infiltration. Another was accused of domestic assault, which may not have impaired his objectivity on the case but did much to impugn his character. Yet another had started a security business on the side without proper approval to do so, and perhaps improperly shared details of this FBI casework to drum up customers (Bensinger & Garrison, 2021). Unlike the prosecutors on the Hutaree case who had to deal with allegations of investigational impropriety during the trial, the Watchmen prosecutors left these agents off the stand for most of the proceedings, likely helping jurors with the perceived integrity of the case.

Attorneys argued the defendants had been "targeted" by informants because of their social media presences where they, including Fox who had an Anarchist flag in his video backgrounds, railed against the government. They told me that on many occasions, "there were more CIs in the room than there were actual members," and that may have literally been true at some points of the investigation given that there were 12 CIs compared to the 14 people who were arrested (Garrison & Bensinger, 2021). Attorneys argued that it was one or more of the CIs who were responsible for making Facebook pages for the group, for encouraging the defendants to recruit others to their social media pages, and even for first suggesting the kidnapping plot as a way to send a message about how members would not tolerate encroaching government tyranny during the pandemic (Bensinger & Garrison, 2021). A promotion for an upcoming podcast about Buzzfeed's incredulous coverage of the trial and its evidence describes the case this way:

> Far from disciplined killers, the men accused of the heinous crime were in fact loudmouth stoner goofballs who spun wild fantasies, focused largely on bodybuilding and drinking beer, and in some cases seemed blissfully unaware that they were even engaged in a plot at all. . . . [T]he FBI built its case on a series of confidential informants who themselves could not stop committing crimes and engaging in bizarre behavior. Even some of the FBI agents themselves were caught in uncomfortable situations. It was ugly and embarrassing all-around.
> (White, 2022)

Most people would, of course, prefer that law enforcement and prosecutors engaged with any case follow the rules and concretely demonstrate their evidence beyond any shadow of a doubt. Those stakes are even higher with defendants who may become martyrs for groups that already fundamentally distrust the government. Any error or appearance of impropriety not only creates further distrust in a single case's outcome but also heightens anger and distrust for government actors across the board. Legal appeals for some of the Watchmen defendants may or may not be successful, but continuing negative coverage of prosecutorial integrity even from relatively liberal media outlets gives fodder for the broader nostalgic group landscape to argue that they are being unjustly targeted by a tyrannical government. It also risks other, currently unaffiliated individuals becoming persuaded by the targeting argument and joining that landscape. We are similarly seeing that January 6th insurrection defendants are claiming the government has victimized them by exaggerating their actions. A nontrivial number of those defendants who have set up GoFundMe or similar donation accounts asking for help with legal fees and other expenses insist upon their innocence alongside descriptions of what good, Christian husbands and fathers they are, attempting to reference the image of persecuted, ideal settler-patriots to bolster their defense (T. Wilson, 2022).

Other Best Practices

In addition to investigation and prosecution integrity, we've seen other areas where criminal justice procedures have fallen short in assessing threats from militias and other nostalgic groups. Law enforcement agencies largely failed to take seriously the social media posts that discussed "Stopping the Steal" before January 6th happened (Goldman & Feuer, 2023), and while some agencies have since ramped up their efforts to monitor social media, this remains a difficult task. Many groups have moved to more secure platforms, some of which have entirely closed or at least limited public footprints that make monitoring difficult. Most groups still seem susceptible to infiltration and observation, but this process takes both time and skill in a way that cannot be easily scaled across the numerous platforms now available. This resource burden could be reduced through improved cross-agency communication channels or, better yet, a centralized database to facilitate tracking and sharing concerns regarding suspect online communications. It is unclear whether there is presently sufficient monitoring of these spaces to meaningfully anticipate and prevent future violence.

Studies of online spaces also cannot happen at the exclusion of in-person interventions. Some units will behave very differently online compared to in person, and in-person communications with LEOs may, in some cases, themselves serve as a deterrent to violent plotting. LEOs should generally be aware of militias that operate in their area and attempt to make contacts for informational purposes; however, those agents must have appropriate training on the range of militia activities and their potential risks. Agents would also benefit from having at least some shared background or other factors with groups in their area because training is less effective than cultural experiences for conveying some contextual information that necessary for quickly and accurately assessing these groups and their statements. Officers should, ideally, work in pairs and be debriefed by other officers to help prevent cases of overidentification between officers and the people they are monitoring.

Lower Barriers to Contact for Legitimate Concerns

At least some law enforcement agencies have open communication channels with established researchers, but researchers who are younger or who are investigating relatively unknown entities may have difficulties in appropriately reporting their concerns. As an example of this problem, in the early days of the Biden administration, a young researcher with whom I had previously been in contact several times asked for advice about a group he had been following that took a radical turn. Based on what he told me, the leader of that group started exhibiting several of the red flags in this chapter, including offering a religious justification to his militia activity, insular practices on a variety of dimensions, and promoting an increasing sense of urgency to lash out against the government. This urgency was driven by the leader's personal problems that he relayed to his members in a way that was designed to stoke empathy, loyalty, and secrecy. Because of my preexisting relationships, I was able to quickly connect that researcher with the relevant agent in his geographical area. When I later followed up with that agent, he affirmed that the facilitation had been helpful because the concern would likely have "sat on a desk" without ever reaching him or being appropriately investigated had the researcher with no previous law enforcement connections attempted to call his office's switchboard. More resources for connecting emerging researchers to existing networks and for more systematically evaluating the qualifications of someone making a report might help identify threats earlier.

What About Communities?

I have talked a lot about law enforcement in this chapter and in other places in this book, but I want to emphasize that there is a history of policies and procedures that may have been created to disrupt violence and outright terrorism from nostalgic groups instead being weaponized against oppressed demographics and social justice–oriented organizations, especially in Black and Muslim communities (Aaronson, 2023; Harris, 2011; Norris & Grol-Prokopczyk, 2015; Williams, 2013, 2015). This is something I knew as someone who has studied and taught social movements for a very long time. My awareness of it became even more acute and personal, however, when I spoke with an agent from a state office of the DHS in the days before the 2020 Presidential election. He had emailed, saying that he wanted to call and chat about my knowledge of any militia activity in his area, but when we talked over the phone, his first questions to me were about the Black NFAC militia, which had recently received media attention for organizing well outside of his jurisdiction. The NFAC seemed to have coalesced for very different reasons than most white militias but were fallaciously seen as substantially more disruptive and threatening due to their Blackness (Carless & Stephens, 2021).

My reservations about working within the existing justice system nonetheless have little power to change that system, especially when there are clear signs of an impending threat. I don't have perfect answers to this problem, but I think that researchers should be looking for more ways to coordinate with civilian leaders of threatened communities to help prevent future violence. One way this can happen is through conversations with existing community or activist organizations. President Biden has initiated network-building efforts at the national level through a program called "United We Stand" (*www.unitedwestand.gov*). It aims to address "hate-fueled violence" through a variety of interventions including allocating prevention resources to communities and schools, improving information literacy, and partnering with my employer, the Center on Terrorism, Extremism, and Counterterrorism, to identify and address extremism on social media. Funding and implementation of programs like this are heavily dependent on political currents, however, and would benefit from additional outside advocacy.

As an example at the more local and immediate level, a coalition called Blueprint North Carolina (*https://blueprintnc.org/*) offers an example. Blueprint has built an impressive network of organizations that have different focuses, ranging from environmental justice to voter registration to AIDS advocacy and beyond. Collectively, and with Blueprint's guidance, these organizations aim to ensure real democracy for all citizens. Blueprint, for example, helped fund and organize barbecues and other community events at polling locations for the 2022 midterm elections. The goal was, as Serena Seabring, the executive director, told me, "to lower temperatures." She observed that if armed individuals show up to what is effectively a party, a celebration of the democratic process, it's much harder to be angry or suspicious, that someone is much less likely to cause trouble if they are met with a smile and someone offering them free food. The impetus for change should not be dumped on people who are oppressed by and suffer from white supremacy, but the reality is that these communities are typically left to fend for themselves against a variety of threats, including police violence, so proactive coalition building may be an effective violence-prevention tool.

Other communities are increasingly developing resources to support their neighbors in a variety of ways that do not involve calling police (*https://dontcallthepolice.com/*), and some of those organizations engage in opportunities to deescalate tensions between opposing groups before they reach a violent threshold. Another place to start might be Community Oversight Boards that usually have the primary job of monitoring police action but, at least in some places, also monitor for other community dangers and tend to be a point of contact for local organizations that are concerned about various dangers and power imbalances where they live. The SPLC has also partnered with the Polarization & Extremism Research & Innovation Lab to produce materials to help community leaders or families who believe they may be seeing signs of radicalization, especially in young people (SPLC, n.d.). The Western States Center similarly provides materials for libraries and other institutions that may be at the front lines of combatting misinformation and disinformation that contribute to radicalization (*Confronting*, n.d.).

Structural and Long-Term Solutions

We can also envision national policies that would help ameliorate nostalgia-inspired violence. As I've noted elsewhere, our educational practices as a general rule neglect to teach a robust version of either history or social studies that allows students to understand the limits of the American Dream. We currently spend an estimated $54 per student on STEM, attempting to have a future work force that can compete economically on the global stage, yet spend only five cents per student on civics (Scribner, 2022). As we've similarly seen with disinvestment in humanities in higher education, we neglect material that helps us contextualize and evaluate the utility and veracity of the natural sciences at our peril. Without fundamental lessons on how to be part of a functional society, our ability to capitalize on those well-funded STEM lessons is questionable as is our ability to maintain a democracy.

Lessons on how to evaluate evidence and identify disinformation and misinformation will also be increasingly crucial as artificial intelligence expands the capacity of bad actors to convincingly mislead and sow discord (ADL, 2023). Educational standards and practices are largely under the purview of the states, which may voluntarily adopt or reject national standards, but making those standards more robust could nonetheless have a positive effect. We also could, theoretically, provide incentives for their adoption through giving increased federal funding or other measures to school districts that opt into those standards.

Even more of a lofty goal, especially during times of heightened political and polarization, is a more inclusive cultural shift that nullifies perceptions of outgroup boundaries and their imagined threats. Promoting alternate versions of successful masculinity that allow men legitimized opportunities for platonic intimacy and that do not exclusively rely on economic success or sexual conquest has the potential to alleviate grievances that are pushing some young men into various violent and misogynistic actions (Messner, 2018; Miller-Idriss, 2020; Perliger et al., 2023). Fostering genuine, not merely token, inclusiveness and programs that help reduce racial prejudice are minimal first steps, not ultimate solutions, that we should be taking to disrupt structural white supremacy and ensure opportunity for everyone. Big, systemic problems require big, paradigm-shifting solutions, and we can aim for these large-scale outcomes even while recognizing the necessity of incomplete and piecemeal programs as intervening steps.

What might be surprising is that I have seen evidence that militia men are open to such lessons. For example, after a training in late summer near the close of my fieldwork, one unit's leader instructed members to rest and hydrate, even if they felt ok, saying he cared about each of them and wanted them to take care of themselves. This led to a discussion about the limits of masculine affection in American masculinity. One man elaborated by recounting how when he was stationed in South Korea, it was common for men to publicly hold hands as a sign of platonic affection. He said that while the practice felt very odd at first, he started to participate and eventually found it quite enjoyable. I watched the other members' faces as they intently listened to his story, and by the end, almost all were nodding their heads in agreement at the notion that men should have more opportunities to care for others without feeling belittled. In a parallel situation, one of my interviewees spoke at length with a member of Detroit's NAACP and told me that he had never really thought about how, in the metaphor of the American Dream as a foot race, Black people have a starting line that is unfairly delayed by slavery and systematic discrimination. He talked about how that conversation really "opened [his] eyes" to the challenges some of his neighbors faced in a way that he had not previously understood.

One-on-one interactions like this are not easily scaled, and we may also have concerns about their durability over time (Paluck et al., 2021). They nonetheless show more openness for change than we sometimes imagine in our current political environment and suggest two things about ameliorating our current polarization. First, facts do matter. There were depressing headlines several years ago that took a preliminary finding from psychology regarding something called the backfire effect and convinced too many people that countering conspiracism or false beliefs with facts always made the believer invest even further in their mistaken ideas. More research has confirmed that this effect is highly situation specific, if it exists at all (Swire-Thompson et al., 2022; Wood & Porter, 2019). Both examples above of impactful lessons include the transmission of factual information about different cultural and historical contexts, respectively, that helped change perceptions about current practices. More broadly, countering disinformation seems important, from my vantage point, not only for the purpose of attempting to convince people with mistaken beliefs but also for preventing others from thinking there are no valid challenges to those misinformed ideas. Speaking up when it is safe to do so, including to elected officials who amplify falsehoods, may be essential for preserving our democracy.

Second, both examples (similar to many other interactions I've observed in online spaces), ultimately hinge on feelings—wanting more and giving more empathy, respectively. Other researchers suggest that empathy-building for out-groups can be an effective foundation for meaningful dialogue and finding common ground (Hochschild, 2018; Moore-Berg et al., 2022). To be clear, this does not remotely mean we should coddle supremacists who intentionally peddle white supremacy. But it does suggest routes for challenging concepts and practices of people who less intentionally enforce structural white supremacy's reach by buying into its false promises and thus do nothing to reduce its impact. Empathy research suggests that finding common ground across people who disagree can serve as a point for restarting the conversation, building perceptions of in-group belonging, and, perhaps eventually, working to productively and factually resolve the original conflict.

Other research rather uncomfortably suggests that bolstering white people's self-esteem before conversations about discrimination may make them more receptive to absorbing anti-racist messages (Fein & Spencer, 1997; Greenwald & Banaji, 1995). This, perhaps, originates in how white people feel personally attacked when confronted with evidence of ongoing discrimination as has been so abundantly visible in anti-CRT dialogue and legislation (*Critical Race Theory*, n.d.) In some cases, this pushback is undoubtedly a thin excuse to avoid changes that would impinge on white supremacy's power. Other people genuinely (though unjustifiably) feel attacked during such discussions because of how their vision of the American Dream and their own accomplishments becomes threatened when confronted with evidence of inequity. This is also complementary to research that shows that white people are more likely to support programs that combat racial discrimination if they believe they will also benefit from those programs (W. J. Wilson, 1990). It is not that, ideally, white peoples' feelings and experiences should be centered in these conversations, but rather that these are considerations that likely must be addressed if change is to be accomplished in our current political landscape.

The takeaways from these examples of effective individual lessons turn us back once more to nostalgic nationalism, but to a different version than currently motivates most of its actors. Boym suggested that, in contrast to the restorative nostalgia that is central to the settler framework of militias and other nostalgic groups, *reflective* nostalgia is contemplative and self-critiquing. She says it works "*in resistance* to paranoiac projections" (emphasis added) (2002, p. 337) that are encapsulated in the threats and conspiracism endemic to its restorative counterpart. Focused on both individual and cultural memory (*ibid.*, p. 49), it is more receptive to corrective histories that, at least in theory, serve as lessons for building a more unified society. It does not, in other words, subsist on "historical amnesia about the country's past" (Braunstein, 2021, p. 12), but rather more honestly analyzes the past. A nationalism rooted in this kind of nostalgia is one that recognizes pitfalls alongside accomplishments so that we can learn from them and try to aim for a society that truly supports the equality of opportunity that is promised in the Dream. Such an approach still risks outgroup formation and problematic exclusion around national boundaries, but like any other large system that contains the seeds of its own destruction, a revised nostalgic nationalism may be at least part of the answer for holding ourselves to a higher standard.

Notes

1. When thinking through the lens of target identification alone, the Hutaree's alleged plot was arguably less threatening because they did not identify a specific police officer to murder or a specific place to ambush an officer before their arrest; nonetheless, police officers making routine traffic stops or having other interactions with Hutaree members could have been at great risk of a violent response.
2. It is worth remembering here how militia founder Norm Olson, a pastor, originally envisioned a much stronger religious element in the militia when he started the Michigan units in the 1990s. He wanted each major unit to have a "militia chaplain," and reported that many did so at the start.
3. This was the man whom one of the Hutaree members later tried to contact to help protect him as others of his unit were being arrested, and I suspect this may have been because he considered that a Muslim would be the last person authorities would suspect of harboring him.
4. It is also worth noting that New Mexico's proposed statute contains an exception for groups that "associate as a military organization solely for historical purposes or fictional performances" (*Legislation*, n.d.). Militia members argue that their actions are rooted in history and in maintaining the nation as the

Founding Fathers thought it should be, thus likely seeing an exception for their actions here as well.
5. In addition to general concerns about the safety of the then-likely first Black President, these inquiries were triggered by a highly publicized arrest of two Tennessee neo-Nazis who plotted to assassinate Barack Obama and kill other Black people (Associated Press, 2008).

References

2023 Regular Session—HB 14. (n.d.). *New Mexico legislature*. Retrieved May 27, 2023, from www.nmlegis.gov/Legislation/Legislation?chamber=H&legtype=B&legno=14&year=23

Aaronson, T. (2023, February 7). The snitch in the silver hearse the FBI paid a violent felon to infiltrate Denver's racial justice movement. *The Intercept*. https://theintercept.com/2023/02/07/fbi-denver-racial-justice-protests-informant/

ADL. (2023, June 6). The dangers of manipulated media and video: Deepfakes and more. *ADL*. www.adl.org/resources/blog/dangers-manipulated-media-and-video-deepfakes-and-more

Agar, J. (2020, October 9). Sheriff who shared stage with militia defends their rights but not alleged governor kidnapping plot. *Mlive*. www.mlive.com/news/grand-rapids/2020/10/sheriff-who-shared-stage-with-militia-defends-their-rights-but-not-alleged-governor-kidnapping-plot.html

Aho, J. (1995). *The politics of righteousness: Idaho Christian patriotism*. University of Washington Press.

Al-Ramahi, M., Elnoshokaty, A., El-Gayar, O., Nasralah, T., & Wahbeh, A. (2021). Public discourse against masks in the COVID-19 era: Infodemiology study of Twitter data. *JMIR Public Health and Surveillance*, 7(4), e26780. https://doi.org/10.2196/26780

Associated Press. (2008, October 27). ATF: Plot by skinheads to kill Obama is foiled. *Msnbc.Com*. www.msnbc.msn.com/id/27405681/ns/politics-decision_08/t/atf-plot-skinheads-kill-obama-foiled/

Baldas, T. (2012, February 16). Lead FBI investigator in Hutaree case says "toothless Tina" e-mail a joke with colleagues. *Detroit Free Press*. www.freep.com/article/20120216/NEWS02/202160522

Bensinger, K., & Garrison, J. (2021, December 17). The FBI said it busted a plot to kidnap Michigan's governor. Then things got complicated. *BuzzFeed News*. www.buzzfeednews.com/article/kenbensinger/fbi-michigan-kidnap-whitmer

Berger, J. M. (2018). *Extremism*. The MIT Press.

Boym, S. (2002). *The future of nostalgia* (Illustrated ed.). Basic Books.

Braunstein, R. (2021). The "right" history: Religion, race, and nostalgic stories of Christian America. *Religions*, 12(2).

Carless, W. (2022, September 7). Extremist Boogaloo Bois back on Facebook since Mar-a-Lago raid as anger toward feds mounts. *USA Today*. www.usatoday.com/story/news/nation/2022/09/07/boogaloo-bois-what-ideology-means-and-why-its-back-facebook/8003317001/

Carless, W., & Stephens, A. (2021, October 8). Black people formed one of the largest militias in the U.S. now its leader is in prosecutors' crosshairs. *The Trace*. www.thetrace.org/2021/10/nfac-black-militia-grandmaster-jay-prosecution/

Churchill, R. H. (2009). *To shake their guns in the Tyrant's face: Libertarian political violence and the origins of the militia movement.* The University of Michigan Press.
Confronting White Nationalism in Libraries: A Toolkit. (n.d.). *Western States Center.* Retrieved July 13, 2023, from www.westernstatescenter.org/libraries
Cooter, A. (2013). *Americanness, masculinity, and whiteness: How Michigan militia men navigate evolving social norms* [Thesis]. http://deepblue.lib.umich.edu/handle/2027.42/98077
Duffy, J. E., & Brantley, A. C. (1997). *Militias: Initiating contact.* www2.fbi.gov/publications/leb/1997/july975.htm
Farris, E., & Holman, M. (2023, January 30). Sheriffs who see themselves as ultimate defenders of the Constitution are especially worried about gun rights. *The Conversation.* http://theconversation.com/sheriffs-who-see-themselves-as-ultimate-defenders-of-the-constitution-are-especially-worried-about-gun-rights-198485
Fein, S., & Spencer, S. J. (1997). Prejudice as self-image maintenance: Affirming the self through derogating others. *Journal of Personality and Social Psychology, 73,* 31–44.
Garrison, J., & Bensinger, K. (2021, July 13). The FBI allegedly used at least 12 informants in the Michigan kidnapping case. *BuzzFeed News.* www.buzzfeednews.com/article/jessicagarrison/fbi-informants-in-michigan-kidnap-plot
Goldman, A., & Feuer, A. (2023, February 1). Bias and human error played parts in F.B.I.'s Jan. 6 failure, documents suggest. *The New York Times.* www.nytimes.com/2023/02/01/us/politics/trump-jan-6-fbi.html
Greenwald, A. G., & Banaji, M. R. (1995). Implicit social cognition: Attitudes, self-esteem, and stereotypes. *Psychological Review, 102*(1), 4–27.
Harris, P. (2011, November 16). Fake terror plots, paid informants: The tactics of FBI "entrapment" questioned. *The Guardian.* www.theguardian.com/world/2011/nov/16/fbi-entrapment-fake-terror-plots
Hochschild, A. R. (2018). *Strangers in their own land: Anger and mourning on the American right.* The New Press.
Jolley, D., Meleady, R., & Douglas, K. M. (2020). Exposure to intergroup conspiracy theories promotes prejudice which spreads across groups. *British Journal of Psychology, 111*(1), 17–35.
Juergensmeyer, M. (2003). *Terror in the mind of god: The global rise of religious violence* (3rd ed.). University of California Press.
Khalel, S. (2020, July 29). Masks to Sharia: QAnon is spreading anti-Muslim ideology via coronavirus opposition. *Middle East Eye.* www.middleeasteye.net/news/masks-sharia-qanon-spreading-anti-muslim-ideology-coronavirus-opposition
Krafcik, M. (2022, March 22). FBI informant said he directed suspects to carry out parts of kidnapping plan. *WPBN.* https://upnorthlive.com/defense-attorneys-continue-to-grill-fbis-key-informant-in-whitmer-kidnaping-case
Lehr, D. (2021). *White hot hate: A true story of domestic terrorism in America's heartland.* Mariner Books.
Levine, M. (2021a, October 31). Inside the making of a domestic terror plot, and an "average guy's" race to stop it. *ABC News.* https://abcnews.go.com/US/inside-making-domestic-terror-plot-average-guys-race/story?id=80643666
Levine, M. (2021b, November 1). Becoming a domestic terrorist: How 3 self-styled "patriots" were led to lethal plot. *ABC News.* https://abcnews.go.com/US/domestic-terrorist-styled-patriots-led-lethal-plot/story?id=80303614

Messner, M. A. (2018). Guns, intimacy, and the limits of militarized masculinity. In *Gun studies* (pp. 224–240). Routledge.

Miller, Z., Colvin, J., & Seitz, A. (2021, April 20). Trump praises QAnon conspiracists, appreciates support. *AP News*. https://apnews.com/article/election-2020-ap-top-news-religion-racial-injustice-535e145ee67dd757660157be39d05d3f

Miller-Idriss, C. (2020). *Hate in the homeland: The new global far right*. Princeton University Press.

Moore-Berg, S. L., Hameiri, B., & Bruneau, E. G. (2022). Empathy, dehumanization, and misperceptions: A media intervention humanizes migrants and increases empathy for their plight but only if misinformation about migrants is also corrected. *Social Psychological and Personality Science, 13*(2), 645–655.

Norris, J. J., & Grol-Prokopczyk, H. (2015). Estimating the prevalence of entrapment in post-9/11 terrorism cases. *The Journal of Criminal Law and Criminology (1973–), 105*(3), 609–677.

Paluck, E. L., Porat, R., Clark, C. S., & Green, D. P. (2021). Prejudice reduction: Progress and challenges. *Annual Review of Psychology, 72*(1), 533–560.

Perliger, A., Stevens, C., & Leidig, E. (2023, January 26). Mapping the ideological landscape of extreme misogyny. *International Centre for Counter-Terrorism*. www.icct.nl/publication/mapping-ideological-landscape-extreme-misogyny

Polantz, K., Carrega, C., & Schneider, J. (2021, October 15). US Capitol Police officer indicted on obstruction of justice charges in connection with January 6. *CNN*. www.cnn.com/2021/10/15/politics/capitol-police-january-6/index.html

Reiter, M. (2012, February 16). Hutaree witness role debated. The *Blade*. www.toledoblade.com/local/courts/2012/02/16/Credibility-of-key-witness-debated-in-Hutaree-case/stories/201202160097

Reynolds, N. (2023, May 9). Republican governor joins Democratic crackdown on militias. *Newsweek*. www.newsweek.com/republican-governor-joins-democratic-crackdown-militias-1799273

Scribner, L. (2022, June 14). *BPC urges congress to act on civics education*. https://bipartisanpolicy.org/press-release/bpc-urges-congress-to-act-on-civics-education/

SPLC. (n.d.). Preventing youth radicalization: Building resilient, inclusive communities. *Southern Poverty Law Center*. Retrieved July 13, 2023, from www.splcenter.org/peril

State Fact Sheets. (2020). *Georgetown Law*. www.law.georgetown.edu/icap/our-work/addressing-the-rise-of-unlawful-private-militias/state-fact-sheets/

Swami, V. (2012). Social psychological origins of conspiracy theories: The case of the Jewish conspiracy theory in Malaysia. *Frontiers in Psychology, 3*. www.frontiersin.org/articles/10.3389/fpsyg.2012.00280

Swire-Thompson, B., Miklaucic, N., Wihbey, J. P., Lazer, D., & DeGutis, J. (2022). The backfire effect after correcting misinformation is strongly associated with reliability. *Journal of Experimental Psychology: General, 151*, 1655–1665.

Temple-Raston, D. (2010, April 12). How the FBI got inside the Hutaree militia. *NPR*. www.npr.org/2010/04/12/125856761/how-the-fbi-got-inside-the-hutaree-militia

White, P. (2022, October 18). Bumbling kidnapping plot of Michigan Gov. Gretchen Whitmer captured in series & podcast in the works from 'Chameleon' producer campside. *Deadline*. https://deadline.com/2022/10/kidnapping-plot-michigan-gov-gretchen-whitmer-series-1235148650/

Why are some White People so Mad about Critical Race Theory? (n.d.). *Psychology in action*. Retrieved June 11, 2023, from www.psychologyinaction.org/white-people-critical-race-theory/

Williams, K. (2013). The other side of the COIN: Counterinsurgency and community policing. In *Life during wartime: Resisting counterinsurgency* (pp. 113–152). Oakland, CA: AK Press. http://archive.org/details/isbn_9781849351317

Williams, K. (2015). *Our enemies in blue: Police and power in America* (Rev. ed.). AK Press.

Wilson, T. (2022, April 11). Jan. 6 defendants raise more than $3.5 million through GiveSendGo. *Rolling Stone.* www.rollingstone.com/politics/politics-features/give-send-riot-jan-6-defendants-have-raised-more-than-3-5-million-through-christian-crowdfunding-website-1332787/

Wilson, W. J. (1990). *The truly disadvantaged: The inner city, the underclass, and public policy* (Reprint ed.). University Of Chicago Press.

Wong, J. C. (2020, August 11). Revealed: QAnon Facebook groups are growing at a rapid pace around the world. *The Guardian.* www.theguardian.com/us-news/2020/aug/11/qanon-facebook-groups-growing-conspiracy-theory

Wood, T., & Porter, E. (2019). The elusive backfire effect: Mass attitudes' steadfast factual adherence. *Political Behavior, 41*(1), 135–163.

Index

Note: Page numbers in *italics* indicate a figure on the corresponding page.

9/11 26, 87, 127, 140, 174
abortion 31, 52, 102, 106, 173
accelerationism 130–133, 157, 171, 179; and Boogaloo 33–34, 134–135; and the Crusaders 147; and the Hutaree 139; and the Watchmen 151–152
Affirmative Action 19
Allen, Curtis 146–149, 178
American Dream 98, 100, 105, 190–191; barriers to 102, 104, 109, 119n5, 155; fallacy of 108, 144, 188–189
antifa 131, 156
anti-government sentiment: as militia purpose 20, 23–25, 59–60, 64–66, 71, 75, 79, 81–82, 135, 169; as motivation for violence 25, 30, 49, 109, 138
Appleseed 28–29, 110, 115
Arbery, Ahmaud 14
Aryan Nations 58–59
Atomwaffen Division 133

back to the land movement 93–94, 126, 160n8; *see also* frontier; land
Biden, Joe 1, 2, 136, 152, 153, 159n4, 186, 187
Black Lives Matter 15, 32, 34, 135, 151
Black Militias 14–15, 47; *see also* Not Fucking Around Coalition (NFAC)
Black Panthers 15, 80–81, 119n15
Blake, Jacob 15, 118, 170

Boogaloo 33–35, 134–136, 139, 151, 153, 160n9
Boy Scouts 93
Brady Bill 63–64; *see also* gun control
Branch Davidians 61–62; *see also* Koresh, David; Waco
Bundy Family 145, 148, 156, 161n18
Bureau of Alcohol, Tobacco, and Firearms (ATF) 59, 61–62, 72
Bush, George H. W. 51–52, 127
Bush, George W. 86–87, 127, 156

Christianity 51, 69n11, 145, 170; appeals to 55, 66, 92, 105–107, 119n7, 128, 138, 147, 173, 185; *see also* white Christian nationalism
Christofascism 129; *see also* fascism
civic duty, community protection 11–12, 20, 26, 29–30, 41, 68, 118, 129, 144, 161n23, 176
Civil Rights Movement 49
Civil War: desired or inevitable 33–34, 134–136, 152, 159n6; historical 5, 18, 46–47, 104
Clinton, Bill 52, 75, 86, 127, 161n20
Clinton, Hillary 146, 148, 159n4
Communism 22, 49, 119n11, 127; *see also* Socialism
Community Oversight Boards 160n7, 188
comradery 10, 110–111
confidential informants (CI) 24, 59, 140–142, 182–185
conspiracy theories 49, 67, 77, 81, 85, 89n12, 113, 127, 131, 157,

159n4, 160n16, 190–191;
in constitutionalist units 23;
in millenarian units 48, 56,
209–210, 221; as motivation
for nostalgic group participation
50, 58, 60–61, 86, 111, 144;
as possible violence indicator
173–174, 176
constitutional militias 23–28, 32–33,
131, 137, 150, 151, 178
constitutional sheriffs *see* sheriffs
COVID-19 pandemic 93, 117;
conspiracies about 26, 32, 67; as
motive for nostalgic group action
14, 21, 102–103, 129–130, 134,
149–150, 153, 171, 174
critical race theory 19, 158, 190
the Crusaders 144–149, 152, 155;
as instructive for violence
prevention 171–173, 177, 182,
184
cultural change: more broadly perceived
as negative 35, 49, 51–52,
99–104, 114; as motivation for
nostalgic group participation
11, 19, 28, 31, 91, 106, 111,
127–129, 145, 152

Democrats 52, 60, 103, 149, 161n20;
as opposing patriotic interests
21–22, 26, 33, 35, 75, 100, 110,
116, 127, 131, 159n4, 174
deplatforming 64, 134, 136–137, 150,
174, 181; *see also* Facebook;
social media
DeSantis, Ron 159
DHS 94, 128, 181, 187
Dobson, James 106

education 49, 101–102, 117; current
efforts to limit 19, 105;
members' educational level 12,
132; militias trying to educate
others 11, 83, 177; as prevention
16, 18, 104, 188–189
enslaved people *see* slavery
extremism 2, 23–28, 175, 179–181;
among veterans 51, 128, 156;
range of action 26–28, 32, 34,
114, 130, 137, 157; subtlety of
85, 154–155
extremist *see* extremism

Facebook 3, 34, 64, 134–137, 150,
174–175, 181; records in
criminal cases 145–146, 148,
184; *see also* deplatforming;
social media
false flag 26, 84–85
fascism 113; *see also* Christofascism;
Trump, Donald
Father Charles Coughlin 49
Federal Bureau of Investigation (FBI)
15, 27, 74–75, 80, 85, 139; in
militia investigations 59–62,
81–82, 140–141, 145, 149, 152,
177, 180–185
Federal Emergency Management Agency
(FEMA) 67
federal government 49, 60, 71; attitudes
toward 20, 41, 50–51, 58,
62–64, 68, 72, 75, 81–88, 93,
116, 145, 182; historical 43–46,
49; *see also* tyranny
Finicum, LeVoy 145
firearms 14, 24, 36n7, 47, 59, 61, 64,
72, 80, 96, 112, 114, 119n15,
138, 140, 142, 153, 160n13,
171–172; centrality to identity
11–12, 28–30, 51, 64, 106, 110,
114–116; historical 41, 44, 46;
see also Second Amendment
Floyd, George 15, 34, 134, 151
Founding Fathers: for Donald Trump
106; as inspiration for modern
militia members 11, 18, 20, 40,
45, 97, 106–107, 111–112, 115,
155; for Norm Olson 56–57, 66
Fox, Adam 150–152, 184
Freedom Church 65–68
Freemen standoff 81–82
frontier 105, 108–109, 114, 117; *see also*
back to the land movement; land

Gadsden flag 113
Gale, William Potter 49–50
Garbin, Ty 152
Great Depression 48–49
Gritz, Bo 60, 81
gun control 24, 26, 51, 66–67, 88n5,
103, 113–114, 116, 127; *see also*
Brady Bill

Harris, Daniel 151–152
Harris, Kevin 59–60, 60

Index

homesteading *see* off-gridders
Hutaree 55, 138–144, 152, 156, 160n11, 160n13, 160n14, 191n1, 191n3; as instructive for violence prevention 172–174, 177, 182–184

imagined communities 99, 154
immigrants 45, 147–148; perceived threats from 33, 35, 100–101, 127, 129, 156; policies about 17, 21, 31, 103–104
Indigenous communities 18, 41, 46, 92, 105, 107–109, 119n10, 160n8
in-groups and out groups 99, 101, 110, 113, 129, 132, 135–136, 138, 154, 170, 173; internal construction of 100, 179, 190

January 6th 1, 13, 15, 17, 32, 137, 153–158; nostalgic group blending during 112, 136; *see also* stop the steal
Jones, Terry 170

Koresh, David 61–62; *see also* Branch Davidians; Waco
Ku Klux Klan (KKK) 47, 48–49, 161n24

land: historical 41, 46; importance of 81, 92–94, 96–98, 105, 107–108, 145; perceived entitlement to federal 145, 156; *see also* back to the land movement; frontier
Law Enforcement Officers (LEO) 50, 67, 118, 138, 170, 180–182, 186; *see also* police
Leaf, Dar 117–118
LGBTQ+ concerns 19, 31, 35, 36n6, 127, 158, 161n19

Malheur National Wildlife Refuge 145
Manifest Destiny 105
masculinity 30, 52, 92–93, 96, 102–103, 106; limits of 189; settler 107–112, 114–115, 127, 147, 155
McVeigh, Timothy 61, 72–74, 79, 84–85, 88n3, 109; *see also* Oklahoma City bombing

military veterans 23, 45, 52, 72; involvement in January 6th 156; participation in nostalgic groups 9, 12, 24–25, 51, 52n2, 58, 128, 142, 157, 176, 178; perceived attacks on 128, 147, 181
millenarian militias 24–28, 32, 150, 157, 170, 178–179; and accelerationism 33–34, 130–133; and Hutaree 138–139
Minutemen 30–31
Moms For Liberty 158
Muslims 169–170, 187, 191n3; and the Crusaders 144–148, 155, 161n19, 173, 177, 184; perceptions of 33, 101–102, 127–128, 149, 160, 174
Mythopoetic Movement 92

National Guard 48, 50, 62, 176, 179
National Rifle Association (NRA) 28, 64, 114–116, 179
neo-Nazis 16, 32, 51, 92, 112, 133, 135, 153, 155; differences from militias 29–31
Nichols, Terry 72–73, 79, 88n4
nostalgia metaphor 31–32, 34–36, 97, 112, 135, 153
Not Fucking Around Coalition (NFAC) 14–15, 187; *see also* Black militias

Oath Keepers 12–13, 52n2, 137, 146, 153, 156–157, 161n23
Obama, Barack 88, 101, 110, 126–129, 145–146, 156, 161n19, 192n5
off-gridders 30–32, 36n7, 87, 92–94, 112, 138, 142, 144, 147–148, 159n2
Oklahoma City bombing 32, 57, 71–76, 84, 109, 119n12, 137, 157; impact on the movement 76–79, 84; *see also* McVeigh, Timothy
Otherization 14, 22, 128, 149

Pence, Mike 156
police 12, 14, 20–21, 55, 118, 120n20, 130, 138–139, 141–142, 170–171, 178, 183, 191n1; and Boogaloo 33–35, 134–135; during January 6th 1, 15, 155; *see also* Law Enforcement Officer (LEO)

police brutality 14–15, 18, 34, 118, 129, 134, 151, 160n7, 170; *see also* Arbery, Ahmaud; Blake, Jacob; Floyd, George
Posse Comitatus 49–51, 71, 138; Act 47, 49–50
preppers *see* off-gridders
Project Appleseed *see Appleseed*
Promise Keepers 92–93
Proud Boys 29–30, 32, 112, 135, 153, 156, 158
Pulse nightclub shooting 145–146

QAnon 26, 159n4, 174

racial threat 34–35, 94, 100, 154, 159, 173, 187; definition 101–3, historical 48, 109; and immigrants 17, 33, 35, 129, 145
racism 16–19, 29, 58–60, 72, 94, 98, 103–105, 115, 118n1; historical 42, 47–49, 51, 109; inside militias 13, 15–16, 73, 81, 95, 126–127, 160n17; Trump and 21, 129, 159
radicalization 2, 34–36, 74, 130, 141, 155, 157, 172, 176–178, 180–181, 186, 188; risk of overlooking 18, 94, 154
Reagan, Ronald 51–52, 98
Red Dawn 55
Reno, Janet 75, 86
Republicans 1–2, 60, 81, 86, 154, 156–157, 159; as patriots 21, 33, 75, 106, 127, 129
Revere, Paul 29, 43, 110
Revolutionary War 41–44, 46, 65, 114–115, 159n6; lessons from 23, 29, 98, 110, 112
Rittenhouse, Kyle 15, 118, 169–170
Ruby Ridge 58–60, 62–64, 69n4, 72, 81–82, 161n18; *see also* Weaver, Randy
rural mentality 91–97, 116–117, 126

Second Amendment 41, 115; as common interest 28, 32, 115, 129; importance of 11–12, 44, 64, 116, 179; *see also* firearms
self-sufficiency 93–96, 118n1
September 11, 2001 *see* 9/11

Settler Colonialism 105, 107, 117, 119n6, 133, 145, 155
sheriffs 20, 71, 116–118, 161n18, 180; and Norm Olson 83, 87; posse comitatus 49–51
slavery 40, 42, 45–46, 105; cooptation of 50, 84, 174; lack of education about 5, 18, 104, 109, 189
Socialism 22, 52, 127; *see also* Communism
social media 2, 19, 114, 135–137, 146, 151, 154, 174–175, 184–187; influence on perceived threat 12, 26, 33, 131, 159; and militia type 23–24; *see also* deplatforming; Facebook
Southwell, Ray 64–65, 73, 75–76, 79, 81; role in militia founding 55, 58, 63, 69n1, 69n3
Sovereign Citizens 50–51, 81, 138
Stein, Patrick 144–145, 148–149, 161n19, 177–178, 184
Stone, David 138, 143, 177
stop the steal 32, 131, 150, 153–155, 157; *see also* January 6th
survivalists *see* off-gridders

Tea Party 92, 143
Thompson, Linda 76–77, 89n8, 140
tokenism 13–14, 189
Trump, Donald 2, 17, 57, 119n15, 161n23; influence on nostalgic groups 28, 32–33, 129–131, 134, 136–137, 146–154, 157, 161n21, 174; stoking perceived threat 21–22, 35, 51, 99–100, 106–108, 156, 159; *see also* Christofascism; fascism
Tulsa Massacre 109
tyranny: broader cultural appeal 26, 33, 60–61, 103, 116; historical perceptions of 43, 77, 86–87; as motivation for action 11, 16, 25, 34, 50–51, 58, 60, 64–67, 75, 80, 88, 112, 114–115, 126, 149–150, 179, 185; *see also* federal government

United Nations (UN) 67, 80, 89n12
United We Stand 2, 187

Index

von Trapp, Debra 74–76

Waco 61–64, 67, 72–73, 75–76, 81–82, 86–87, 89n8, 140; *see also* Branch Davidians; Koresh, David
Washington, George 43–44
Weaver, Randy 58–63; *see also* Ruby Ridge
Weaver, Sara 59
white Christian nationalism 5, 109, 132, 190; *see also* Christianity
whiteness 15–16, 41, 94, 106–108, 115, 128, 173
white supremacy 15–17, 32, 103–107, 109, 151, 155, 170, 188–190, 199n6; historical 42, 46–49
Whitmer, Gretchen *14*, 88, 109, 117, 137, 149–151, 171

"woke" 16–17, 22–23
"wokeness" *see* "woke"
Wolverine Watchmen 137–138, 149–153, 161n21; as instructive for violence prevention 171–172, 174, 178, 184–185
women: involvement in nostalgic groups 13, 29, 94, 107, 119n4, 172; perceptions of 5, 13, 30, 49, 75, 92, 99, 102–103, 173
Wright, Gavin 144–149, 152, 155, 161n20, 184

Y2K 82–87, 126, 132

Zello 137, 160n10